CENTRAL FISHE
IRISH ANGLI

GW00370838

GameAngling

GILL AND MACMILLAN

Gill and Macmillan Ltd
Goldenbridge
Dublin 8
with associated companies throughout the world
© Central Fisheries Board 1993
0 7171 1827 4
Index compiled by Gabrielle Noble
Design and Artwork by Design Image, Dublin
Printed by ColourBooks Ltd, Dublin
The maps are based on the Ordnance Survey by permission of the
Government (Permit No. 5552)
All rights reserved. No part of this publication may
be copied, reproduced or transmitted in any form or by
any means, without permission of the publishers.
A catalogue record is available for this book from the
British Library.

CONTENTS

GAME ANGLING

CENTRAL FISHERIES BOARD
IRISH ANGLING GUIDES

A totally comprehensive series of handbooks on every aspect of angling in Ireland. Compiled by and published in association with the Irish Fisheries Boards, each Guide provides all the most recent and accurate information required by the angler to make the most of Ireland's superb angling opportunities.

The series comprises three books:
Sea Angling
Coarse Angling
Game Angling

THE FISHERIES BOARDS

The Central and seven Regional Fisheries Boards were established to protect, develop and promote all forms of sport fishing in Ireland. They are non-profit-making bodies and all income, including the royalties from this book, is devoted to fishery improvement and conservation. The Central Board employs specialist Coarse, Game and Sea angling staff whose main function is the collection and dissemination of angling information such as is included here.
The Board wishes to thank its colleagues all over the country, the thousands of anglers, the boat operators, club secretaries, fishery owners and all those interested and involved in the sport without whose co-operation these guides could not be produced.

INFORMATION

The nature of angling is such that the information provided must be viewed as being as accurate as possible at the time of going to print.
The Fisheries Boards provide maps, brochures and some local guides and Bord Failte, the Irish Tourist Board, provide a set of three brochures titled 'Only The Best' Coarse, Game and Sea Angling.
The Irish Tourist Board also inspects accommodation, registering and approving only the premises meeting its high standards. The Fisheries Boards recommend that anglers stay only at such approved accommodation. Guides and lists are available from any tourist office.

INTRODUCTION

Ireland is widely regarded internationally as the outstanding angling destination in Europe. The vast variety and quality of our fishing has given the country a reputation of which we are justly proud.

Ireland is an island approximately 300 miles long and 200 miles wide, with a very high ratio of inland waters to land. There are 14,000 miles of fish-bearing rivers, and thousands of lakes. The climate is perfect for fishing. It is temperate and kind to the angler, with moderate summers, mild winters, and adequate rainfall throughout the year. The warm waters of the North Atlantic Drift lap the south and west coasts, giving a milder climate than our geographical location would suggest. The result is a fabulous mixture of cold and warm-water fish species, capable of exciting the specialist angler or the casual fisherman on annual family holiday.

An interesting fact about Ireland's freshwater fish is that only the game fish species – salmon, sea trout, brown trout, and char – are truly indigenous. Apart from the eel and gudgeon, all the others – bream, pike, roach, rudd, tench, carp, and the rest – were introduced over the centuries; most were brought in by monks who travelled widely on the Continent.

To most Europeans, Irish game angling is a new and wonderful experience. It is the world of natural wild salmon and trout. The salmon you catch in Ireland have just returned from their great feeding migrations across the top of the North Atlantic Ocean. Few countries in the world can still offer this – and at such reasonable prices.

In most countries, fishing for wild brown trout is now a rarity. Virtually every stream, river and lake in Ireland holds brown trout to a lesser or greater extent. Our sea trout are renowned for their spectacular sporting qualities. At the moment, the sea trout population is going through a rough period in the Connemara area (of which more later), but the remainder of the country's sea trout fisheries are in top condition and offer a great sporting challenge.

Within the text, the following symbols are used to denote the start and end of river systems:

■	Main river and its tributaries
▬▬▬▬	Ends that section
❏	A tributary and its system
❖ ❖ ❖ ❖ ❖ ❖	Ends that section
☐	A channel of a tributary and its system
★ ★ ★ ★ ★ ★	Ends that section.

THE SPECIES

Ireland's game fisheries are based on Atlantic salmon, sea trout, and brown trout. Arctic char are present in some lakes but are not significant in angling returns. In some areas where there is a shortage of readily available trout fishing the local fisheries board operates regulated fisheries. These are maintained to a high standard by regular stocking of native brown and introduced rainbow trout.

■ ATLANTIC SALMON *(SALMO SALAR)*

IRISH RECORD: 57 lb.

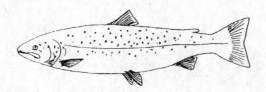

Irish: bradán. French: saumon. German: lachs. Dutch: zalm. Italian: salmone de reno. Spanish: salmón.

Salmon are 'anadromous'. They spawn in the gravel of a river bed in the depths of winter, and the eggs hatch out in March. The little fry, or 'parr', remain in the relatively poor rivers and streams for one, two or more years, when they 'smoltify' (turn silver) and migrate to sea, travelling to the rich feeding grounds of the North Atlantic to grow and mature. Some return to their natal rivers after one year and are known as 'grilse' or 'peel'. They range in weight from 2 to 8 lb, but the average is about 5.5 lb. Grilse constitute the major proportion of Irish rod-caught salmon, and, though they can be caught over many months, the runs peak from mid-June to mid-September.

Other salmon remain at sea, growing and feeding for more than one year. They usually weigh from 8 lb upwards, and, depending on when they return, they can be called 'spring salmon' or 'summer salmon'. Occasionally some may stay at sea for up to four years and can weigh 20 lb or more.

■ SEA TROUT *(SALMO TRUTTA)*

IRISH RECORD: 16 lb 6 oz.

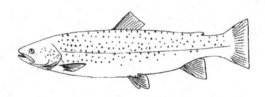

Irish: breac geal. French: truite de mer. German: meerforelle. Dutch: zeeforel. Italian: trota di mare. Spanish: trucha.

Sea trout are also anadromous, but they seldom travel far from the mouth of the estuary, preferring to range up and down the coastline. They go to sea in May and the majority return the following July and August; they average about .75 lb and are known as 'finnock'. A few fisheries get a run of multi-sea-winter sea trout which will average about 3 lb.

The sea trout population in one area, Connemara, has shown a dramatic reduction in recent years. Research into the problem is continuing. As a temporary conservation measure, a bye-law has been introduced that prohibits the killing of sea trout in the area between Clew Bay and Galway Bay; if caught on rod and line in this area, they must be returned alive to the water.

■ BROWN TROUT *(SALMO TRUTTA)*

IRISH RECORD: 26 lb 2 oz.

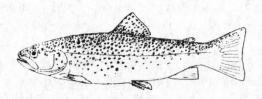

Irish: breac donn. French: truite. German: forelle. Dutch: bruine forel. Italian: trota. Spanish: trucha.

Sea trout and brown trout share the same ancestry, but the brown trout spend their entire life in fresh water. They are the most widely distributed game fish species in the country. Some spend their entire life in the river in which they were spawned, while others migrate down to the lakes in the system, where they grow to maturity. Their size can vary according to the waters they live in. They live for about six or seven years, but on some of the richer river systems the average age can be as low as four years.

Lough trout tend to weigh 1 to 2 lb, and the river trout are usually somewhat smaller. Some of the larger loughs, notably Lough Corrib, Lough Mask, and Lough Leane, have a population of 'ferox' trout that can reach 20 lb or more. They are normally taken trolling. On Lough Melvin, Co. Leitrim, there are two additional strains, the sonnaghan and gillaroo, both of which readily take flies.

■ DISTRIBUTION

The geology of the country directly affects the productivity of our waters in many respects, including fish stocks and fish growth rates. Ireland has a central plain of carboniferous limestone; the outer margins are composed of denser rock, with the harder, more acid granite rocks making up the coastline.

The rich limestone waters are capable of growing fish to maturity and sustaining them into their old age, and they produce the best brown trout fisheries. The midland lakes and tributaries of the Shannon system and the great western lakes of Lough Corrib, Lough Mask and Lough Conn are all limestone lakes with a high pH or alkalinity. The average weight in some of these lakes can be over 2 lb. Some of the great limestone rivers, such as the Suir and the Boyne, are also top-class trout fisheries. Brown trout, however, can be found virtually everywhere. Even in the poorest mountain acid lakes they can be numerous but small, lively, and eager to take a fly.

Sea trout are found in virtually every river system around the coast to varying degrees. They are usually found in the tidal waters and lower reaches of the big limestone rivers of the east and south coasts. They seldom venture upstream in such waters, preferring the poorer acid waters (low pH) coming off the coastal mountains; in the acid waters of the western seaboard they are likely to inhabit the entire river system. Cos. Kerry, Galway, Mayo and Donegal are considered to have the most productive waters.

Salmon are more widespread than their smaller cousins, the sea trout. To a varying degree, salmon enter almost every river in Ireland that they can navigate upstream, though some systems have shown a reduction in recent seasons. The larger systems naturally produce the biggest numbers, but some of the smaller rivers can be very productive for angling purposes. Grilse run all Irish salmon rivers, often in great numbers, but the larger multi-sea-winter fish are not so readily available.

Whereas they probably enter most systems, only a few of the larger rivers get fish in sufficient numbers to warrant serious fishing. Many salmon fisheries keep records, and the best way of ascertaining the quality of the fishing is to get the relevant catch data from individual fisheries, going back over a few years. Even then the size of the runs tend to fluctuate on certain river systems from one season to the next.

■ SEASONS

All Irish game angling is restricted to seasons. There are statutory opening and closing dates for each fishery district, and the season may differ for salmon, sea trout and brown trout angling – even in the same river. The opening and closing dates are listed with each fishery, but these may change from time to time, particularly in relation to the closing dates. If in doubt, it is always best to check. Of course, the statutory open season is not necessarily the same as the best fishing period. Some of the early salmon rivers fish well for spring salmon as early as January, but the more numerous grilse runs can be expected from mid-June to mid-September.

A relatively small number of systems get a run of big sea trout in April and May, but the main run begins in late June or early July, and the sea trout continue running into the systems in lesser or greater numbers until the closing date at the end of September or early October.

Brown trout can be fished right through the season, from the statutory opening date, which is usually in March, to the closing date in late September or early October. However, certain times of the year are better. Brown trout angling is considered to peak in the second half of May for around a month, and again in September.

Early in the season, in March and April, the best of the fishing is usually close to midday, when the temperatures are highest. During May and June there is often brown trout activity and good fishing extending right through the day.

From late June to July and August, the best brown trout fishing is usually found late in the evening or early in the morning. By September, the fishing reverts to daytime fishing.

■ FISHERIES ADMINISTRATION

The Minister for the Marine has the ultimate responsibility for Ireland's inland fisheries. The Central Fisheries Board and the seven regional fisheries boards (see map on page 21) were established to develop, protect and promote angling, and they are responsible to the Minister for the Marine. The boards also manage and control a number of important salmon and sea trout fisheries, and manage and develop brown trout fishing on a number of well-known rivers and lakes.

Legislation was recently enacted for the establishment of fisheries development societies. The function of these co-operative societies will be to raise and distribute, for the public benefit, funds for the development of trout and coarse fishing in their fisheries region. The co-ops may, from time to time, decide that the holding of a co-op share certificate will be required before fishing for trout or coarse fish. Before fishing, please enquire from a local tackle shop, fisheries board, or angling accommodation centre. The certificates cost £12 (annual), £5 (twenty-one days), or £3 (three days).

■ OWNERSHIP, PERMITS, AND LICENCES

All game fisheries in Ireland (salmon, sea trout and brown trout fisheries) are owned: there is no public right to game fishing. In this guide, reference is made to 'free fishing' on numerous waters; this may mean that the legal owners or riparian owners do not exercise their rights to exclude or to charge anglers, or it may be that positive ownership of a fishery has not been asserted. Where rights are established, the owners may be a state organisation, an angling club, a company, or a private individual, who do not necessarily own the adjoining land.

Angling clubs and associations may either own or lease fishing rights. There are a few fisheries, particularly good salmon stretches, that are retained exclusively by their owners; but on most waters it is possible to get permission to fish, and visiting anglers are welcomed. On club waters it may be possible to fish by joining the club, by becoming an associate member, or by purchasing a day permit. Other private fisheries are let in a variety of ways, depending on whether it is a river or lake. The fishing on rivers is let by the day, by the week, or occasionally by the season. The cost may include the services of a 'gillie' or guide. On lakes there are differing charges for bank fishing, the use of a boat, of a boat and engine, or of boat, engine, and gillie. Charges vary according to the exclusivity and productivity of the water, but daily permits on good privately owned salmon waters can vary from £10 to £50, while on the quality 'free fisheries', such as Loughs Conn, Corrib, Leane, and Currane, there is no charge. Needless to say, each visitor should enquire about permit costs before booking a salmon rod.

The better-known trout fisheries, particularly the loughs, are either free or are controlled by the fisheries boards. The following is a schedule of permit prices for brown and rainbow trout fishing on all Central Fisheries Board and regional fisheries board waters, except for stocked fisheries controlled and developed by the South-Western Regional Fisheries Board.

Ordinary annual permit	£5
Ordinary day permit	£2
Pensioner or juvenile annual permit	£2
Pensioner or juvenile day permit	50p

South-Western Regional Fisheries Board Permit Charges

Adult annual permit	£20
Three-week permit	£10
Adult daily permit	£3

STATE LICENCES

A state licence is required by law before one can fish for salmon or sea trout on any water, irrespective of any permit issued by a fishery owner, and is not included in the permit price unless stipulated. No licence is required for brown trout or rainbow trout angling.

Salmon and sea trout licences can be purchased from fisheries boards and from approved licence distributors, such as tackle shops, hotels and guesthouses, and fishery officers.

Season: all-district licence	£25	
Season: single-district licence	£12	
Juvenile (under-18) licence	£8	(all districts)
21-day licence	£10	(all districts)
One-day licence	£3	(all districts)

■ FISHING METHODS

SALMON

Salmon can be fished using a variety of methods. Tactics include fly fishing, spinning, trolling, worm, and the natural shrimp. The methods or combination of methods allowed can vary from fishery to fishery.

A double-handed fly rod will be required on some of the bigger, fast-flowing rivers and on some of the smaller rivers when they are in spate. There are many locations too where a single-handed rod will be adequate, and sometimes preferable to the big rod. Floating, sinking-tip or intermediate fly lines may be appropriate depending on conditions, and leader strength can range from 6 to 8 lb, depending on the fishing conditions and the average size of the fish.

The tackle can vary from a 9 foot rod matched to a no. 7 floating line to an 18 foot rod and a no. 12 fast-sinking line. The flies will range in size too, depending on the location, and local conditions can dictate anything from a size 12 single salmon fly to a 3 or 3.5 inch brass or copper tube fly.

Salmon fly reels should be big enough to accommodate the fly line and at least 150 yards of 25 lb breaking strain backing line.

A single fly is normally used when fly fishing a river. In certain circumstances two flies may be used or indeed may be advantageous. In fast, streamy water the fly is cast at 45° to the stream and fished around by the pull of the current. In dead water the fly line and fly are retrieved by hand. In lake fishing, the flies are cast and retrieved in front of a drifting boat. It is usual to use a single-handed rod (though on some lakes a double-handed salmon rod is used) and a team of two or three flies fished on a floating, sinking or sink-tip line.

There are hundreds of salmon fly patterns to choose from. Some of the most popular and useful in Ireland are Blue Charm, Garry Dog, Black Pennell, Green Peter, Hairy Mary, Thunder and Lightning, Stoat's Tail, Silver Stoat's Tail, Silver Doctor, Black Doctor, Black Goldfinch, Willie Gunn, Silver Rat, General Practitioner, Curry's Red Shrimp, and Green Highlander. Individual fisheries may have their own favourite patterns.

Spinning is an effective method of taking grilse on a river, as is trolling in a lake. A wide range of light baits is used, including spoons, spinners, and minnows, such as the Lane Minnow.

A ledgered worm or worms can be an effective bait, as is a natural shrimp, which can be either fished from a float or spun.

Spring salmon can be fished in both river and lake. On rivers they are caught spinning, fly fishing (usually with a double-handed rod and sinking line), worm fishing, or on a natural shrimp. On the lakes the most usual fishing methods are trolling, fly fishing, and spinning.

Spinning on rivers and trolling on lakes are probably the most popular spring salmon fishing methods. A strong 9.5 to 11 foot rod with a progressive action is required. For reels, the choice is between a multiplier and a big fixed-spool reel capable of holding at least 150 yards of 18 to 20 lb monofilament. The most popular baits are the Devon Minnow and Irish Rubber Tail Spinner; they can be fished in a range of sizes and colours, depending on water conditions. The size will range from 2 to 4 inches, and among the most popular patterns for rivers are Yellow Belly, Brown and Gold, and Blue and Silver. A selection of leads and swivels will also be required.

Worms and natural shrimp can also be fished with this tackle.

The gillie, where available, usually supplies the landing net. If the angler wishes to bring his own it should be big enough to accommodate a large salmon; or, alternatively, a tailer or gaff – if allowed by the regulations – may be used. It is always well to ascertain in advance the tackle requirements of particular fisheries, as these can vary greatly for both spring salmon and grilse fishing.

Each fishery has its own regulations regarding fishing methods. Some allow all legitimate methods, in which case flies, worms, maggots and spinners are allowed.

SEA TROUT

Sea trout also can be caught by a variety of methods. Worms and spinning are more generally used after a flood. In estuaries or in the sea they are regularly taken spinning, and bait fishing and free lining sand-eel in an estuary can be very effective.

For sea trout, tackle requirements will usually be either light spinning tackle or single-handed fly rods matched to sinking or floating-fly lines.

Fly fishing is by far the most popular method for sea trout. Fly fishing tactics vary from fishery to fishery, and even between daylight and dusk. Daytime fishing can consist of wet or dry fly fishing, and under certain conditions both can be used. With wet flies, floating or sinking lines can be used. Fly fishing can be very successful at dusk and can continue right through the night till dawn.

On the lakes, wet fly is the most common method used, either from a drifting boat or from the banks of smaller lakes. Depending on conditions, two, three or four flies may be fished on the leader. Some of the most useful wet fly patterns are Alexandra, Bibio, Black and Peacock Spider, Black Pennell, Black Widow, Blae and Black, Bloody Butcher, Butcher, Blue Bottle, Blue Zulu, Bog Fly, Claret Bumble, Claret and Mallard, Claret Murrough, Connemara Black, Daddy Long-Legs, Green Peter, Delphi, Donegal Blue, Duckfly, Fiery Brown, Rogan's Gadget, Gold and Claret, Invicta, Jacob's Ladder, Kill-Devil Spider, Kingfisher Butcher, Kingsmill, Bruiser, Claret Bumble, Fiery Brown Bumble, Golden Olive Bumble, Magenta Bumble, Peter Ross, Silver Doctor, Silver Invicta, Thunder and Lightning, Wickham's Fancy, and Zulu. The most useful sizes are 8, 10, and 12.

Dapping for sea trout on lakes is another good method. The equipment needed for this form of fishing is a long, light rod (about 16 feet), and a reel filled with monofilament or fine backing line to which is attached about 4 feet of light synthetic blow line or floss. A 4.5 foot leader is attached to the floss. If natural insects are used, a box or other container will be required to store them. The most common natural insects used are crane fly (daddy long-legs) and grasshoppers. Artificial Daddys, Green Peters, Murroughs and even Mayflies can also be used.

BROWN TROUT

Lake fishing for brown trout falls into five distinct categories: wet fly, dry fly, nymph, dapping, and trolling.

For fly fishing, the rod used should have an easy action and can vary in length from 9 to 12 feet. A floating or sinking line may be used, depending on the fishing conditions.

Wet fly fishing can be practised from the bank or from a boat. It consists of casting a team of two, three or four flies onto the water and retrieving them under the surface.

The choice of flies is dictated by the feeding pattern of the trout at a particular time, and on the angler's preferences. Traditional wet flies are suggestive of trout food, and thousands of trout are caught on them every season. The list given for sea trout could easily be used for brown trout, with a few additional patterns added, such as the March Brown, Sooty Olive, and various Mayfly patterns.

The dry fly can be used when trout are taking their food off the surface. Trout feed on adult midges, the duns and spinners of olives and mayflies, black gnats, sedges, and terrestrial flies. Dry fly fishing calls for a high standard of skill in fly casting and boat handling and in hooking and playing trout. The artificial fly being used should match the natural fly that is being imitated, and it should be treated with a good fly flotant well before being used so that the flotant has plenty of time to dry and waterproof the hackle and wings and body of the artificial.

Nymph fishing is most effective during hatches of chironomids. It works both in a ripple and in calm water, and the secret of success is finding an area of the lake with trout feeding at the surface and presenting nymph or pupa patterns close in size and colour to those the trout are feeding on.

Dapping is one of the oldest methods of fishing the mayfly hatch on a lake. The equipment required is described in the sea trout section. It is also effective for fishing terrestrials on a lake in August and September. The most commonly used insects at this time are crane flies and grasshoppers, but bushy artificial flies such as Green Peters and Murroughs, and other purpose-tied dapping flies, can also be used.

The large ferox trout are invariably caught by trolling, which is also used early in the season for ordinary trout. Spring trolling is generally done over the shallows, whereas trolling for large trout takes place over deeper water and later in the season. It is probably true to say that trolling can be effective at various depths from 6 to 30 feet with the bait or spoon being fished about 2 feet off the lake bottom.

Brown trout rivers vary greatly in character and fall into a number of categories, depending on the underlying rock formation. The most important category of all from a trout fisher's point of view is the limestone river or stream, that is, one with a high alkalinity. These rivers and streams provide wet fly fishing and dry fly fishing. Wet flies are generally cast across and down the river; dry flies are cast upstream to imitate the natural insects hatching at a particular time. Trout can easily weigh up to 3 lb on a limestone river, and the average in some of these rivers will be as high as 1 lb or more.

Fly hatches are quite prolific on limestone rivers and provide a valuable source of food for trout. They also provide the key to the information an angler requires to catch these trout on fly. Some of these flies have different stages of development, such as nymph, dun, and spinner, and to be successful the angler has to be acquainted with them and know the matching artificials. The most commonly found flies on Irish rivers are *Baetis rhodani*, *Baetis tenax*, *Baetis tumilus*, *Simulium* spp., *Procloeon rufulum*, *Centroptilum luteolum*, *Ephemerella ignita*, *Ephemerella notata*, *Ephemera danica*, *Chironomidae*, *Caddis* spp., *Simulium* spp., and various terrestrial flies, the most common of which are *Bibio marci* and *Bibio johannis*.

Daytime fishing can be with the nymph, wet fly, or dry fly. It is most often practised from March to late May and during September. Evening fishing is likely to give best results from early June to the end of July.

Fly rods for river fishing are very much a matter of the angler's personal choice, but 8.5 feet is a good average length. The fly line may be double-tapered and the reel big enough to hold the line and about 75 yards of backing line. Tapered leaders are best for dry fly fishing, and the tip should be just strong enough to land the average river trout – usually 2.5 to 4 lb.

■ ENVIRONMENTAL CHANGES

Freshwater river systems throughout the western world are coming under increasing pressure from industrial and agricultural developments. Ireland is no exception. Some damage has been done in the past by arterial drainage and pollution. However, with recent legislation, improved planning, and increased co-operation between the fisheries boards and the appropriate authorities, significant advances have been made in preventing further damage to our fisheries. Indeed, several fisheries that were severely threatened a few years ago are now re-established and have every appearance of providing top-class fishing for years to come. 'Eutrophication' or enrichment of some systems, caused principally by land fertilisation, can still create excessive plant growth in some slow-flowing rivers, making angling difficult, particularly in June and July.

■ SERVICES

A range of services is generally on offer by fishery owners and operators who service tourist anglers. On lakes these services usually take the form of boats for hire, boats and outboard motors for hire, or boats, outboard motors and gillies for hire. On rivers the services generally take the form of gillies for hire. In some instances it is possible either in fishing-tackle shops or at certain private fisheries to hire fishing tackle and wet-weather clothing. Enquiries about all such services should be made in advance.

THE WATERSIDE CODE OF BEHAVIOUR FOR FISHERMEN

◆ Leave no litter. Gather up the plastic bags, the fishing line, and the bait bags, and bring them home.
◆ Never cross lands that are not signposted and that have no fishing structures.
◆ When in doubt, ask permission to cross lands.
◆ Do not drive cars into fields.
◆ Do not cross meadows. Always walk along the waterside.
◆ Close all gates, and light no fires.
◆ Respect the landowner's property.

Special Notes
◆ Look out – look up! Do not fish near overhead electricity wires.
◆ In the interests of disease prevention, visiting anglers are advised to disinfect their nets, waders etc. before using them on Irish waters.

■ SPECIMEN AND RECORD FISH

The Irish Specimen Fish Committee consists of representatives of the various angling federations, Government departments and official organisations with an interest in angling. Its objective is to verify, record and publicise the capture on rod and line of record and 'specimen' fish in Irish waters. A list of specimen fish is published annually and is available from the honorary secretary of the Irish Specimen Fish Committee at the Central Fisheries Board, Glasnevin, Dublin 9. Only fish that can be fully vouched for as to weight and species can be accepted.

Specimen awards are presented annually, usually at functions in Dublin and Belfast. Claim forms are available from the committee or from local clubs and tackle shops. The following is a schedule of record and specimen weights.

FRESHWATER SPECIES

SPECIES	WEIGHT LBS. OZ	DATE OF CAPTURE	PLACE OF CAPTURE	CAPTOR
Salmon	57 0	1874	River Suir	M. Maher
Sea Trout	16 6	29.10.1983	Shimna River, Co. Down	Thomas McManus
Brown Trout (River)	20 0	22.2.1957	River Shannon, Corbally	Major Hugh Place
Brown Trout (Lake)	26 2	15.7.1894	Lough Ennel	Wm Mears
Bream	11 12	1882	River Blackwater (Monaghan)	A. Pike
Carp	26 2	28.5.1989	The Lough, Cork	Kieron V. Bend
Dace	1 2	8.8.1966	River Blackwater Cappoquin	John T. Henry
Perch	5 8	1946	Lough Erne	S. Drum
Pike (River)	42 0	22.3.1964	River Barrow	M. Watkins
Pike (Lake)	38 9	15.12.1991	Monaghan	Jim Doyle
Roach	2 13½	11.8.1970	River Blackwater, Cappoquin	Lawrie Robinson
Rudd	3 4	27.5.1991	Annaghmore Lough	Steve Wilks
Rudd/Bream Hybrid	6 4	5.3.1990	Monalty Lake	Peter Walsh
Roach/Bream Hybrid	2.06 kg	2.7.1989	Drumreask L.	Philip Arthur
Tench	7 13¼	25.5.1971	River Shannon, Lanesboro	Raymond Webb
River Eel	6 15	12.6.1979	L. Droumenisa, Bantry	J. Murnane

SCHEDULE OF SPECIMEN WEIGHTS (REVISED)

FRESHWATER FISH	IRISH RECORD LBS OZ		SPECIMEN WEIGHT LBS KG	
Salmon *(Salmo salar)*	57	0	20	9.072
Sea Trout *(Salmo trutta)*	16	6	6	2.721
Brown Trout *(Salmo trutta) (River)*	20	0	5	2.268
Brown Trout *(Salmo trutta) (Lake)*	26	2	10	4.536
Slob Trout *(Salmo trutta)*	–	–	10	4.536
Bream *(Abramis brama)*	11	12	7½	3.402
Carp *(Cyprinus carpio)*	26	2	10	4.536

Dace (Leuciscus leuciscus)	1	2		1	.454
Perch (Perca fluviatilis)	5	8		3	1.361
Pike (Esox lucius) (Lake)	38	9		30	13.608
Pike (Esox lucius) (River)	42	0		20	9.072
Roach (Rutilus rutilus)	2	13½		2	.907
Rudd (Scardinius erythrophthalmus)	3	1		2¼	1.021
Rudd/Bream hybrid	6	4		3	1.361
Roach/Bream hybrid	2.065 kg			3	1.361
Tench (Tinca tinca)	7	13¼		6	2.721
Eel (Anguilla anguilla)	6	15		3	1.361

USEFUL ADDRESSES

Department of the Marine
Fisheries Administration
Leeson Lane
Dublin 2
Telephone (01) 6785444
Abbotstown Laboratories
Telephone (01) 210111

Central Fisheries Board
Balnagowan House
Mobhi Boreen
Glasnevin
Dublin 9
Telephone (01) 379206/7/8/9

Eastern Regional Fisheries Board
Balnagowan House
Mobhi Boreen
Glasnevin
Dublin 9
Telephone (01) 379209

Southern Regional Fisheries Board
Anglesea Street
Clonmel, Co. Tipperary
Telephone (052) 23624

South-Western Regional Fisheries Board
1 Neville's Terrace
Masseytown
Macroom, Co. Cork
Telephone (026) 41221/2

Shannon Regional Fisheries Board
Thomond Weir
Limerick
Telephone (061) 455171

Western Regional Fisheries Board
Weir Lodge
Earl's Island
Galway
Telephone (091) 63118/9/0

North-Western Regional Fisheries Board
Ardnaree House
Abbey Street
Ballina, Co. Mayo
Telephone (096) 22623

Northern Regional Fisheries Board
Station Road
Ballyshannon, Co. Donegal
Telephone (072) 51435

Irish Specimen Fish Committee
Balnagowan House
Mobhi Boreen
Glasnevin
Dublin 9
Telephone (01) 379206

Federation of Irish Salmon and Sea Trout Anglers
Jim Maxwell
Dunscollub
Leap, Co. Cork
Telephone (028) 33266

Trout Angling Federation of Ireland
Vinnie O'Reilly
Headford, Co. Galway
Telephone (093) 35499

Irish Trout Fly Fishing Association
J. J. McNally
Cullies, Co. Cavan
Telephone (049) 31626

National Anglers' Representative Association
Paddy Byrne
21 College Park
Droichead Nua, Co. Kildare
Telephone (045) 33068

Bord Fáilte
Baggot Street Bridge
Dublin 2
Telephone (01) 6765871

Bord Fáilte Angling Representative
Paul Harris
47 The Crescent
Brinklow, Warwickshire CU23 0LG
England
Telephone (0786) 833203

■ SEQUENCE OF THIS GUIDE

This guide follows a geographical sequence, starting in the north-east and moving south, then west, and finally northwards, using river systems as units of reference. The guide is divided into chapters representing the fisheries regions, then into districts and river systems. See note on page 2 regarding symbols.

FISHERIES BOARDS AND DISTRICTS

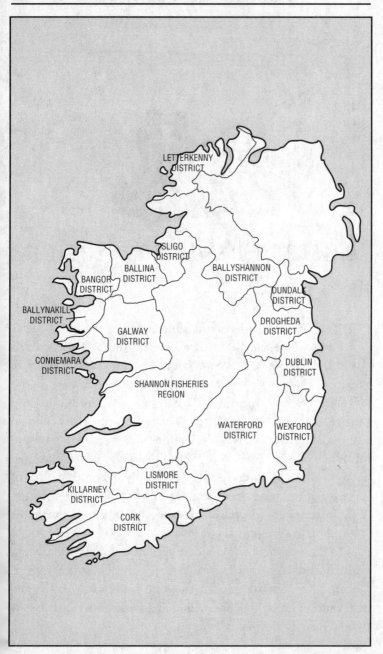

Eastern Fisheries Region

The Eastern Fisheries Region extends from the River Blackwater, which forms the border with Northern Ireland, along the east coast to the point of Kiln Bay, Co. Wexford. The principal game fisheries in this region are on the larger rivers entering the Irish Sea, such as the Boyne, the Liffey, and the Slaney. Although the region has few natural trout lakes, many waters are maintained as fisheries by the introduction of catchable brown trout, largely as a result of the demand for angling exceeding the supply. About one-fifth of the sixty or so brown trout angling clubs in the Eastern Region have introduced restrictions on membership as a means of controlling the pressure on our waters.

The Eastern Region is divided into the Dundalk, Drogheda, Dublin and Wexford Districts, with the headquarters in Dublin. Anglers are served through a network of licence distributors throughout the region and by fisheries board staff located near all the major fisheries.

The Dundalk Fisheries District comprises parts of Cos. Louth, Cavan, and Monaghan, together with as much of the River Blackwater and its tributaries as lie within Co. Monaghan.

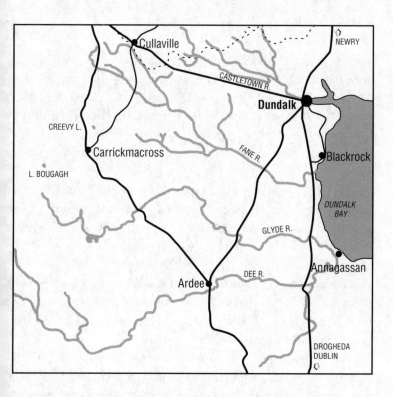

CASTLETOWN RIVER
Open Season
Salmon and sea trout: 1 February to 30 September;
brown trout: 1 March to 30 September.
The Castletown River flows into the head of Dundalk Bay. This system holds wild brown trout, sea trout, and salmon, and is also stocked with brown trout. There is a five-mile stretch of brown trout fishing here, mainly to wet fly in April. The sea trout fishing can be good from late July to the end of

September. The salmon run in early July and from then to the end of the season. For information on the fishing or on day tickets, contact:

◆ *Mr John Dollard*, 23 Parnell Park, Dundalk, Co. Louth.

FANE RIVER
Open Season
Salmon and sea trout: 1 February to 12 October;
brown trout: 1 March to 30 September.

The Fane River enters the sea at Blackrock, Co. Louth. The chief tributaries of interest to the game fisher are the Clarebane, Mullaghduff, Frankfort and Drumleak Rivers. All these tributaries are brown trout fisheries, and the fishing is free.

The river gets a good run of late summer and autumn salmon, and the distance they make upstream during the angling season depends entirely on water levels. The river also gets a run of sea trout and finnock, which enter the river in July and August.

There is brown trout fishing on the Fane at various points from Cullaville all the way downstream to within a mile of Fane Valley Bridge. The quality of the fishing varies, and the typical size fluctuates from 0.5 to 0.75 lb.

The brown trout, salmon and sea trout fishing is nearly all tightly controlled, either by the riparian owners or angling clubs and associations on the river. Enquiries about fishing and club membership should be made to:

◆ *Dundalk Salmon Anglers' Association:* Mr Patrick Wehrly, Jenkinstown, Co. Louth
◆ *Dundalk Brown Trout Anglers' Association:* Mr John Dollard, 23 Parnell Park, Dundalk, Co. Louth
◆ *The Village Anglers' Club, Inishkeen:* Mr Arthur Campbell, Monavallet, Co. Louth.

In certain instances, applications to fish can be made to individual riparian owners.

MILLTOWN LOUGH

Open Season

1 March to 30 September.

Milltown Lough is a 100 acre lake about two miles north of Castleblayney. It is heavily stocked by Castleblayney and District Anglers' Association with brown trout. The average size of the trout is 1 lb.

Enquiries about club membership and day tickets can be made to:

◆ *Mascot Shop*, Main Street, Castleblayney, Co. Monaghan.

DRUMGANNY AND TREAGH LAKES

Open Season

1 May to 30 September.

These two small lakes are stocked with trout by the Village Anglers' Club, Inishkeen, Co. Monaghan. Day tickets are available, and enquiries should be made to:

◆ *Mr Arthur Campbell*, Monavallet, Co. Louth.

MONAGHAN BLACKWATER

Open Season

1 March to 30 September

The Monaghan Blackwater rises in Co. Tyrone and flows through Co. Monaghan back to the border at Middletown. This river has undergone an arterial drainage scheme; a rehabilitation programme is planned, and when it is completed the river should revert to being a good trout stream.

There is an angling club with interest on the river; contact the secretary:

◆ *Mr G. Hughes*, Killygowan, Monaghan.

GLYDE RIVER

Open Season

Salmon and sea trout: 1 February to 20 August;
brown trout: 14 February to 20 August.

The Glyde River rises on the Monaghan-Cavan border and joins the Dee River at Annagassan, Co. Louth. Its main tributaries are the Tubbermannin, the Killanny and the Lagan Rivers. These tributaries are mainly regarded as brown trout fisheries.

The whole system underwent one of the first arterial drainage schemes in the country. The main channel was deepened considerably, and the banks are impossibly high in places. These banks have now become overgrown and are difficult to fish, with overhanging branches in many places.

The Glyde River gets a small run of spring salmon, and these are generally taken between February and May.

The sea trout stocks have declined, and few sea trout now run the river. The river is said to hold good stocks of brown trout in some areas, and the average size is about 1 lb.

Much of the fishing is private or subject to permission from riparian owners. There is salmon fishing available at Castlebellingham; apply to:

◆ *The Manager, Bellingham Castle Hotel,* Castlebellingham, Co. Louth.

The Dee and Glyde Development Association has a stretch of the lower river, and application for membership should be made to:

◆ *Mr Padge Reilly,* Cappocksgreen, Ardee, Co. Louth.

CREEVY LAKE
Open Season
Brown trout: 1 April to 30 September.

This small lake, two miles north of Carrickmacross, is managed as a 'put and take' fishery. It is fished from the bank only, and all legitimate fishing methods are allowed. Enquiries about fishing should be made to:

◆ *Mr Gordon Sweetnam,* Main Street, Carrickmacross, Co. Monaghan; telephone (042) 61219
◆ *Carrickmacross Sports Shop,* Main Street, Carrickmacross, Co. Monaghan.

LOUGH BOUGAGH

Open Season

Brown trout: 1 March to 30 September.

This is a small lake stocked with brown trout and rainbow trout by Carrickmacross Anglers' Club. It lies about three miles from Carrickmacross on the Kingscourt road. It is bank fishing only. Enquiries about fishing and permits should be made to:

- ◆ *Mr Gordon Sweetnam*, Main Street, Carrickmacross, Co. Monaghan
- ◆ *Carrickmacross Sports Shop*, Main Street, Carrickmacross, Co. Monaghan.

EMY LOUGH

Open Season

Brown trout: 1 March to 30 September.

Emy Lough is situated near Emyvale, Co. Monaghan. The lake is developed by the Eastern Regional Fisheries Board as a brown trout fishery. It holds a fair stock of wild trout and is regularly stocked with takeable brown trout. Boats are available for hire from:

- ◆ *Mr Pat McMahon*, Emy Lough, Emyvale, Co. Monaghan; telephone (047) 87598.

Anglers fishing the lough should be in possession of a regional fisheries board trout angling permit.

DEE RIVER

Open Season

Salmon and sea trout: 1 February to 30 September;
brown trout: 14 February to 30 September.

The Dee River enters Dundalk Bay at Annagassan, where it shares a common estuary with the Glyde. It was one of the first rivers in the country to have an arterial drainage scheme, and that scheme has left the banks impossibly high in some places.

At present it is regarded as a good brown trout, sea trout and salmon fishery. The river gets a run of spring salmon, and it is estimated that up to 200 spring fish are taken in a season. The spring salmon fishing is considered to extend upstream from the tide for approximately ten miles to Ardee, and the fishing lasts from February to May. The summer grilse fishing can best be described as patchy.

It is generally agreed that the Dee gets a good run of sea trout from mid-July to August or September. The best of the sea trout fishing is from the tide to a point about one mile above Whitemill Bridge. All legitimate fishing methods are allowed on the river for sea trout fishing.

The Dee holds a big stock of brown trout, and there are a lot of trout averaging from 0.75 lb to 1.5 lb. This brown trout fishing extends all the way from Drumcar upstream almost to Whitewood Lake. The early season fishing is usually to wet flies, and the river is said to have hatches of March browns, dark olives, iron-blues, blue-winged olives, alders, black gnats, mayflies, and various sedges. The evening fishing to sedges, especially in July, is considered to be important.

There are numerous fishery owners on the river, and the fishing is available through riparian owners, private owners, and angling clubs. Salmon and sea trout fishing is available at Willistown Weir; enquiries should be made to:

◆ *Mr Peter Harmon*, Strand Road, Annagassan, Co. Louth
◆ *Mr Peter McGuinness*, Woodenstown, Castlebellingham, Co. Louth.

The Dee and Glyde Development Association has extensive stretches of brown trout, salmon and sea trout fishing on the river. Enquiries about fishing permits and club membership should be made to:

◆ *Mr Padge Reilly*, Cappocksgreen, Ardee, Co. Louth
◆ *Mr Thomas Durigan*, Stickillin, Ardee, Co. Louth.

St Mary's School, Drumcar, Co. Louth, has good spring salmon fishing, and some grilse fishing and sea trout fishing are available. Permits are available from:

◆ *St Mary's School*, Drumcar, Co. Louth; telephone (041) 51211.

The Cappoge fishery is a good sea trout, spring salmon and summer salmon fishery. Information on the fishing is available from:

◆ *Mr Enda O'Callaghan,* Main Street, Ardee, Co. Louth.

Nobber Trout Angling Club has fishing on both banks, from Rockfield Bridge upstream to Whitewood Lake, except for one short stretch. This is a brown trout fishery, and the club encourages fly fishing and spinning only. For information on the fishing apply to:

◆ *Mr Michael O'Reilly,* 6 O'Carolan Park, Nobber, Co. Meath
◆ *Mr Bert Onions,* Main Street, Nobber, Co. Meath.

DROGHEDA DISTRICT

The Drogheda Fisheries District comprises the River Boyne and all its tributaries, the River Nanny, and the Delvin River.

■ RIVER BOYNE SYSTEM

Open Season
Salmon and sea trout: 1 February to 15 September;
brown trout: 15 February to 15 September.
There is a 9 inch (229 mm) statutory size limit for trout.

The River Boyne and its tributaries drain most of Co. Meath. The river has fifteen large tributaries, and at least twelve of these are of interest to the game fisher; these are the Kells Blackwater, Skane River, Tremblestown and Athboy River, Enfield Blackwater, Barora River, Moynalty River, Martry River, Stonyford River, River Deel, Yellow River, Knightsbrook River, and Riverstown River.

The Boyne flows over limestone and has all the fly hatches associated with a limestone river, including mayfly in places and prolific hatches of sedges.

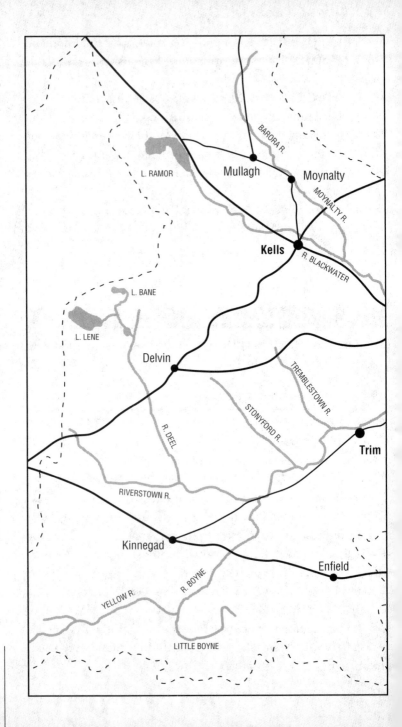

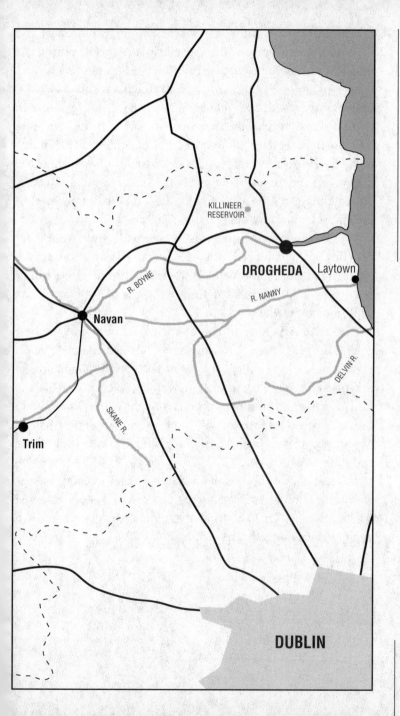

KILLINEER
RESERVOIR

R. BOYNE

DROGHEDA Laytown

R. NANNY

DELVIN R.

Navan

SKANE R.

Trim

DUBLIN

The major part of the river system is characterised by the fact that it underwent an arterial drainage scheme that drastically altered the character of the river's environment, and it now exhibits all the signs of a drained river: high banks, uneven river bed, long canalised stretches, fast run-off in floods, excessive vegetation growth in summer and autumn, and low flow regimes in the tributaries in summer. The fifteen-mile stretch from Navan to Drogheda was untouched by the drainage scheme and retains its original characteristics. A rehabilitation scheme is now in progress on the drained part of the main channel and many of the tributaries.

The Boyne system is one of the premier brown trout river fisheries in the country, with good stocks dispersed along the main channel and on several of the tributaries. It gets a run of sea trout, and the best of this fishing is from just below Oldbridge up to Slane.

The river gets a small run of spring salmon, and the best fishing is from Navan downstream on the main channel and on the last mile of the Kells Blackwater. The spring salmon season is February to late May or early June.

The grilse and summer salmon fishing is mainly confined to the fisheries downstream of Slane, with occasional fish to Navan and further upstream. The grilse season is June to the end of the season.

Almost all the good fishing water both on the main channel and in the tributaries is privately owned and is either reserved by the owners, let to individual anglers, or let or leased to angling clubs or syndicates.

Fisheries on the Main Channel

Drogheda and District Angling Association has a number of fishing stretches leased between Drogheda and Newgrange. This water offers summer salmon, sea trout and brown trout fishing. For information on club membership or day tickets, contact:

◆ *Mr Martin Carolan*, Fairgreen, Drogheda, Co. Louth
◆ *Mr Seán Keenan*, Military Connection, Laurence Street, Drogheda, Co. Louth.

Rossin-Slane Angling Club has a number of fishing stretches leased between Slane and Drogheda. These fisheries offer summer salmon fishing, sea trout and brown trout fishing. For information on club membership and availability of fishing, contact:

◆ *Mr Barry Flood*, 'Waterunder', Drogheda, Co. Louth; telephone (041) 38514.

The Oldbridge fishery is a renowned summer salmon fishery, and it can offer sea trout and brown trout fishing too. For information on the availability of fishing, contact:

◆ *Mr Jack Marry*, Dowth, Co. Louth.

The Ballinacrad fishery is a spring salmon fishery with some summer salmon and brown trout. For information on the fishing, contact:

◆ *Mrs Ita McDonnell*, Dowth, Co. Louth.

The Slane Castle fishery comprises extensive fishing from Beauparc downstream to below Slane Bridge. It holds occasional spring salmon, summer salmon, and some sea trout, and offers the prospect of good brown trout fishing. The fishing is not let at present.

Mr B. G. Dean's fishery offers single-bank fishing on a stretch midway between Slane and Navan. It offers spring salmon and brown trout fishing. For information on the availability of fishing, contact:

◆ *Mr B. G. Dean*, Bonshaw, Navan, Co. Meath.

Navan and District Angling Club has leased several fisheries both upstream and downstream of Navan, giving it nearly six miles of fishing. The best of the spring run is now in April and May. The brown trout stocks are good, but visitors should be aware that the river weeds up badly from midsummer. For information on club membership or day tickets, apply to:

- ◆ *The Sports Den*, Trimgate Street, Navan, Co. Meath; telephone (046) 21130
- ◆ *Mr Michael Connor*, Cill Ard, Abbey Road, Navan, Co. Meath.

Dalgan Angling Club has a stretch close by Dalgan Park College and downstream of Ballinter. It holds occasional spring salmon and has a good stock of brown trout. For information on club membership apply to:

- ◆ *Mr Joseph Lenehan*, Clonardon, Garlow Cross, Navan, Co. Meath
- ◆ *Mr Joseph Kinsella*, Kilcarn, Co. Meath.

Bective Angling Club has various stretches on both banks upstream and downstream of Bective Abbey near Navan. The waters hold occasional spring salmon and brown trout. For information on club membership apply to:

- ◆ *Mr Charles Woods*, Tribley Road, Bective, Navan, Co. Meath; telephone (046) 22936.

Trim, Athboy and District Angling Club has access to various fisheries on the Boyne. The waters hold occasional spring salmon and good stocks of brown trout. For information on club membership, apply to:

- ◆ *Mr Gerard Lee*, Loman Street, Trim, Co. Meath
- ◆ *Mr Liam Henry*, Dunlever, Trim, Co. Meath.

Longwood Angling Club has extensive fishing rights on the Boyne. At various points along this water there are stretches that hold good stocks of brown trout. Further rehabilitation work is planned here. For information on club membership, apply to:

- ◆ *Mr Michael Bird*, Castlerickard, Longwood, Co. Meath.

KELLS BLACKWATER

The Kells Blackwater is one of the major tributaries of the Boyne, joining it at Navan. This is a medium-sized river, which has undergone major arterial drainage works, with the exception of a few stretches in the middle reaches and at the Mollies at Navan. It holds a small number of spring salmon between Kells and Navan. There are fair to good stocks of brown trout at various locations downstream from Lough Ramor all the way to the Boyne.

In some places the banks are very high, and anglers should exercise care, especially along the deeper stretches.

The fishing is virtually all privately owned, and anglers wishing to fish should apply to the angling clubs that have fishing rights.

Kells Angling Club has fishing in the vicinity of Kells and Carnaross, extending upstream towards Lough Ramor. For information on club membership and day tickets, apply to:

◆ *Mr Thomas Murray*, Farrell Street, Kells, Co. Meath.

Kilbride Angling Club is based in Dublin and has fishing in the middle reaches of the river. The club water produces the occasional spring salmon and can give good sport for trout. For information on club membership, apply to the honorary secretary:

◆ *Mr Des Johnston*, 43 Avondale Park, Raheny, Dublin 5.

Navan and District Angling Club has access to extensive fishing on the Blackwater at various points from Navan upstream. The river at Navan produces a few spring salmon, and the rest of the water is best known as a brown trout fishery. For information on club membership, apply to:

◆ *The Sports Den*, Trimgate Street, Navan, Co. Meath;
  telephone (046) 21130
◆ *Mr Michael Connor*, Cill Ard, Abbey Road, Navan,
  Co. Meath.

LOUGH RAMOR

Lough Ramor, near Virginia, Co. Cavan, is a medium-sized lake and holds occasional salmon, together with brown trout and coarse fish. The trout fishing takes place usually at mayfly time, from mid-May to mid-June. There is a boat quay at Virginia, and it is possible to gain access with permission at a hotel on the Virginia–Kells road.

MOYNALTY RIVER

The Moynalty River is a tributary of the Kells Blackwater. It holds good stocks of brown trout, the average size being 8 oz. For information on club membership, apply to:

◆ *Mr Gerard Farrell,* Moynalty, Co. Meath.

BARORA RIVER

The Barora River joins the Moynalty River midway between Mullagh and Moynalty. The banks are very high, just like the Moynalty River, and difficult to fish. It holds a good stock of brown trout to over 1 lb in suitable stretches. Enquiries about fishing and membership of Barora Angling Club should be made to:

◆ *Mr Gerard Farrell,* Moynalty, Co. Meath.

ATHBOY RIVER
TREMBLESTOWN RIVER

These are tributaries of the River Boyne. The Tremblestown River is the extension of the Athboy River, and meets the Boyne a mile upstream of Trim. It holds a big resident stock of trout up to 12 oz.

Fishing is strictly by riparian owners' permission; Trim, Athboy and District Angling Club has access to fishing stretches. For information on this fishing and club membership, apply to:

◆ *Mr Gerard Lee,* Lomond Street, Trim, Co. Meath
◆ *Mr Liam Henry,* Dunlever, Trim, Co. Meath.

STONYFORD RIVER

The Stonyford River joins the Boyne five miles west of Trim. Some rehabilitation following arterial drainage work has been carried out, and fish stocks have recovered well. The average size of the trout is around 10 oz.

Some of the fishing is strictly by permission of the riparian owners. Information about membership of Stonyford Angling Club is available from:

◆ *Mr Thomas Conlon*, 5 Killallon Road, Clonmellon, Co. Westmeath.

RIVER DEEL

The River Deel flows south through the village of Raharney to the Boyne. It holds brown trout to 0.75 lb at various points along its course; in the upper reaches the trout are smaller. Enquiries about membership of the Deel and Boyne Angling Club should be made to:

◆ *Mr Jack Shaw*, Riverdale, Raharney, Co. Westmeath.

RIVERSTOWN RIVER

The Riverstown River is a tributary of the River Deel. It holds fairly plentiful stocks of brown trout to 0.75 lb. The fishing is at its best early in the season. Enquiries about membership of the Deel and Boyne Angling Club should be made to:

◆ *Mr Jack Shaw*, Riverdale, Raharney, Co. Westmeath.

WHITE LAKE
Open Season
Brown trout: 1 May to 30 September.

The White Lake is four miles east of Castlepollard, Co. Westmeath. It is stocked with both rainbow and brown trout. There is a 10 inch (254 mm) size limit, and a bag limit of six trout.

This lake is managed by White Lake Anglers' Association. A permit is required to fish here, and may be obtained from:

◆ *Mr Patrick Farrelly*, 18 Ard na Gréine, Kells, Co. Meath.

LOUGH LENE

Lough Lene is a large, shallow limestone lake that holds a stock of quite large brown trout. There is an angling club associated with the lake, and enquiries about fishing should be made to:

◆ *Mr Thomas Fagan*, Innisfree, Collinstown, Co. Westmeath.

YELLOW RIVER

The Yellow River flows through Co. Offaly to join the Boyne north of Edenderry. It holds a small stock of good trout, and the best fishing is early in the season. Edenderry Anglers' Association claims fishing rights on the river, and enquiries should be made to the honorary secretary:

◆ *Mr Sidney Hopkins*, 66 JKL Street, Edenderry, Co. Offaly.

LITTLE BOYNE

The Little Boyne rises near Carbury, Co. Kildare, and flows to join the Boyne near Edenderry. The banks are extremely high in places because of drainage works. It holds a small stock of good trout. Enquiries about the fishing should be made to the honorary secretary of Edenderry Anglers' Association:

◆ *Mr Sidney Hopkins*, 66 JKL Street, Edenderry, Co. Offaly.

ENFIELD BLACKWATER

The Enfield Blackwater is a rich limestone river that flows north to join the Boyne. In places the banks are very high and difficult to fish. The river holds substantial stocks of brown trout up to 0.75 lb.

Enquiries about membership of Longwood Angling Club and about fishing should be made to the honorary secretary:

◆ *Mr Michael Bird*, Castlerickard, Longwood, Co. Meath.

SKANE RIVER

The Skane River joins the Boyne at Ballinter. It holds a fair stock of trout up to 10 oz.

Enquiries about membership of Dalgan Angling Club should be made to:

◆ *Mr Joseph Lenehan*, Clonardon, Garlow Cross, Navan, Co. Meath
◆ *Mr Joseph Kinsella*, Kilcarn, Co. Meath.

KILLINEER RESERVOIR

Open Season

Brown trout: 15 February to 15 September.

Killineer is a small reservoir to the west of the Drogheda–Dunleer road, two miles from Drogheda, stocked with brown trout. It is fly fishing only, and there is a bag limit of two trout.

Permission to fish is available from:

◆ *Mr Seán Keenan*, Military Connection, Laurence Street, Drogheda, Co. Louth
◆ *Mr Martin Carolan*, Fairgreen, Drogheda, Co. Louth.

RIVER NANNY
Open Season
Sea trout: 12 February to 15 September;
brown trout: 15 February to 15 September.
The River Nanny flows east to the sea at Laytown, Co. Meath. It holds a small stock of wild trout and is stocked annually with brown trout. It also gets a small run of sea trout. The peak of the trout fishing is in May and June.

There are three angling clubs on the river. Membership is limited. Information on the fishing is available from:
◆ *Duleek Angling Club:* Nichola's Newsagent, Main Street, Duleek, Co. Meath
◆ *Drogheda Angling Club:* Mr Seán Keenan, Military Connection, Laurence Street, Drogheda, Co. Louth.

DELVIN RIVER
Open Season
Sea trout: 12 February to 15 September; *brown trout:* 5 February to 15 September.
This little river enters the sea north of Balbriggan and is stocked annually with brown trout. This is a small, narrow river, quite overgrown and difficult to fish with fly. It gets a small run of sea trout from July onwards.

Day tickets for the waters of Gormanston and District Angling Club are available at:
◆ *The Sail Inn,* North Road, Balbriggan, Co. Dublin
◆ *Donnelly Electric,* Shopping Centre, Balbriggan, Co. Dublin.

The Dublin Fisheries District comprises Co. Dublin and parts of Cos. Wicklow, Meath, and Kildare, and embraces all rivers flowing into the sea between Skerries and Wicklow Head. The use of night lines is prohibited in the district, and there is an 8 inch (203 mm) size limit for brown trout.

The principal waters are the Broad Meadow, Tolka, Liffey, Dodder, Dargle, and Vartry.

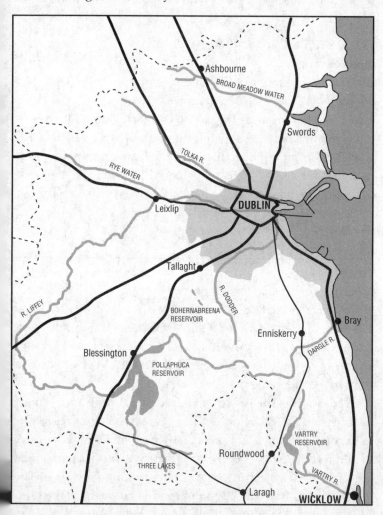

BROAD MEADOW WATER

Open Season

Sea trout: 1 February to 12 October;

brown trout: 1 March to 30 September.

The Broad Meadow Water runs off very quickly because of a drainage scheme, and holds only occasional sea trout in its lower reaches. The secretary of the Broad Meadow Angling Club is:

◆ *Mr Kenneth Rundle*, 119 Orlynn Park, Lusk, Co. Dublin.

TOLKA RIVER

Open Season

Sea trout: 1 February to 12 October;

brown trout: 1 March to 30 September.

The Tolka River enters the sea at Clontarf, Dublin. It rises in open country but flows mainly through urban areas. It holds some wild trout but is drained, polluted, and eutrophic, and is really a 'put and take' fishery stocked by the Tolka Anglers' Club. Information on fishing is available from the secretary:

◆ *Mr Thomas Foley*, 34 Virginia Park, Dublin 11.

■ RIVER LIFFEY SYSTEM

Open Season

Salmon and sea trout: 1 January to 30 September;

brown trout: 1 March to 30 September.

The River Liffey flows for 82 miles before entering the sea at Dublin Bay. It flows over different geologies, and fishery scientists have observed some of the fastest-growing brown trout in Ireland in the river at Lucan.

A dam has been constructed at Pollaphuca, near Blessington, Co. Wicklow, to form one of the largest reservoirs in Europe, and there is a second reservoir and dam at Leixlip. Water abstraction is a problem on the river; furthermore, there are three hydro-electric power stations along its course. The lower reaches from the city to beyond Leixlip tend to be deep and sluggish. The river takes on a more lively character beyond Celbridge. Upstream of Straffan to Ballymore Eustace a lot of bank clearance and building of stiles has been carried out by the Eastern Regional Fisheries Board.

Spring salmon can be taken from early January, and grilse run from June. July is a peak month. Most of the spring fish are taken at Islandbridge, Dublin. The grilse are mainly taken up near Leixlip.

The river gets a small run of sea trout. The best of the fishing is in July at the Dublin and District Salmon and Trout Anglers' water immediately above and below Islandbridge.

Fishing is prohibited between Lucan Weir and the bridge below it, and between Leixlip Dam and the confluence of the Liffey and the Rye Water.

Brown trout are found from Islandbridge upstream, but the best of the brown trout fishing is upstream of Leixlip and all the way to Ballymore Eustace. The average weight of the trout at Clane is about 10 oz. Anglers believe that the weight of the trout increases the further one goes downstream. The Liffey has all the usual fly hatches associated with a limestone river.

Most of the fishing on the Liffey system is controlled by clubs or private interests. There is free fishing at the Memorial Park at Islandbridge and on the left bank immediately upstream of Leixlip Bridge to the Rye Water confluence. Dublin and District Salmon and Trout Anglers' Association has extensive fishing water on the river at Islandbridge and other places. Membership is open and may be obtained at:

◆ *Rory's Fishing Tackle*, 17A Temple Bar, Dublin 2.

Chapelizod Anglers' Association has fishing on the river at Chapelizod; the honorary secretary is:

◆ *Mr Paul Devereux*, 23 St Lawrence's Road, Dublin 20.

Lucan Anglers' Association has fishing on the river at Lucan; the honorary secretary is:

◆ *Mr Alan Byrne*, 46 Newtown, Leixlip, Co. Dublin.

Kilbride Anglers' Club has fishing on the upper Liffey from the Sally Gap down to below Ballysmuttan Bridge. The honorary secretary is:

◆ *Mr Des Johnston*, 43 Avondale Park, Raheny, Dublin 5.

Ballymore Eustace Anglers' Club has about four-and-a-half miles of fishing on the river at Ballymore Eustace. The honorary secretary is:

◆ *Mr Thomas Deegan*, 928 Briencan, Ballymore Eustace, Co. Kildare.

Kilcullen Anglers' Association has fishing on the river at Kilcullen for wild and stocked brown trout. Enquiries about fishing should be made to:

◆ *Mr E. Delahunt*, Bishop Rogan Park, Kilcullen, Co. Kildare.

North Kildare Trout and Salmon Anglers' Association has fishing on the river from Kilcullen all the way down to Millicent Bridge. This fishing is for both wild and stocked brown trout. Enquiries about the fishing should be made to:

◆ *Mr Patrick Byrne*, 21 College Park, Droichead Nua, Co. Kildare.

Clane Anglers' Association has fishing on the river upstream of Straffan. Enquiries about fishing should be made to:

◆ *Mr Anthony Doherty*, Raheen, Rathcoffey, Naas, Co. Kildare.

Dublin Trout Anglers' Association has trout fishing on the river downstream of Straffan House. Enquiries about membership and day tickets should be addressed to:

◆ *Mr Dan O'Brien*, New Road, Blackhall, Clane, Co. Kildare
◆ *Mr Sylvester Gallagher*, Reeves, Straffan, Co. Kildare.

RYE WATER

The Rye Water joins the Liffey at Leixlip. It has the ability to grow big brown trout. Much of the fishing is private, but where the river flows through housing estates, access can be gained to the water's edge from the linear park alongside. The banks are well shaded, and this river has all the fly hatches one associates with a rich limestone river, excluding mayfly.

Leixlip Anglers' Association controls fishing downstream of Carton Estate to the junction with the River Liffey. For information, contact:

◆ *Mr Aidan Crean*, Westmantown Lodge, Lucan, Co. Dublin.

POLLAPHUCA RESERVOIR
Open Season
Brown trout: 1 March to 30 September.

This is the largest reservoir in Ireland, and is over six miles long. It holds a small stock of natural trout and is heavily dependent on artificial stocking. The average size of the trout is about 0.75 lb. There are good seasonal hatches of duckfly, buzzers, and sedges, and the water sometimes gets a big fall of terrestrial flies during the summer.

Anglers may put a boat on the water after obtaining a boat permit and a number from the ESB. Permission to fish the reservoir may be obtained from:

◆ *Electricity Supply Board*, 13 Lower Fitzwilliam Street, Dublin 2
◆ *Miley's Bar*, Main Street, Blessington, Co. Wicklow.

Day tickets and season tickets are available from tackle shops in Dublin.

RIVER DODDER
Open Season
Brown trout: 17 March to 30 September.

The Dodder is a remarkable river in that it flows through the city of Dublin and yet is worth fishing for brown trout and sea trout. In all there are about seven or eight miles of brown trout fishing from Firhouse down to Ballsbridge. The sea trout can give quite good fishing in July, August, and September. Access is reasonably good, with public parklands on both banks.

The Dodder Anglers' Club has a special interest in the river, and has a policy of making visitors welcome for a day's fishing. Membership is open to all, and cards are available at:

◆ *The Kiosk*, Orwell Bridge, Ballsbridge, Dublin 4

♦ *Rory's Fishing Tackle*, 17A Temple Bar, Dublin 2
♦ *Watts Brothers Ltd*, 18 Upper Ormond Quay, Dublin 7
and most fishing tackle shops on the south side of the city and in Tallaght.

BOHERNABREENA RESERVOIRS
Open Season
Brown trout: 1 March to 30 September.
The Bohernabreena Reservoirs are south of Tallaght, Co. Dublin, and access to them is off the Firhouse–Brittas road beyond the Fort Bridge. The fishing on both reservoirs is by fly only, and this is by ministerial order. The lower reservoir is small, and the average size of the trout here is just over 0.5 lb. The upper reservoir is much bigger and nearly a mile long. The same angling regulations apply. Here the trout are much smaller but much more plentiful and come at about four to the pound.

Permission to fish the reservoir may be obtained from:
♦ *Waterworks Department*, 68 Marrowbone Lane, Dublin 8; telephone (01) 543444, ext. 318 or 319.

Members of Dublin Trout Anglers' Association and the Dodder Anglers' Association may fish the reservoirs, and membership cards of these associations may be purchased in most Dublin fishing tackle shops. Access to the reservoirs cannot be obtained until the gatekeeper inspects the angler's fishing permit.

VARTRY RESERVOIRS
Open Season
Brown trout: 1 March to 30 September.
Dublin City Council issues tickets for bank fishing on the south reservoir; boat fishing is let to Wicklow Anglers' Association. These reservoirs hold brown trout. The trout in the upper reservoir are wild; trout stocks in the lower reservoir are augmented by occasionally stocking with small trout that become naturalised. The average size of the trout here is 0.75 lb.

Permission to fish the reservoirs may be obtained from:

◆ *Waterworks Department*, 68 Marrowbone Lane, Dublin 8; telephone (01) 543444, ext. 318 or 319.

DARGLE RIVER
Open Season
Salmon: 1 February to 30 September; *sea trout:* 1 February to 12 October; *brown trout:* 1 March to 30 September.

The Dargle River flows east through Enniskerry to enter the sea at Bray. It is one of Ireland's prime sea trout rivers. The big sea trout come in May, and runs of smaller fish arrive in June, July, and August.

The river also gets a good run of salmon. The peak of the spring run is at the end of April and in early May. The grilse fishing can be good in a wet season, and the best of the fishing is said to be in the month of August.

Mr Hugh Duff has a private fishery on the river and offers season tickets and day tickets; enquiries should be made to:

◆ *Mr Hugh Duff*, Tinnehinch House, Enniskerry, Co. Wicklow; telephone (01) 2868652.

The Dargle Anglers' Club has extensive fishing on the river. Membership application forms are available from:

◆ *Mr Alyn Turne*, 47 Ardmore Park, Bray, Co. Wicklow
◆ *Jet Filling Station*, Dublin Road, Bray, Co. Wicklow.

VARTRY RIVER
Open Season
Sea trout: 1 February to 12 October;
salmon: 1 February to 30 September.

The Vartry River joins the sea at Broad Lough, just north of Wicklow. It is primarily a sea trout river, and the trout run late. The only fishing available on the river is from the Vartry Angling Club, and club membership is limited. Details are available from:

◆ *Mr Ray Dineen*, Tara House, Redcross, Co. Wicklow; telephone (0404) 41645.

The Wexford Fisheries District comprises parts of Cos. Wexford, Wicklow, and Carlow, and embraces all rivers flowing into the sea between Wicklow Head and Kiln Bay, Co. Wexford. The principal rivers are the Slaney, the Owenavorragh, and the Avoca.

■ AVOCA RIVER SYSTEM

Open Season
Salmon, sea trout, and brown trout: 15 March to 30 September.
The Avoca River has been ruined by the run-off from disused copper mines, and for the last seven miles it is virtually a dead river.

AVONMORE RIVER
The Avonmore River flows through the villages of Laragh and Rathdrum to join the Avoca River. It holds big stocks of small brown trout. Some of the best fishing is said to be in Avondale Forest Park downstream of Rathdrum. The best of the fishing is usually after a flood.

Rathdrum Angling Club is active on the river, and the secretary is:
◆ *Mr Christopher Bolton*, 5 Ballinderry Road, Rathdrum, Co. Wicklow.

AVONBEG RIVER
The Avonbeg River joins the Avonmore upstream of Avoca. It holds big stocks of small brown trout.

AUGHRIM RIVER
The Aughrim River joins the Avoca River downstream of Wooden Bridge. It is a big river by Wicklow standards, with deep, dangerous pools. The average size of the trout is about 0.5 lb,

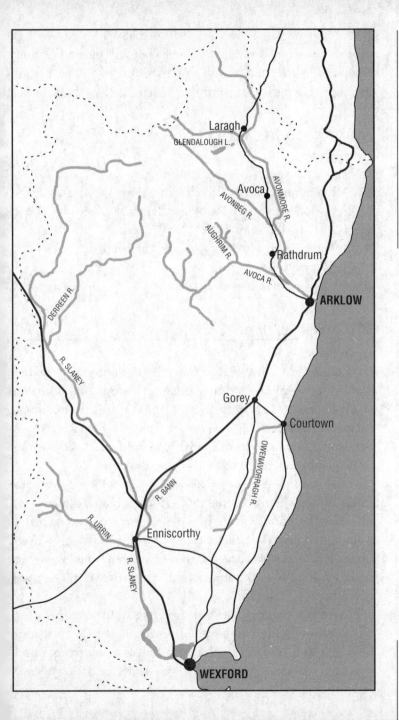

Laragh
GLENDALOUGH L.
Avoca
AVONBEG R.
AVONMORE R.
AUGHRIM R.
Rathdrum
AVOCA R.
ARKLOW
DERREEN R.
R. SLANEY
Gorey
Courtown
OWENAVORRAGH R.
R. BANN
R. URRIN
Enniscorthy
R. SLANEY
WEXFORD

49

with occasional fish up to 0.75 lb or better. This river has probably the most prolific fly hatches of any of the Wicklow rivers, especially olives and sedges. Some of the best trout fishing is to sedges on summer evenings.

GLENDALOUGH LAKES
Open Season
Brown trout: 1 March to 30 September.
The Glendalough Lakes hold small brown trout. The lower lough is stocked with brown trout annually. Enquiries about the fishing should be made to:
◆ *Mr Frank Byrne,* 110 Bellview Park, Greystones,
   Co. Wicklow.

■ RIVER SLANEY SYSTEM

Open Season
Salmon and sea trout: 26 February to 15 September for the Slaney and tributaries downstream of its junction with the Bann River, 26 February to 31 August for the remainder, including the Bann River; *brown trout:* 26 February to 16 September downstream of Enniscorthy Bridge, 26 February to 30 September upstream of Enniscorthy Bridge.

The Slaney rises in Co. Wicklow and flows south to Enniscorthy, where it is tidal to Wexford. It is a medium-sized, fast-flowing river, and is one of Ireland's premier spring salmon fisheries. The peak of the spring salmon fishing is from opening day on 26 February to the end of March, and there can be fair fishing in April and indeed into early May. The river gets a poor run of grilse.

There is a by-law that limits angling to fly only between Ballycarney Bridge and Achade Bridge after 1 April and between Enniscorthy Bridge and Ballycarney Bridge and upstream of Achade Bridge after 1 May. Gaffs are not permitted.

The majority of the fishing is held by private owners. A number of angling associations have stretches on the river, and they offer day tickets. For information on the private fisheries, contact the honorary secretary of the Slaney Rod Anglers' Association:

◆ *Mr John O'Gorman,* Knocknagan House, Tullow, Co. Carlow.

The following clubs offer day tickets on their fisheries:

◆ *Tullow Salmon and Trout Anglers' Association:* Mr Joe O'Neill, Carlow Road, Tullow, Co. Carlow

◆ *Enniscorthy and District Anglers' Association:* Mr Joe Cash, Tomnalosset, Enniscorthy, Co. Wexford

◆ *Salsboro Angling Club:* Mr Patrick Lacey, Mile House Road, Armstrong's Range, Enniscorthy, Co. Wexford

◆ *Island Angling Club:* Mr William Cash, 6 Bellefield Terrace, Enniscorthy, Co. Wexford.

The stretch downstream of the bridge in Enniscorthy offers free fishing for both salmon and sea trout.

BANN RIVER

The Bann River is a tributary of the Slaney. It is regarded primarily as a sea trout fishery, and the best of the fishing is from Camolin downstream. By statutory regulation, fishing is fly only after 1 May from the Railway Bridge downstream. There is an angling club on the water; contact:

◆ *Mr Anthony Breen,* Milltown, Ferns, Co. Wexford.

DERREEN RIVER

The Derreen River is regarded primarily as a trout stream, and the brown trout average about 0.5 lb. The best of the fishing is in March, April, May, and June. For information on the fishing in the Hacketstown area, contact:

◆ *Mr Dermot Doyle,* 26 Mountain View, Hacketstown, Co. Carlow.

RIVER URRIN

The River Urrin joins the Slaney south of Enniscorthy. It is regarded primarily as a sea trout fishery, and the sea trout run from the first week in July. There is one angling club on the river, and enquiries about day tickets should be made to:

◆ *Mr John Horgan,* Ballybrannish, Enniscorthy, Co. Wexford.

OWENAVORRAGH RIVER

Open Season

All species: 15 March to 30 September.

This river is eighteen miles long and is relatively featureless and slow-flowing. It holds some salmon after the first flood in August, and gets a good run of sea trout. The best of the sea trout fishing is from mid-June to August. The Owenavorragh Angling Club stocks the river with brown trout, and leases part of the stretch from the tide up to a point about one mile upstream of Boleaney Bridge. Day tickets are available on the angling club water from:

◆ *Whitmore's Jewellery Shop,* Main Street, Gorey, Co. Wexford.

Southern Fisheries Region

The Southern Fisheries Region comprises Cos. Kilkenny and Laois and parts of Cos. Waterford, Carlow, Kildare, Offaly, Tipperary, Wexford, Cork, Kerry, and Limerick. It embraces all rivers flowing into the sea between Kiln Bay, Co. Wexford, and the most southern point of Ballycotton Bay, Co. Cork.

The principal river systems in the region are the Barrow, Nore, and Suir (known as the Three Sisters), and the Cork Blackwater. It comprises two fishery districts: Waterford and Lismore. The River Suir is noted for its brown trout fishing. The Cork Blackwater has spring salmon and grilse, while some of its tributaries hold good stocks of brown trout.

WATERFORD DISTRICT

The Waterford Fisheries District comprises Cos. Kilkenny and Laois and parts of Cos. Waterford, Carlow, Kildare, Offaly, Tipperary, and Wexford. It embraces all the rivers flowing into the sea between Kiln Bay, Co. Wexford, and Helvick Head, Co. Waterford. The principal rivers in the district are the Barrow, Nore, and Suir.

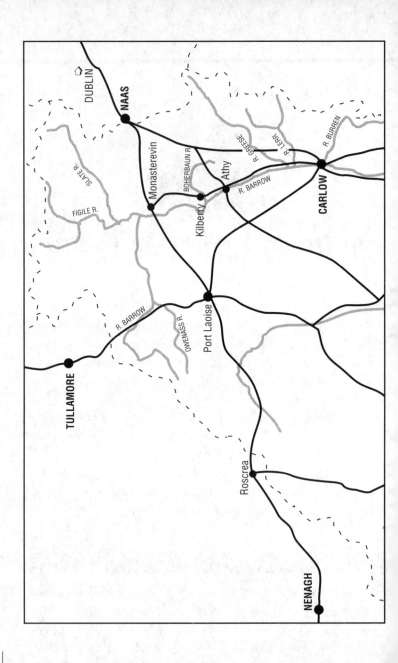

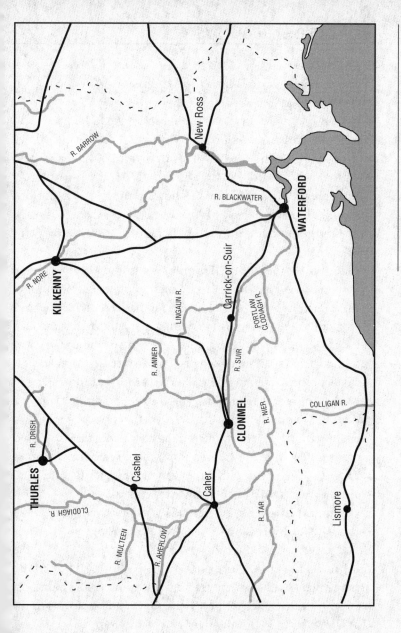

Open Season

Salmon and sea trout: 1 February to 30 September;
brown trout: 1 March to 30 September.

(This season applies to all the tributaries of the River Barrow.)

The River Barrow rises on the northern slopes of the Slieve Bloom Mountains and flows north and then east past Mountmellick and Portarlington to Monasterevin. At Monasterevin it turns south and flows through Athy, Carlow, and Leighlinbridge, past Muine Bheag, Goresbridge, Borris, and Graiguenamanagh, before reaching the tide at Saint Mullin's.

The Barrow is about 120 miles long and drains a huge catchment area consisting of mountain, bog, pastureland, and tillage farming. It is a river that has had recurring serious water pollution problems in recent times, and fish kills have occurred. Some of the tributaries and part of the upper river have had arterial drainage schemes carried out in the past.

The Grand Canal joins the river at Athy, and from there to the tide the river is navigable. The conversion of the river to a navigable channel involved the construction of locks and weirs, which have notably altered the character of the river and have resulted in much ponding and deep water upstream of each weir. The passage of boats can at times disturb feeding trout and be a source of annoyance to anglers.

Ownership of fishing rights on the river has been established only in a limited number of cases, and there is much uncertainty about rights on certain stretches. Some of the fishing is regarded as free. Angling clubs have made arrangements with riparian owners regarding access along the banks of the river, where necessary, and it is this arrangement that allows them to fish the river and its tributaries.

The salmon fishing is generally regarded as poor, and what fish are taken are mostly grilse, taken either during the summer or late in the season.

The brown trout fishing is fair to good and even very good in places, the average weight ranging from 0.5 to 1.25 lb, depending on location. The development of the brown trout fishing on the river is mainly carried out by angling clubs.

The use of night lines is prohibited by law, as is angling for 50 yards downstream of Clashganna Weir. Angling is also forbidden for 210 yards below the top lock gate at Lodge Mills and in the tail-race of Lodge Mills discharging into the canal.

Saint Mullin's Angling Club has about four miles of fishing extending downstream from the weir at Saint Mullin's. The river here holds a variety of fish, including brown trout, occasional salmon, bream, and pike. The average size of the brown trout is 0.5 lb, and they are regarded as being plentiful in this area. Salmon run from April, but the best of the fishing is said to be in September, with occasional fish arriving in small numbers in June. Permits for the fishing at Saint Mullin's are available from:

◆ *Mr Nicholas Blanchfield*, Saint Mullin's, Co. Carlow;
  telephone (051) 24745.

Graiguenamanagh Angling Club has fishing extending downstream from Clashganna, past Graiguenamanagh to Bahana Wood and on the right bank downstream of Ballyteiglea Bridge. The average weight of the trout here is said to be about 10 oz, and the stocks are regarded as being good. The best of the grilse fishing is in June and September. Worm is the most common angling method used. Enquiries about the fishing should be made to:

◆ *Mr Liam Foley*, Turf Market, Graiguenamanagh, Co. Carlow.

Borris Angling Club has about three miles of fishing, extending downstream from Ballyteiglea. This is a mixed trout, salmon and coarse fishery. The brown trout fishing is said to be good. Enquiries about the fishing and permits should be made to:

◆ *Mr Frank Hynes*, Cournellan, Borris, Co. Carlow;
  telephone (0503) 73423.

There is about a quarter of a mile of trout fishing at Milltown. Grilse are occasionally taken here too from June to September. Enquiries about the fishing should be made to:

◆ *Mr Michael Fenlon*, Milltown, Borris, Co. Carlow.

Milford Angling Club has a short stretch of water between Carlow and Leighlinbridge. It holds a good stock of brown trout. Enquiries about the fishing should be made to:

◆ *Mr Bobby Quinn*, The Locks, Milford, Co. Carlow.

Carlow-Graiguecullen Angling Club has about eight miles of fishing extending downstream from Maganey Bridge. The trout fishing on this stretch is only fair. This is regarded as 'open fishing', and a permit to fish is not usually required from the club.

Vickerstown Angling Club has fishing on the main channel of the Barrow itself, on the Stradbally River, and on the Killiney River, a very small tributary of the Barrow and feeder to the canal. The trout stocks are said to be poor. Further enquiries should be made to:

◆ *Mr James Crean*, Vickerstown Inn, Vickerstown, Port Laoise, Co. Laois; telephone (0502) 25189.

For information on brown trout fishing in the Muine Bheag area, contact:

◆ *Mr D. J. Rea*, The Parade, Muine Bheag, Co. Carlow.

The trout fishing at Goresbridge is said to be good. There is about four miles of fishing here, and the waters are usually stocked by Goresbridge Salmon and Trout Angling Association. For further information, contact:

◆ *Mr John Murphy*, Barrack Street, Goresbridge, Co. Carlow; telephone (0503) 75194.

Kilberry-Cloney and Boherbaun Angling Club has approximately three miles of fishing on the Barrow and five miles on a tributary, the Boherbaun River. The fishing on the Barrow is mainly for salmon late in the season, and the brown trout fishing here is poor. Enquiries to:

◆ *Mr Larry Foy*, 553 Kilberry, Athy, Co. Kildare.

The Boherbaun River enters the Barrow near Kilberry, four miles north of Athy. This is regarded as a good trout river, and the average size is big, with good numbers of fish in excess of 1 lb.

Athy and District Anglers' Club has access to extensive fishing on the Barrow upstream of the town and to Maganey Lock south of the town. This is mostly a mixed fishery, with coarse fish, brown trout, and some salmon. The trout fishing is said to be fair, and the peak of the season is generally between May and August. The river can cater for between fifty and a hundred anglers. The annual membership fee of the club covers all costs; information is available from:

◆ *Mr Dennis Whelan*, 29 Graysland, Carlow Road, Athy, Co. Kildare; telephone (0507) 37537
◆ *Mr Brendan Murphy,* Leinster Street, Athy, Co. Kildare
or from local tackle shops.

Portarlington Angling Club has extensive fishing on the Barrow. The club waters extend from Kilnahown Bridge to a point some four miles south of the town. The Barrow is a medium-sized river at Portarlington, lying on a limestone base. The Portarlington water holds a few salmon late in the season. The club waters hold good stocks of wild brown trout and are stocked with farmed trout also. The average weight is probably 0.75 lb, and trout to 4 lb are taken occasionally. Visitors enquiring about fishing should apply to:

◆ *Mr Michael Finlay*, Finlay's Bar, Bracklone Street, Portarlington, Co. Laois
◆ *Mr Joe Hargrove,* Barrow Bank, Portarlington, Co. Laois
◆ *Mr Dominick Ryan*, Kilmalogue, Portarlington, Co. Laois.

OWENASS RIVER

The Owenass River enters the Barrow downstream of Mountmellick. It holds a large stock of small brown trout with occasional trout to 1 lb. Enquiries about fishing rights should be made from riparian owners or from Mountmellick Anglers' Club:

◆ *Mr Brian Lynch*, Wolfe Tone Street, Mountmellick, Co. Laois.

FIGILE RIVER

The Figile River joins the Barrow north of Monasterevin. It holds occasional trout to about 2 lb. The river has undergone severe drainage works recently, and much of it is not worth fishing.

SLATE RIVER

The Slate River joins the Figile two miles south of Bracknagh. This river has undergone drainage work, and the banks are high and difficult in many places. It runs low in summer but can provide good fly fishing over moderate stocks of trout early in the season.

RIVER GREESE

The River Greese is a clear limestone river that rises near Dunlavin, Co. Wicklow, and joins the Barrow north of Carlow. It holds a good stock of wild brown trout. The trout fishing is controlled by two angling clubs, the River Greese Anglers' Association and the Barrow Angling Club. Visitors wishing to fish the Greese Anglers' Association waters should get in touch with:

◆ *Mr Patrick Leigh*, Wood Hill, Narraghmore, Co. Kildare; telephone (0507) 26611
◆ *Mr Michael Lawlor*, Corner House, Ballitore, Co. Kildare.
    Anglers wishing to fish the Barrow Anglers' Club water can get in touch with the secretary:
◆ *Mr Éamonn Moore*, Chapelstown, Carlow
or make arrangements with riparian owners.

RIVER BURREN

The River Burren joins the Barrow at Carlow. It is a rich limestone river with a good stock of brown trout, and has all the usual hatches of fly one expects to find on a limestone river, including mayfly. The Barrow Angling Club has extensive fishing on the river, and enquiries about membership should be made to:

- ◆ *JB Motor and Sport*, Castlehill Centre, Carlow
- ◆ *Mr Éamonn Moore*, Chapelstown, Carlow.

RIVER LERR

The River Lerr joins the Barrow upstream of Carlow. It holds a small stock of brown trout. The Barrow Angling Club controls some of the water, and enquiries should be made to

- ◆ *JB Motor and Sport*, Castlehill Centre, Carlow
- ◆ *Mr Éamonn Moore*, Chapelstown, Carlow.

■ RIVER NORE SYSTEM

Open Season
Salmon and sea trout: 1 February to 30 September;
brown trout: 1 March to 30 September.

The River Nore rises in Co. Tipperary and flows eastwards through Borris-in-Ossory and then south through Co. Kilkenny, passing through or close by the towns of Durrow, Ballyragget, Kilkenny, Bennettsbridge and Thomastown to join the River Barrow upstream of New Ross, Co. Wexford. It is tidal from Inistioge Bridge to its confluence with the Barrow. It is basically a limestone river with very rich fly life. Much of the catchment is given over to tillage, pastureland, and bloodstock. Mill weirs are a feature of the river, and these give rise to long, deep stretches and slow-flowing water. The banks are high in places, and there is an excessive amount of tree cover and vegetation in many places, which makes fishing difficult.

The salmon fishing on the Nore is said to be patchy, and what fishing there is on the river is confined to the stretch from the tide upstream to the confluence with the River Dinin.

The Nore holds good stocks of brown trout in some areas, and the best of the fishing on the main channel is upstream of

Thomastown and on the King's River. The river has prolific fly hatches. There are sedges in profusion, and olives and stone-flies are also very common.

The ownership of the fisheries is well defined, and most of the rights are either exercised by private owners or leased to angling clubs.

The first fishery up from the tide is controlled by Inistioge Anglers' Association. This is a short stretch of water and is primarily a low-water salmon fishery. It holds salmon early in the season. Permits are available from:

◆ *The Castle Inn*, The Square, Inistioge, Co. Kilkenny.

Cotterell's fishery consists of two-thirds of a mile of fishing downstream of Brown's Barn Bridge. This is mainly a low-water fishery and can produce salmon even very early in the season. Season tickets and day tickets are available from:

◆ *Mr Andy Cotterell*, Kilmacshane, Inistioge, Co. Kilkenny; telephone (056) 58403.

Kilkenny Angling Club has extensive fishing on the Nore and also on the lower reaches of the Dinin. A limited number of salmon day tickets are available from:

◆ *Mr Ed Stack*, Bleach Road, Kilkenny; telephone (056) 65220.

Trout fishing day permits can be obtained from any of the tackle shops in Kilkenny, including:

◆ *Mr Paul Campion*, Dean Street, Kilkenny

◆ *The Sports Shop*, High Street, Kilkenny.

Trout fishing day tickets are also available at hotels in Kilkenny.

Gillies are available on the Kilkenny waters by prior arrangement; contact:

◆ *Mr Ed Stack*, Bleach Road, Kilkenny; telephone (056) 65220.

Thomastown Angling Club has four miles of double-bank fishing on the Nore. This is said to be some of the best salmon fishing; the water also holds good stocks of brown trout. There is a club regulation that permits brown trout fishing only from 1 April, and then only fly fishing and worm fishing for trout are allowed. Day tickets are available both for salmon and trout fishing, and can be obtained at:

◆ *John Synnott's Shop,* The Quay, Thomastown, Co. Kilkenny.

The borough of Kilkenny has ancient riparian rights on the Nore, extending for about seven miles from the town, some of it on both banks; this fishing is regarded as free.

Mount Juliet House has three miles of double-bank fishing on the Nore upstream of Thomastown and a further mile on the King's River. The fishing on the Nore is divided into 'beats'. These waters hold salmon and brown trout. Salmon rods are let by the day, and there are evening permits for trout fishing. Gillies are available by prior arrangement, and there is fishing tackle for hire at Mount Juliet House. Enquiries should be made to:

◆ *The Fishery Manager,* Mount Juliet House, Thomastown, Co. Kilkenny; telephone (056) 24455.

Durrow and District Anglers' Association has extensive fishing on the River Nore, the Erkina River, the River Goul, and the Owveg River. The Nore holds good stocks of brown trout at this point. The Erkina River has good stocks of trout, but the best of the fishing is early in the season. The River Goul joins the Erkina River; it holds fair stocks of trout up to 1.25 lb. The Owveg is a tributary of the Nore; it holds fair stocks of brown trout and fishes best early in the season. Permits to fish all these waters are available from:

◆ *Mr William Lawlor,* The Square, Durrow, Co. Laois; telephone (0502) 36234.

Rathdowney Angling Club has about two-and-a-half miles of trout fishing on the Erkina River. The trout stocks are said to be good at this point. Permits are available from:

◆ *Mr Michael White,* Moorville, Rathdowney, Co. Laois.

Abbeyleix Angling Club has about four miles of fishing on the Nore. The river holds fair to good stocks of brown trout at this point, up to 1 lb. Permits are available from:

◆ *Mr Victor Bowell,* Sandymount, Abbeyleix, Co. Laois.

Mountrath and District Angling Club has fishing on the River Nore, the Delour River, and the Mountrath River. Permits to fish for trout are available from:

◆ *Mr Thomas Watkins,* 6 St Finian's Terrace, Mountrath, Co. Laois.

Callan and District Anglers' Association has approximately five miles of trout fishing on the King's River, which flows east through Callan to join the Nore north-west of Thomastown. This is a rich limestone river, and the average size of the trout is quite big. The river was subjected to an arterial drainage scheme some years ago, and the banks are very high in places. For fishing permits and information, contact:

◆ *Mr Chris Vaughan,* Green Street, Callan, Co. Kilkenny.

■ RIVER SUIR SYSTEM

Open Season

Salmon and sea trout: 1 February to 30 September;
brown trout: 1 March to 30 September.

Fishing is prohibited north of Suir Island at Clonmel between Oldbridge and a line drawn across the river in continuation of the west side of Abbey Street, and in the mill tail-races discharging into the River Suir within those limits. This prohibition does not apply to fishing with single rod and line from that part of the north bank of the river known as Old Quay.

The River Suir and its tributaries drain most of Co. Tipperary. The Suir is one of the premier trout angling rivers in the country and is much loved by trout anglers. Most of the channel is characterised by a series of shallow and deep glides, interrupted occasionally by shallow riffles. Many of its major tributaries drain large areas of limestone too, as does the main river, and this gives to the river many of the best characteristics of a chalk stream, with prolific fly hatches and big stocks of trout.

Downstream of the headwaters, in the Templemore area, arterial drainage work was carried out in 1989, and this section is not recommended to the trout angler.

The Suir holds large numbers of trout, because of the ideal nature of the habitat and the absence of predators and competitors. The average size of the trout in the Suir is less than 1 lb, but there are areas, especially around Caher and Clonmel and in the Drish and Nier tributaries, where trout up to 3 lb and over can be encountered.

The dominant fly hatches consist of various species of olives and sedges.

Chest waders and a wading staff are an essential part of the angler's tackle when fishing the main channel of the Suir.

The best of the salmon fishing on the Suir extends downstream from Ardfinnan towards Carrick-on-Suir. The Suir mainly gets a run of grilse and summer fish, and the two best fishing months are probably June and September.

In the Templemore area, severe arterial drainage works have been carried out on the river in recent times, and the fishing at this point cannot be recommended.

Between Thurles and Holycross the river is deep and meandering, with the shallows limited to areas near the bridges. It holds some big trout and pike. Fishing here is by permission of the riparian owners.

RIVER DRISH

The River Drish joins the Suir at Turtulla, east of Thurles. It is a clean, slow-flowing lowland river. The Drish is a well-balanced wild brown trout fishery, holding good stocks of fish. Further information is available from:

- ◆ *Mr Michael Mockler*, Ballycahill, Co. Tipperary
- ◆ *Mr William O'Gorman*, publican, Bohernacrusha Crossroads, Holycross, Co. Tipperary
- ◆ *Reception Desk, Hayes Hotel*, The Square, Thurles, Co. Tipperary.

CLODIAGH RIVER

The Clodiagh River joins the Suir downstream of Two Fords Bridge. It offers limited trout fishing on its lower reaches. From its confluence with the Suir upstream to the Railway Bridge the fishing is controlled by Thurles-Holycross-Ballycamus Angling Association; fishing in all other areas is by permission of riparian owners. Permits for club waters are available from:

◆ *Mr Michael Mockler*, Ballycahill, Co. Tipperary
◆ *Mr William O'Gorman*, publican, Bohernacrusha Crossroads, Holycross, Co. Tipperary
◆ *Hayes Hotel*, The Square, Thurles, Co. Tipperary.

The fishing from Holycross Bridge to Killeen Flats varies, depending on the stretch of river. The stretch upstream of Agent's Flats is affected by a diversion of water to a hydro-electric plant. In summer, low water levels result in excessive vegetation, which limits fish stocks in this area.

From Agent's Flats to Two Ford Bridges is a good wet and dry fly area, with good stocks of trout up to 1.5 lb.

From the place known as the Meetings to Ballycamus Ford is an excellent dry fly section, which at times holds good stocks of trout. This water is controlled by Thurles-Holycross-Ballycamus Angling Association, and permits may be obtained from:

◆ *Mr Michael Mockler*, Ballycahill, Co. Tipperary
◆ *Mr William O'Gorman*, publican, Bohernacrusha Crossroads, Holycross, Co. Tipperary
◆ *Hayes Hotel*, The Square, Thurles, Co. Tipperary.

It should be noted that on the Thurles-Holycross-Ballycamus Angling Association waters the fishing is restricted to fly fishing only. There is a lower size limit of 250 mm (9.8 inches) and a daily bag limit of six trout.

Ardmayle House fishery is one mile long. It offers brown trout fishing, and anglers are catered for at Ardmayle House.

For information on the fishing, apply to:

◆ *Ardmayle House*, Cashel, Co. Tipperary;
   telephone (0504) 42399.

Cashel-Golden-Tipperary Angling Association controls both banks from Camus Bridge to Suir Castle, and shares the west bank from Suir Castle to New Bridge with Caher Angling Club. Downstream of Camus Bridge the river is wide and shallow and holds reasonable stocks of trout. From Castlelake to Mantle Hill and from Golden to Athassel Abbey is prime trout angling water, which holds very good stocks of trout. Athassel Abbey to New Bridge is an excellent trout angling section. Fishing permits are available from:

◆ *Mr Myles O'Keeffe*, Golden, Co. Tipperary
◆ *The Bridge House*, Golden, Co. Tipperary
◆ *Mrs Ryan's Shop*, Friar Street, Cashel, Co. Tipperary
◆ *O'Rahelly's Sports*, Main Street, Tipperary
◆ *Columb's Furniture*, Tipperary
◆ *Drumm's Sports*, Tipperary.

MULTEEN RIVER

The Multeen River joins the Suir from the west near Cashel. It holds big stocks of trout, averaging 0.5 lb in the middle and lower reaches. Fishing is by permission of the landowners.

RIVER ARA
RIVER AHERLOW

The Ara and Aherlow Rivers join before entering the Suir from the west, four miles north of Caher.

The Ara provides trout fishing from Kilshane downstream to its confluence with the Aherlow River. It supports large numbers of trout, averaging 10 oz, with some up to 2 lb. This is a good trout fishery, with some excellent dry fly water. Fishing on the river is controlled by Ara Angling Club; permits to fish may be obtained from:

- *Mr W. G. Evans*, Tackle Shop, Main Street, Tipperary
- *Mr Peter Keenan*, Ara Angling Club, Tipperary.

The Aherlow River flows through the Glen of Aherlow, and it holds large numbers of small trout. The best angling sections are in the Galbally area, Rossadrehid, and downstream of Cappagh Old Bridge. There is an angling club on the river, and permits for the club waters are available from:

- *Morrisey's Bar*, Castle Street, Caher, Co. Tipperary.

Caher and District Angling Club controls the right bank from 400 m downstream of New Bridge to the Bakery Weir and from Swiss Cottage to Carrigataha. The river here is broad and meandering, with fast, shallow glides, riffles, and occasional deep pools. It holds a good stock of trout up to 12 inches, and even larger in certain areas. The section from the Swiss Cottage to Rochestown is an excellent trout fishing area. The trout fishing on all these waters is restricted to fly fishing only. Permits to fish club waters may be obtained from:

- *Morrisey's Bar*, Castle Street, Caher, Co. Tipperary;
  telephone (052) 41516.

Gillies are available, and enquiries should be made at the same address.

The Shamrock Lodge Fishery is upstream of Rochestown. It is about a quarter of a mile long and offers good trout fishing. Permits are available from:

- *Mr Joe O'Connor*, Shamrock Lodge, Caher, Co. Tipperary;
  telephone (052) 66202.

The Suir from Ardfinnan Bridge downstream to Clocully is a fast, meandering river, holding good stocks of brown trout. The shallow areas near the mouth of the Tar and the bridge at Newcastle hold moderate stocks of takeable trout. The deeper channel upstream of the weir at Ardfinnan holds moderate stocks of trout. Much but not all of the fishing in this area is controlled by Ardfinnan Angling Club, and permits to fish these waters are available from the honorary secretary:

- *Mr John Maher*, Greenview, Ardfinnan, Co. Tipperary.

A limited number of rods are available at the Cloghardeen fishery. Apply to:

◆ *Mr P. F. Mason,* Cloghardeen Farm, Ardfinnan,
   Co. Tipperary; telephone (052) 66236.

RIVER TAR

Two rivers, the Shanbally and the Duag, join near Clogheen to form the Tar. This is a a major tributary of the Suir, coming in from the west near Newcastle. All three rivers hold good stocks of trout, up to 270 mm, found chiefly in the deeper pools. There is an angling club on the river, and further information about the fishing is available from:

◆ *Mrs Eileen Ryan,* Clonanav Farm, Ballymacarbry,
   Co. Waterford; telephone (052) 36141.

Clonmel Area

The Suir from its confluence with the River Nier to Kilmanahan is 40 m wide. It consists of fast water and some long glides. This area holds moderate to good stocks of trout up to 300 mm. Downstream of Kilmanahan to Knocklofty Bridge is slower, deep water with good dry fly fishing for trout. From Knocklofty Bridge down to Marlfield is a wide, shallow river of long, fast glides and riffles. It has good stocks of trout and provides both wet and dry fly fishing. From Marlfield to Clonmel the river is 30 to 40 m wide and consists of pools and glides. Within the town the river holds good stocks of brown trout.

Clonmel and District Salmon and Trout Anglers' Association controls the fishing on both banks from Deerpark to Kilmanahan Castle. Fishing is by fly only, and chest waders are not allowed. Permits to fish both trout and salmon are available from:

◆ *Mr John Kavanagh,* The Sports Shop, Westgate, Clonmel,
   Co. Tipperary.

Clonmel and District Angling Club has fishing on the right bank from Knocklofty Bridge downstream for about one mile. Fly fishing only is allowed. Permits are available only for brown trout fishing; apply to:

◆ *Mr John Carroll*, Lindville House, Kilsheelan, Co. Tipperary; telephone (052) 33450.

The fishing upstream of Knocklofty Bridge is reserved by Knocklofty House Hotel for its guests; enquiries can be made to:

◆ *Knocklofty House Hotel*, Knocklofty, Clonmel, Co. Tipperary; telephone (052) 38222.

The Marlfield fishery offers good trout fishing and occasional salmon fishing. Apply to:

◆ *Marlfield Lodge*, Clonmel, Co. Tipperary; telephone (052) 25234.

The fishing on some stretches in the Clonmel-Newcastle area is leased by Mrs Eileen Ryan. These stretches offer good brown trout fishing and occasional salmon fishing late in the season. For information on the fishing, gillie service, tackle hire, and accommodation, apply to:

◆ *Mrs Eileen Ryan*, Clonanav Farmhouse, Ballymacarbry, via Clonmel, Co. Waterford; telephone (052) 36141.

Fishing is also available from:

◆ *Mr Frans Beckers*, Kilmanahan, Co. Waterford; telephone (052) 36433.

The fishing between the bridges in the town of Clonmel is free.

RIVER NIER

The River Nier is a tributary of the Suir. It is a clean, spate mountain stream with cascades, riffles, glides, and deep pools. There are good stocks of trout up to 420 mm in the middle and lower reaches of this river. Further information on the fishing and gillies is available from:

◆ *Mrs Eileen Ryan*, Clonanav Farmhouse, Ballymacarbry, via Clonmel, Co. Waterford; telephone (052) 36141.

Clonmel-Kilsheelan Area

The River Suir downstream of Clonmel is broad and deep with productive shallow glides. From Clonmel to Tikincor Bridge it holds moderate to good stocks of brown trout; from Tikincor to Kilsheelan it holds good stocks of relatively large trout. Much of the fishing in this area is controlled by Clonmel and District Angling Club, and enquiries should be made to:

◆ *Mr John Carroll*, Lindville House, Kilsheelan, Co. Tipperary; telephone (052) 33450.

Kilsheelan Angling Club has fishing on the left bank of the Suir upstream from Kilsheelan Bridge for about one mile; enquiries should be made (after 5.00 p.m.) to:

◆ *Mr Jonathan Moriarty*, Kilsheelan, Co. Tipperary.

RIVER ANNER

The Anner enters the Suir east of Clonmel. The upper and middle reaches hold good stocks of trout, but the fishing is reserved for members of Fethard and Killusty Angling Club.

From Thorney Bridge to where it joins the Suir the river holds moderate stocks of trout up to 300 mm. Visitors can fish this section with the permission of the riparian owners, except for the Anner Castle fishery, which is private.

The Glencastle fishery on the Suir is downstream of Kilsheelan. It is about two miles long and offers good trout and salmon fishing. Information about the fishing is available from:

◆ *Mrs Maura Long*, Glencastle, Kilsheelan, Co. Tipperary; telephone (052) 33787.

Carrick-on-Suir Angling Club has fishing downstream of Duff Castle. This section holds a good stock of trout, but they are quite small. Permits to fish are available from:

◆ *Mr John O'Keeffe*, OK Cycles and Sports, New Street, Carrick-on-Suir, Co. Tipperary.

Coolnamuck fishery consists of four miles of south-bank fishing immediately upstream of tidal waters, holding both salmon and trout. Permits are available from:

- *Mr John O'Keeffe*, OK Cycles and Sports, New Street,
  Carrick-on-Suir, Co. Tipperary.

    Boats and boatmen are also available for hire at the same address.

PORTLAW CLODIAGH RIVER

The Portlaw Clodiagh River joins the Suir east of Portlaw. It has moderate stocks of trout, up to 1 lb. Fishing is available from riparian owners outside the boundary of Curraghmore Estate.

RIVER BLACKWATER

The River Blackwater enters the Suir north of the city of Waterford. It has good stocks of trout up to 10 inches between Kilmacow and Mullinavat. Enquiries about the fishing should be made locally.

LINGAUN RIVER

The Lingaun River joins the Suir two miles downstream of Carrick-on-Suir. It holds good stocks of trout up to 10 inches. Enquiries about the fishing can be made to:

- *Mr John O'Keeffe*, OK Cycles and Sports, New Street,
  Carrick-on-Suir, Co. Tipperary.

COLLIGAN RIVER

Open Season

Salmon and sea trout: 1 February to 30 September;
brown trout: 1 March to 30 September.

The Colligan River flows into Dungarvan Bay. It is a spate river and holds both salmon and big sea trout. The first runs of sea trout enter the river in June, and July sees the majority of sea trout enter the system. The river also gets a run of grilse in July and larger summer salmon in September. The local angling club controls the fishing; permits are available from:

- *Boumann's Jewellers*, Main Street, Dungarvan,
  Co. Waterford.

COMERAGH MOUNTAIN LAKES
Open Season
Brown trout: 1 March to 30 September.

These five small lakes lie in the Comeragh Mountains and can be approached from a car park in the Nier Valley. They hold small wild brown trout. A gillie or guide is available by contacting:

◆ *Mrs Eileen Ryan*, Clonanav Farmhouse, Ballymacarbry, Co. Waterford; telephone (052) 36141.

GLENAHIRY LAKE
This is a small pond in the Nier Valley, stocked with brown trout. Enquiries about the fishing should be made to:

◆ *Mrs Eileen Ryan*, Clonanav Farmhouse, Ballymacarbry, Co. Waterford; telephone (052) 36141.

BAY LOUGH
Open Season
Brown trout: 15 March to 30 September.

This is a small mountain lough in the Knockmealdown Mountains, holding trout up to 12 oz. The fishing is regarded as free. There is parking at a lay-by a short distance from the lough.

BALLYSHONOCK RESERVOIR
Open Season
Brown trout: 15 March to 30 September.

Ballyshonock Reservoir is 500 m off the Waterford–Cork (N25) road near Kilmacthomas. It holds a big stock of wild brown trout averaging 0.5 lb, with some larger trout up to 4 lb. It is also stocked with rainbow trout. Enquiries about the fishing should be made to:

◆ *Carroll's Cross Inn*, Kilmacthomas, Co. Waterford.

KNOCKADERRY RESERVOIR
Open Season
Brown trout: 1 March to 30 September.

This reservoir is four miles off the Waterford–Cork (N25) road, about six miles from Waterford. It holds a stock of wild brown trout averaging 1 lb and is occasionally stocked with rainbow trout. Enquiries about the fishing and boat hire should be made to:

◆ *Mr Jack Connolly*, Knockaderry, Co. Waterford;
   telephone (051) 84107.

LISMORE DISTRICT

The Lismore Fisheries District comprises parts of Cos. Cork, Kerry, Limerick, and Waterford, and embraces all the rivers flowing into the sea between Helvick Head, Co. Waterford, and Ballycotton, Co. Cork. The principal waters of the district are the River Blackwater and its tributaries.

■ CORK BLACKWATER SYSTEM

Open Season
Salmon and sea trout: 1 February to 30 September;
brown trout: 15 February to 30 September.

There is a statutory size limit of 7 inches for salmon and trout, and gaffs are not permitted. No fishing is allowed from the Mill Dam at Clondulane or for 30 yards below it.

The Munster Blackwater rises in Co. Kerry and flows for over 100 miles through Cos. Cork and Waterford to the tide at Cappoquin. It is Ireland's fourth-longest river and is noted for its big run of salmon. The average size of the brown trout is rather small. Spinning and fly fishing for salmon are the methods allowed on all fisheries, but on some fisheries the use of a worm or shrimp is allowed.

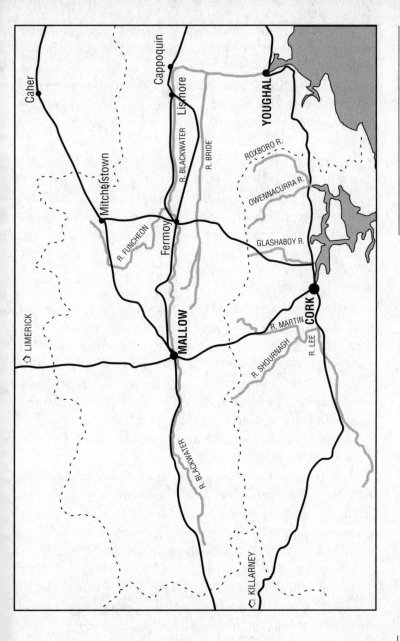

Clondulane Weir, downstream of Fermoy, is a dominant feature on the river and controls the run of spring fish in low, cold-water conditions.

The Careysville fishery consists of one-and-three-quarter miles of double-bank fishing. February is regarded as the most productive month for spring salmon, and June sees the peak of the grilse run. Applications for fishing should be made to:

◆ *The Manager, Careysville Fishery,* Fermoy, Co. Cork; telephone (025) 31094.

The Dempster fisheries have ten beats in the section of the river between Ballyduff and Ballyhooly. These fisheries hold spring fish, and the grilse run begins in early June. Enquiries about the fishing should be made to:

◆ *Peter Dempster Ltd,* Carrigeen Hill, Conna, Co. Cork; telephone (058) 56248; fax (025) 31813.

The Blackwater Lodge Hotel has eighteen beats spread along the river, from the lowest beat, which is only three miles above the tide, to Mallow, some forty miles upstream. The beats are rotated daily and average about three-quarters of a mile each. The number of rods is limited to four per beat. Gillies are available and should be reserved in advance. Enquiries about the fishing should be made to:

◆ *Blackwater Lodge Hotel,* Ballyduff, Co. Waterford; telephone (058) 60235; fax (058) 60162.

Fox's Fishery at Killavullen is three-quarters of a mile long, ten miles upstream of Fermoy. It takes four rods, and all legitimate fishing methods are allowed. A gillie can be arranged. Enquiries about the fishing should be made to:

◆ *Mr Dan O'Donovan,* 32 Woodlands, Kerry Pike, Cork; telephone (021) 872322.

Ballymaquirk Fishery and Lodge is between Kanturk and Banteer, Co. Cork. It consists of three-quarters of a mile of single-bank fishing on the Blackwater and a quarter of a mile on the Allow River. It generally holds grilse and brown trout. It is let with three rods, and there is a lodge that offers self-catering accommodation. Enquiries about the fishing should be made to:

◆ *Mr B. Murphy O'Connor,* Greybrook House, Waterfall, Co. Cork; telephone (021) 502555; fax (021) 502376

◆ *Ballyhooley Castle Fishery:* Mrs Merrie Greene, Ballyvolane House, Castlelyons, Co. Cork; telephone (025) 36349.

Lombardstown and District Trout Anglers' Club has access to about four miles of trout fishing on the Blackwater between Waterloo Bridge and Roskeen Bridge. Enquiries should be made to:

◆ *Lombardstown and District Trout Anglers' Club,* Lombardstown, Co. Cork.

Millstreet Anglers' Association has fishing on about ten miles of the Blackwater, the Finnow River, and the Aubane River. These waters hold occasional salmon late in the season and a good stock of brown trout. The fishing can be very good, especially in April for brown trout, and the trout range in size from 0.25 to 0.5 lb. Day tickets are available from:

◆ *Mr Dermot O'Keeffe,* Main Street, Millstreet, Co. Cork.

RIVER FUNCHEON

The River Funcheon joins the Blackwater just downstream of Fermoy. It is a good brown trout river and very suitable for the dry fly. There are four angling clubs on the river: Mitchelstown, Kildorrery, Glanworth, and Kilworth. Membership of the clubs is open, and the river is signposted with information about permits. Enquiries can be made to:

◆ *Mr Seán Dennehy,* Fermoy Road, Kildorrery, Co. Cork; telephone (022) 25497

◆ *Mrs Peter Collins,* Fermoy Road, Kildorrery, Co. Cork; telephone (022) 25205.

South-Western Fisheries Region

The South-Western Fisheries Region includes all the rivers flowing into the sea between Kerry Head, Co. Kerry, and Ballycotton, Co. Cork. It covers the greater part of Cos. Kerry and Cork.

The underlying rock formation is about equally divided between old red sandstone and various limestones. The region has a varied menu of game fishing on offer. It is well known for the quality of its salmon and sea trout fishing.

Lough Currane has a proud reputation for spring salmon fishing and is internationally recognised as one of the top sea trout lakes in Ireland. There are many other river systems in the region too that offer the prospect of sport with salmon. The River Maine gets grilse; the River Laune, Lough Leane and its upper lakes and tributaries hold both spring salmon and grilse. The Caragh River and Lough Caragh are noted for the quality of their salmon fishing; the Owenmore and most of the small rivers on the Dingle Peninsula get a grilse run, as does the Inny

River; the Blackwater west of Kenmare has grilse; and the Sheen River and the Roughty River have both salmon and grilse. The Cloonee system has grilse, and the Glanmore system salmon and grilse. Glengarriff and Coomhola get good runs of salmon and grilse on spates. The River Ilen and the Bandon River have salmon and grilse, and the River Lee in Cork gets a big run of both.

Sea trout are to be found in profusion in the region, with virtually every river that enters the sea getting a run of fish; the River Lee is probably the only river that does not have a significant run. The brown trout fishing is confined mainly to the rivers in the east of the region: the River Lee and its tributaries and the Bandon and Owennacurra. The Laune holds significant stocks too.

The lakes in the area all hold greater or lesser stocks of brown trout of various sizes, but the average size is small. A special feature of this region is the number of lakes that are stocked with rainbow trout to cater for the local and tourist angler alike. These lakes are spread all over the region, and nearly all of them hold numbers of double-figure rainbow trout.

The region has two districts – the Cork District and the Killarney District – and the regional headquarters is at 1 Neville's Terrace, Masseytown, Macroom, Co. Cork; telephone (026) 41222.

CORK DISTRICT

The Cork Fisheries District extends from Ballycotton to Galley Head, and the principal river systems within the district are the Owennacurra, the Glashaboy, the Lee, the Owenboy, the Bandon, the Argideen, the Ilen, the Merlach, the Ouvane, the Coomhola, the Glengarriff, and the Adrigole.

There is a 7 inch size limit for trout in the Cork District.

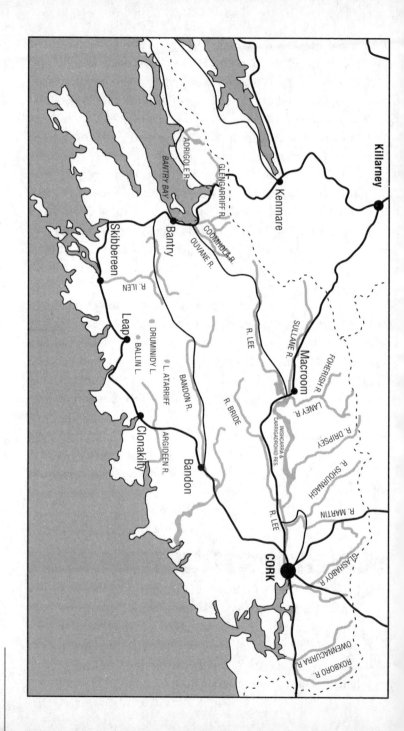

LOUGH ADERRA
Open Season
Brown trout: 1 April to 30 September.

Lough Aderra is sixteen miles east of Cork, adjoining the Cork–Youghal road. It is stocked regularly by the regional fisheries board with brown trout and rainbow trout. There are six boats for hire. Boats and permits are available from the waterkeeper, Mrs M. Higgins, beside the lake. The open season usually runs from 1 April to 30 September.

OWENNACURRA RIVER
Open Season
Salmon: 1 February to 30 September; *sea trout:* 1 February to 12 October; *brown trout:* 15 February to 12 October.

The Owennacurra River flows through Midleton into Cork Harbour. It is primarily a sea trout fishery, and the best of the fishing is in July, August, and September. It also holds small brown trout, and is occasionally stocked by the local angling club with 1 lb brown trout. Midleton and District Angling Association has the goodwill of the fishing, and up-to-date information is available from:
◆ *TH Sports*, Main Street, Midleton, Co. Cork.

ROXBORO RIVER
Open Season
Salmon: 1 February to 30 September; *sea trout:* 1 February to 12 October; *brown trout:* 15 February to 12 October.

The Roxboro River is a small river that rises north of Dungourney and flows south and west to the sea. It holds occasional good brown trout and gets a small run of sea trout. The goodwill of the fishing is controlled by Midleton and District Angling Association, and information and permission to fish is available from:
◆ *TH Sports*, Main Street, Midleton, Co. Cork.

GLASHABOY RIVER

Open Season

Salmon: 1 February to 30 September;

sea trout: 1 February to 12 October.

The Glashaboy River gets a run of sea trout from the middle of June. The numbers of fish have decreased considerably in recent years. Enquiries about the fishing should be made to the secretary of the local club:

◆ *Mr Bobby Seward,* Glanmire and District Salmon and Trout Angling Association, Glanmire, Co. Cork.

■ RIVER LEE SYSTEM

Open Season

Salmon: 1 February to 30 September;

brown trout: 15 February to 12 October.

The River Lee rises above Gougane Barra, Co. Cork, and flows east into Cork Harbour. The valleys downstream are now flooded and form reservoirs because of the erection of dams for hydro-electric power stations. Fishing is prohibited for 50 yards downstream of the powerhouse of Cork Waterworks.

The ESB stocks up to 150,000 salmon smolts annually into the river. The bulk of the salmon fishing now takes place in the nine-mile stretch of river downstream of Inishcarra Dam. The peak of the salmon fishing is from late March, and the grilse fishing is usually in full swing by early July.

The river holds a fair stock of brown trout, averaging 0.5 lb but with some fish up to 1 lb or better. The best fishing is during the day in May and June, and there is good evening fishing during the summer.

The regional fisheries board's fisheries are at the top and bottom of the river; booking can be made through:

◆ *South-Western Regional Fisheries Board,* 1 Neville's Terrace, Masseytown, Macroom, Co. Cork; telephone (026) 41222

◆ *Inishcarra Fishery Office;* telephone (021) 873976

◆ *Tackle Shop,* Lavitt's Quay, Cork; telephone (021) 272842.

Cork Salmon Anglers' Association Ltd lets day tickets, and they are available from:

◆ *Mr John Buckley*, Raheen House, Carrigrohane, Co. Cork; telephone (021) 872137.

The Lee Salmon Anglers' Club lets day tickets, and they are available from Monday to Friday from:

◆ *Mr Percy Cole*, Auto Factor, Douglas Street, Cork; telephone (021) 311082.

Permission to fish for brown trout is also required from the fishery owners, except at the Lee Fields, upstream of the waterworks weir. This is mainly a slow, deep section of water, and restocking with brown trout by the regional fisheries board takes places from time to time. The fishing rights on the reservoirs are owned by the ESB, and an annual trout fishing permit is available at a nominal charge.

RIVER MARTIN

The River Martin flows through Blarney to join the River Shournagh, a tributary of the Lee. It holds stocks of brown trout that average about 4 oz. The fishing is regarded as free.

RIVER SHOURNAGH

The River Shournagh joins the Lee at Leemount Bridge. It holds a good stock of brown trout up to 9 inches. Much of the river is overgrown, but there are clear areas where fly fishing can take place. The best fishing months are said to be April, May, and June.

RIVER BRIDE

The River Bride flows through Crookstown, Ryecourt and Ovens to join the Lee. It holds excellent stocks of brown trout, and the average size is about 6 oz. It is heavily fished in spring. This river occasionally gets a small run of salmon in September. The fishing is regarded as free.

OWENNAGERAGH RIVER

The Owennageragh River joins the Shournagh west of Blarney. It holds a good stock of brown trout, and the fishing is regarded as free.

RIVER DRIPSEY

The River Dripsey holds a big stock of small brown trout. It flows into Inishcarra Reservoir, and the fishing is regarded as free.

LANEY RIVER

The Laney River joins the Sullane River east of Macroom. It is a fast-flowing stream that holds reasonably good trout. The banks are overgrown in places. The best of the fishing is from Morrison's Bridge upstream to Bawnmore Bridge, where the banks are reasonably clean, or from Morrison's Bridge downstream.

The fishing is regarded as free, but Macroom and District Fly Anglers' Association has a conservation interest in the river and should be supported.

FOHERISH RIVER

The Foherish River is a tributary of the Sullane and holds small brown trout; the banks are very overgrown in places. The fishing is considered free, but Macroom and District Fly Anglers have a conservation interest in the river and should be supported.

SULLANE RIVER

The Sullane River flows east through Ballyvourney and Macroom into Carrigadrohid Reservoir. It is a moorland river and holds a good stock of brown trout averaging 6 oz. It fishes well through the season, and the fly fishing is particularly good on summer evenings in July and August. The fishing is regarded as free; Macroom and District Fly Anglers have a conservation interest in the river.

THE MIDDLE LEE

This is the section of river above the Old Gearagh Forest at the upper end of Carrigadrohid Reservoir. This is a strong moorland river with attractive stretches above and below Drumcarra Bridge. It holds small numbers of brown trout and gets a run of large reservoir trout to 2 or 3 lb in late summer.

INISHCARRA AND CARRIGADROHID RESERVOIRS

These reservoirs to the west of Cork hold a small stock of wild brown trout. The best trout fishing areas are at the north arm of the mouth of the River Dripsey, the wide shallow area east of Carrigadrohid, and along the northern shore east of the mouth of the River Dripsey. Up-to-date information and maps of these mixed fisheries, which also hold pike, bream, and perch, are available from:

◆ *South-Western Regional Fisheries Board*, 1 Neville's Terrace, Masseytown, Macroom, Co. Cork; telephone (026) 41222.

A permit is required from the ESB, which is available at a nominal charge. At present an annual trout permits costs £2, and is available from:

◆ *Inishcarra Generating Station*
◆ *South-Western Regional Fisheries Board*
◆ *ESB offices*, Macroom, Co. Cork.

GOUGANE BARRA LAKE
Open Season
Brown trout: 15 February to 12 October.
Gougane Barra Lake holds a stock of brown trout averaging 4 oz. Boats are available from:

◆ *Gougane Barra Hotel*, Ballingeary, Co. Cork;
   telephone (026) 47069.

BANDON RIVER
Open Season
Salmon, sea trout, and brown trout: 15 February to 30 September.
Fishing is prohibited on a 100 yard section immediately
downstream of the weir in Bandon.

The Bandon offers a great variety of game fishing. It gets a
good run of salmon, including both spring fish and grilse, and
has an excellent run of sea trout, and the brown trout fishing is
regarded as being quite good.

The salmon fishing extends all the way upstream from
Innishannon to Togher Castle, depending on water conditions.
The sea trout fishing begins in July and is concentrated on the
lower part of the river. The brown trout fishing is spread
throughout the river, and the average size is 6 oz.

The majority of the fishing is controlled by private owners
or angling associations:

◆ *Mr Chambre Good,* Belmont, Innishannon, Co. Cork;
telephone (021) 75261

◆ *Ms Angela or Ms Patricia Blanchfield,* Blanchfield House,
Ballinhassig, Co. Cork; telephone (021) 885167.
For Bandon Salmon and Trout Anglers' Association:

◆ *Mr Michael O'Regan,* Oliver Plunkett Street, Bandon,
Co. Cork; telephone (023) 41674.
For Ballineen and Enniskean Anglers' Association:

◆ *Mr Tom Fehilly,* Bridge Street, Ballineen, Co. Cork

◆ *Mr David Lamb,* Kilcolman Park, Enniskean, Co. Cork;
telephone (023) 47279.
For Dunmanway Salmon and Trout Anglers' Association:

◆ *Mr Patrick McCarthy,* Yew Tree Bar, Main Street,
Dunmanway, Co. Cork

◆ *South-Western Regional Fisheries Board,* 1 Neville's Terrace,
Masseytown, Macroom, Co. Cork; telephone (026) 41222.

ARGIDEEN RIVER
Open Season
Salmon: 15 February to 30 September;
sea trout and brown trout: 15 February to 12 October.

The Argideen River is primarily regarded as a sea trout fishery. The river is jointly managed by Argideen Anglers' Association and the South-Western Regional Fisheries Board, and there are two private stretches that are not let. Visitors' tickets are available from:

◆ *Mr Peter Wolstenholme,* Courtmacsherry Ceramic, Courtmacsherry, Co. Cork; telephone (023) 46239
◆ *South-Western Regional Fisheries Board,* 1 Neville's Terrace, Masseytown, Macroom, Co. Cork; telephone (026) 41222
◆ *The Fishing Office,* Inchy Bridge, Courtmacsherry, Co. Cork.

NEASKIN LOUGH
CHAPEL LAKE
BALLYNACARRIGA LOUGH
CURRAGHALICKEY LAKE
LOUGH ATARRIFF

These small lakes are in west Cork and hold a mixture of brown trout with some of them also containing rudd, tench, and pike. For information on the fishing, contact Dunmanway Salmon and Trout Anglers' Association:

◆ *Mr Pat McCarthy,* Yew Tree Bar, Dunmanway, Co. Cork.

RIVER ILEN
Open Season
Salmon: 1 February to 30 September;
sea trout: 1 February to 12 October.

The River Ilen is a medium-sized river that flows in a southerly direction to the tide at Skibbereen. It gets a run of spring salmon and grilse, and is said to get a good run of sea trout. The spring fish enter the river from March, and the grilse come in June, while the sea trout fishing begins to pick up in July.

The ownership of the rights on the river is fragmented. Fishing is available in some instances from the riparian owner. The River Ilen Anglers' Club has approximately four miles of fishing; day tickets and weekly tickets are available from:

◆ *Mr Tony Kelly*, Fallon's Sports Shop, North Street, Skibbereen, Co. Cork; telephone (028) 21435.

GARRANES LAKE
Open Season
Brown trout: 1 May to 31 August.

Garranes Lake is three miles south-west of Dunmanway. It is regularly stocked with rainbow trout. Boats and fisheries board permits are available from:

◆ *Mr Gene Carolan*, shop and filling station, Garranes, Drimoleague, Co. Cork; telephone (028) 31514.

BALLIN LOUGH
Ballin Lough is by the roadside two miles north of Leap. It is stocked with brown trout by the local angling club. Day tickets are available from:

◆ *Mrs Mary Williamson*, Ballin Lough Anglers' Club Ltd, Leap, Co. Cork; telephone (028) 33266.

SHEPPERTON LAKES
Open Season
1 April to 30 September.

The Shepperton Lakes are three miles east of Skibbereen, and managed and stocked with rainbow trout by the regional fisheries board. Four boats are available for hire; boats and fisheries board permits are available from:

◆ *N. Connolly*, Shepperton, Skibbereen, Co. Cork; telephone (028) 33328.

DRUMINIDY LAKE
Open Season
1 May to 31 August.
Druminidy Lake is three miles south-east of Drimoleague. It is stocked regularly with rainbow trout, and fishing is from the shore. Fisheries board permits are available from:
◆ *Mr Con O'Donoghue*, Druminidy Lake, Drimoleague,
   Co. Cork; telephone (028) 31597.

OUVANE RIVER
Open Season
Salmon: 17 March to 30 September;
sea trout: 17 March to 12 October.
The river gets a small run of grilse and sea trout. It fishes best on a spate.

COOMHOLA RIVER
Open Season
Salmon: 17 March to 30 September;
sea trout: 17 March to 12 October.
The Coomhola River drains into the top of Bantry Bay. It gets a good run of grilse every season; it also gets a small run of sea trout in July and August.

GLENGARRIFF RIVER
Open Season
Salmon: 17 March to 30 September;
sea trout and brown trout: 17 March to 12 October.
The Glengarriff River enters the sea at Glengarriff, and gets a run of grilse and sea trout. The fishing usually begins in late June or early July. Permission to fish can be obtained from Glengarriff Anglers' Association:
◆ *Mr Bernard Harrington*, The Maple Leaf, Glengarriff,
   Co. Cork; telephone (027) 63021.

ADRIGOLE RIVER
Open Season
Salmon: 17 March to 30 September;
sea trout: 17 March to 12 October.
This small river gets a small run of grilse and sea trout in June. Permission to fish may be obtained from Kenmare Anglers' Association:
◆ *Mr John O'Hare,* fishing tackle shop, Main Street, Kenmare, Co. Kerry.

SCHULL RESERVOIR
Open Season
15 June to 31 August.
Schull Reservoir is a joint development between the South-Western Regional Fisheries Board and the local development association. It holds a small stock of wild brown trout and is stocked with adult rainbow trout. Permission from the regional fisheries board is required to fish; permits can be purchased from:
◆ *Ms K. Newman,* Schull, Co. Cork.

LOUGH BOFINNE
Open Season
1 April to 30 September.
Lough Bofinne is three miles east of Bantry, and the development of the lough is a joint venture between Bantry Anglers' Association and the South-Western Regional Fisheries Board. The lough is regularly stocked with adult rainbow trout. Boats are available for hire; for permits and boat hire, contact:
◆ *Mr P. Spillane,* Lough Bofinne, Bantry, Co. Cork.

CAHA MOUNTAIN LOUGHS
The Caha Mountain Loughs are on the Caha Mountains on the Beara Peninsula to the south-west of Glengarriff in Co. Cork. There are about twenty loughs in all, and virtually all of them

can be fished from the shore. Some hold brown trout to 1 lb, although there are some loughs that hold no trout at all. Access to the loughs is quite difficult and requires a steep climb.

LOWER LOUGH AVAUL
Open Season
1 April to 30 September.

Lower Lough Avaul is two miles south-west of Glengarriff. There is a joint development project between Glengarriff Anglers' Association and the South-Western Regional Fisheries Board. The lough holds a stock of wild brown trout and is regularly stocked with large rainbow trout by the fisheries board. Fisheries board permits are available from:

◆ *Mr Bernard Harrington*, publican, Glengarriff, Co. Cork
◆ *Mr Dan O'Sullivan*, Upper Lough Avaul, Glengarriff, Co. Cork.

UPPER LOUGH AVAUL
Open Season
1 April to 30 September.

Upper Lough Avaul is half a mile beyond Lower Lough Avaul. The lake holds small brown trout and is stocked regularly with big rainbow trout. There is a boat for hire. Fisheries board permits are available from:

◆ *Mr Bernard Harrington*, publican, Glengarriff, Co. Cork
◆ *Mr Dan O'Sullivan*, Upper Lough Avaul, Glengarriff, Co. Cork.

GLEN LOUGH
Glen Lough is two miles north-east of Adrigole, and access to it is off the road. It holds small brown trout and sea trout and occasional salmon from July. Enquiries about the fishing should be made to Kenmare Trout Anglers' Association:

◆ *Mr John O'Hare*, fishing tackle shop, Kenmare, Co. Kerry.

The Killarney Fisheries District consists of the old fishery board districts of Kenmare, Waterville, and Killarney. It includes part of Co. Kerry, and embraces all the rivers flowing into the sea between Crow Head and Dunmore Head, including the Blasket Islands.

GLENBEG LOUGH
LOUGH FADDA

Bearhaven Anglers' Association has a lease on these loughs and on a number of other small lakes in the Ardgroom area. They hold small brown trout. Enquiries about the fishing should be made to:

◆ *Mr Michael Harrington,* Churchgate, Castletown Bearhaven, Co. Cork; telephone (027) 70011.

DERRYVEGGAL LAKE
Open Season

15 June to 31 August.

Derryveggal Lake is three miles west of the village of Ardgroom. It holds a good stock of wild brown trout, and adult rainbow trout are stocked regularly. This is a joint development between the fisheries board and the local anglers' association. Fisheries board permits and boats are available from:

◆ *Mr Joe O'Sullivan,* The Bungalow, Ardgroom, Co. Cork
◆ *Mr Michael Harrington,* Church Gate, Castletown Bearhaven; telephone (027) 70011.

CROANSAGHT RIVER
GLANMORE LOUGH
Open Season

Salmon: 15 March to 30 September;
sea trout: 15 March to 12 October.

The Croansaght River drains Glanmore Lake. It gets a small run of spring salmon, and the grilse come in June; the sea trout run in August. There is one boat for hire on the lake. Permission to fish and information about boats are available from:

◆ *Craigie's Hotel*, Castletown Bearhaven, Co. Cork; telephone (027) 70379.

CLOONEE SYSTEM

The Cloonee System consists of a short river and two loughs south of Kenmare. The loughs hold an excellent stock of brown trout, with some sea trout from late July and occasional grilse. There are boats for hire. For permission to fish, apply to:

◆ *Mrs Mary O'Shea*, Lake House, Cloonee, Kenmare, Co. Kerry; telephone (064) 84205.

URAGH LOUGH

Uragh Lough is south of Kenmare and holds small brown trout and occasional sea trout in August. Enquiries about the fishing should be made to Kenmare Angling Association:

◆ *Mr John O'Hare*, fishing tackle shop, Main Street, Kenmare, Co. Kerry.

INCHIQUIN LAKE
Open Season
Sea trout and brown trout: 15 March to 12 October.

Inchiquin Lake is south of Kenmare. It is noted mainly as a brown trout and sea trout fishery but also holds char and salmon. Most of the fishing is done from a boat. Enquiries about the fishing should be made to:

◆ *Estate Office*, The Square, Kenmare, Co. Kerry; telephone (064) 41341
◆ *Cheveley Johnston and Company*, 27 Wellington Road, Cork; telephone (021) 501109.

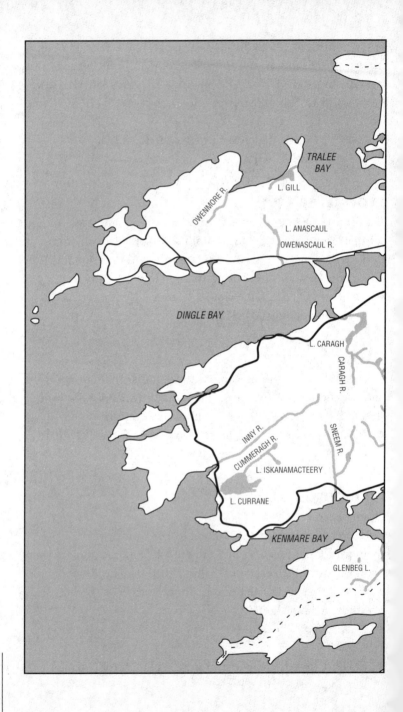

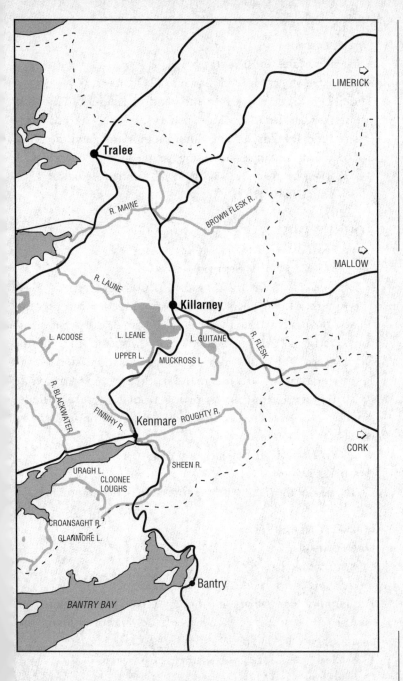

SHEEN RIVER
Open Season
Salmon: 15 March to 30 September;
sea trout and brown trout: 15 March to 12 October.

The Sheen River flows into the head of Kenmare Bay. It is primarily regarded as a salmon fishery, and the sea trout run is less prolific. It holds spring salmon from March, and the grilse arrive in June. Enquiries about the fishing should be made to:

◆ *The Manager, Sheen Falls Lodge Hotel,* Kenmare, Co. Kerry; telephone (064) 41600.

ROUGHTY RIVER
Open Season
Salmon: 15 March to 30 September;
sea trout and brown trout: 15 March to 12 October.

The Roughty River flows in a westerly direction through the village of Kilgarvan into the top of Kenmare Bay. It gets a small run of spring salmon and a good run of grilse; the sea trout run has declined. The banks are very overgrown and undeveloped. The fishing rights are fragmented; there is one stretch at Ardtully Castle that is the property of Kenmare Salmon Angling Ltd, and another stretch at Kilgarvan on which day tickets can be obtained from:

◆ *John O'Hare,* fishing tackle shop, Main Street, Kenmare, Co. Kerry.

The rest of the fishing is by permission of the landowners.

FINNIHY RIVER
Open Season
Salmon: 15 March to 30 September;
sea trout and brown trout: 15 March to 12 October.

The Finnihy River flows into Kenmare Bay. It is a small river that produces a few grilse every season. Enquiries about the fishing should be made to:

◆ *Estate Office,* The Square, Kenmare, Co. Kerry; telephone (064) 41341.

BLACKWATER RIVER (KENMARE)
Open Season
Salmon: 15 March to 30 September;
sea trout: 15 March to 12 October.

The River Blackwater enters Kenmare Bay seven miles west of the town of Kenmare. It drains a large area, including three loughs. It gets a small run of spring salmon, an excellent run of grilse, and a good run of sea trout. This is a productive river but has its problems which include gravel extraction. Enquiries about the fishing should be made to:

◆ *Estate Office*, The Square, Kenmare, Co. Kerry; telephone (064) 41341

◆ *Maj. Waller*, Dromore Castle, Blackwater, Kenmare, Co. Kerry.

SNEEM RIVER
Open Season
Salmon: 15 March to 30 September;
sea trout: 15 March to 12 October.

The Sneem River drains a number of lakes. It gets a small run of grilse and sea trout in July and August. It is very much a spate river. It is usually let together with a holiday cottage; enquiries should be made to:

◆ *Mr Henry Cooper*, Sneem, Co. Kerry.

HUMPHRY LAKES

These small lakes are in the mountains of east Kerry. They are not very accessible, and the trout are said to range between 1 and 4 lb. The fishing can be difficult, and permission is not usually required.

BARFINNIHY LAKE
Open Season
15 June to 31 August.

Barfinnihy Lake is six-and-a-half miles from Kenmare, near Moll's Gap. It is developed by the regional fisheries board and holds a good stock of wild brown trout, and adult rainbow trout are stocked regularly. Information and permits are available at:

- *Cremin's Tourist Shop*, Moll's Gap, Kenmare, Co. Kerry
- *Mr John O'Hare*, fishing tackle shop, Main Street, Kenmare, Co. Kerry.

LOUGH FADDA
Open Season
15 June to 31 August.

Lough Fadda lies eleven miles south-west of Kenmare and three miles from the village of Sneem. It holds a good stock of rainbow trout, and adult rainbow trout are stocked regularly. It is developed by the regional fisheries board, and boats and permits are available from:

- *Mrs O'Sullivan*, Direenamackion, Tahilla, Co. Kerry
- *Mrs N. Hussey*, Sneem, Co. Kerry.

■ WATERVILLE SYSTEM

Open Season
Salmon: 17 January to 30 September; *sea trout:* 17 January to 12 October. There is a 9 inch size limit for trout.

WATERVILLE RIVER
The Waterville River drains Lough Currane and the entire Waterville system to the sea. It produces spring salmon and grilse. This is a private fishery on which rods are let occasionally; enquiries about the fishing should be made to:

- *Waterville House*, Waterville, Co. Kerry;
  telephone (0667) 4244.

CUMMERAGH RIVER
The Cummeragh River drains a large catchment area and ten loughs into Lough Currane. It holds occasional spring salmon

and is a noted grilse and sea trout fishery. The fishing is private; enquiries should be made to:

◆ *Waterville House,* Waterville, Co. Kerry;
   telephone (0667) 4244
◆ *Mr Robert Noonan,* Dromkeare Lodge, Waterville, Co. Kerry.

LOUGH CURRANE

Lough Currane is noted for its big sea trout, and produces a good number of spring salmon and grilse every season as well. The fishing is free, and there is public access at the Bog, the Bridge, and Water-Lily Bay. There are numerous private access points as well.

The big sea trout arrive in April, and the peak of the sea trout fishing is around mid-June. The fishing can vary from then until the end of the season but is generally quite good in September. The spring salmon fishing begins on opening day – 17 January – and the peak of the spring salmon fishing is in late March and April. The peak of the grilse run is in June.

Boats and crews can be arranged through:

◆ *Mr Michael O'Sullivan,* The Lobster Bar, Waterville,
   Co. Kerry; telephone (0667) 4183
◆ *Mr Brod O'Sullivan,* Stella Mara, Waterville, Co. Kerry;
   telephone (0677) 4749
◆ *Mr Frank Donnelly,* Lake Road, Waterville, Co. Kerry;
   telephone (0667) 4303
◆ *Mr Vincent O'Sullivan,* Waterville, Co. Kerry; telephone
   (0667) 4255
◆ *Mr Terence Wharton,* Ballybrack, Waterville, Co. Kerry;
   telephone (0667) 4264
◆ *Mr John M. Donnelly,* Lake Road, Waterville, Co. Kerry;
   telephone (0667) 4139
◆ *Mr Michael Donnelly,* Raheen, Waterville, Co. Kerry
◆ *Mr Tom O'Shea,* Tarmons, Waterville, Co. Kerry.

LOUGH NA MONA
DERRIANA LOUGH
LOUGH ISKANAMACTEERY
CAPPAL LOUGH

These are all mountain loughs on the Waterville system. Some of them hold small brown trout, others relatively good brown trout, and all of them hold sea trout and salmon later in the season after the first floods take the fish up. The sea trout fishing can be particularly good on these loughs late in the season, especially in September and October. Enquiries about the fishing should be made to:

◆ *Butler Arms Hotel*, Waterville, Co. Kerry;
   telephone (0667) 4156
◆ *Waterville House*, Waterville, Co. Kerry;
   telephone (0667) 4244.

INNY RIVER
Open Season
Salmon: 17 January to 30 September;
sea trout: 17 January to 12 October.

The Inny River drains the mountains west of Waterville. It is an extreme spate system, and the fishing is confined to spate conditions and rarely lasts for more than a day. It is mainly a grilse fishery, with the fish running on every flood from mid-June to September. The removal of gravel from the river is a serious problem and has greatly disrupted the physical character of the channel.

The ownership of the fishing rights is fragmented; enquiries about fishing should be made to:

◆ *Butler Arms Hotel*, Waterville, Co. Kerry; telephone (0667) 4156
◆ *Jim Sugrue*, Moulnahone, Mastergeehy, Co. Kerry
◆ *Dónal O'Sullivan*, Inchiboy, Mastergeehy, Co. Kerry
◆ *James O'Connell*, Foildrenagh, Mastergeehy, Co. Kerry
◆ *John O'Shea*, Killenleigh, Mastergeehy, Co. Kerry
◆ *Mr Frank Donnelly*, Lake Road, Waterville, Co. Kerry;
   telephone (0667) 4303

- *Michael J. O'Sullivan*, The Lobster Bar, Waterville, Co. Kerry; telephone (0667) 4255
- *Michael Gass*, Kylemore House, Waterville, Co. Kerry; telephone (0667) 4225
- *Waterville House*, Waterville, Co. Kerry; telephone (0667) 4244.

■ CARAGH RIVER SYSTEM

Open Season

Salmon: 17 January to 30 September; *sea trout:* 17 January to 12 October; *brown trout:* 15 February to 12 October.

The Caragh River drains a large catchment area and about six lakes before entering Lough Caragh. On leaving the lough it flows for two miles to the sea.

The Caragh River is a classic spate system. It gets a good run of spring salmon and grilse, and the lower river is noted as a sea trout fishery. The spring fish run in February, March, and April; the grilse begin running at the end of May; and the sea trout run from mid-August.

Enquiries about the fishing should be made to:

- *KRD Fisheries Ltd*, Killorglin, Co. Kerry; telephone (066) 61106
- *Glencar Hotel*, Glencar, Co. Kerry; telephone (066) 60102
- *Mr Johnnie Mangan*, Glencaragh Anglers' Association; telephone (066) 60146.

LOUGH CARAGH

Lough Caragh is noted for its spring salmon fishing and grilse fishing, and to a lesser extent as a brown trout and sea trout fishery. The fishing is regarded as free. The season is as for the Caragh River.

There is one public access point to the lake at the outflowing river. Boats and boatmen are available for hire along the north and west shores or can be arranged through:

- *Glencar Hotel*, Glencar, Co. Kerry; telephone (066) 60102.

LOUGH ACOOSE, CLOON LOUGH, LOUGH REAGH

These three loughs are on the Caragh system, and they hold brown trout and occasional salmon. Enquiries about the fishing should be made to:

◆ *Glencar Hotel*, Glencar, Co. Kerry; telephone (066) 60102

and for Lough Acoose also to:

◆ *Mr Johnnie Mangan*, Glencaragh Anglers' Association; telephone (066) 60146.

LOUGH NA KIRKA

Open Season

15 June to 31 August.

Lough na Kirka lies six miles south-west of Killorglin. It is a small lake holding an excellent stock of small brown trout and is stocked with rainbow trout by the regional fisheries board. Permits are available from:

◆ *Cappanalee Outdoor Education Centre*, Killorglin, Co. Kerry

◆ *Mr Dermot Foley*, The Bridge, Killorglin, Co. Kerry.

OWENMORE RIVER

Open Season

Salmon and sea trout: 1 April to 30 September.

This is a small spate river on the Dingle Peninsula that drains nine loughs. It gets a run of sea trout from April, and grilse from June. Enquiries about the fishing should be made to:

◆ *Mr Gerry Connor*, Bridge Cottage, Cloghane, Co. Kerry; telephone (066) 38244

◆ *Mr Bertie Brosnan*, Mitchell's Road, Tralee, Co. Kerry.

OWENASCAUL RIVER
LOUGH ANASCAUL

Open Season

Salmon: 17 March to 30 September;

sea trout: 17 March to 12 October.

The Owenascaul River drains into Dingle Bay. It is believed to be worth fishing for grilse and sea trout from June. The fishing is regarded as free. Lough Anascaul holds sea trout and occasional grilse. Enquiries about the fishing should be made locally.

LOUGH GILL

Lough Gill holds brown trout averaging 0.5 lb. The fishing is regarded as free. A boat is necessary to fish the lough; boats are available from:

◆ *Mrs Kelleher*, The Guesthouse, Loubeg, Castlegregory, Co. Kerry
◆ *Mrs Agnes Reidy*, Goulane House, Stradbally, Dingle, Co. Kerry.

LOUGH CAUM

Open Season

15 June to 31 August

Lough Caum, in Glenteenasig Forest, Aughacashla, holds a good stock of small brown trout and is regularly stocked with adult rainbow trout by the regional fisheries board. Permits and boats are available from:

◆ *Keane's Foodmarket*, Aughacashla, Castlegregory, Co. Kerry; telephone (066) 39186.

■ RIVER LAUNE SYSTEM

Open Season

Salmon: 17 January to 30 September; *sea trout:* 17 January to 12 October; *brown trout:* 15 February to 12 October.

The River Laune drains the lakes of Killarney. It gets a good run of spring salmon and grilse; the best of the spring salmon is early in the season, and the grilse run peaks in June. The sea trout stocks have declined, but the river holds a good stock of brown trout. It is possible to get permission to fish the river by contacting:

◆ *South-Western Regional Fisheries Board*, 1 Neville's Terrace, Macroom, Co. Cork; telephone (026) 41222
◆ *Park Superintendent, Knockrear Estate Office*, Killarney, Co. Kerry; telephone (064) 31246

- *Mr Ted O'Riordan*, secretary, Laune Salmon Anglers' Association, 50 Oak Park Demesne, Tralee, Co. Kerry; telephone (066) 24690
- *Mr John Mangan;* telephone (066) 61393.

Daily and weekly permits are also available from fishing tackle shops in Killarney, from the shop at Beaufort Bridge, and from:

- *Mr Pat O'Grady*, Hillside House, Glenbeigh, Co. Kerry; telephone (066) 68228 who also lets tickets on the Caragh River.

RIVER FLESK

The River Flesk drains into Lough Leane at Killarney. It gets a run of spring salmon early in the season, and the grilse run in late May and early June. Permission to fish can be obtained from:

- *Cahernane Hotel*, Killarney, Co. Kerry; telephone (064) 31895.

Lough Lein Anglers' Association has fishing on this water; permits are available from:

- *The Handy Shop*, Kenmare Place, Killarney, Co. Kerry
- *O'Neill's Tackle Shop*, Plunkett Street, Killarney, Co. Kerry.

Clonkeen Anglers' Association has fishing on the river; enquiries should be made to:

- *Clonkeen Post Office*, Killarney, Co. Kerry.

LOUGH LEANE

Lough Leane is noted for its brown trout and salmon fishing. It holds spring salmon from opening day and grilse from June; it also holds an excellent stock of brown trout. Boats are available for hire from:

- *Mr Henry Clifden*, Ross Castle, Killarney, Co. Kerry; telephone (064) 32252
- *Mr Alfie Doyle;* telephone (064) 33652.

MUCKROSS LAKE

Muckross Lake holds an excellent stock of spring salmon from early in the season. The brown trout are small, and the best fishing is usually in September. Boats are available for hire from private operators at Muckross House, and bank fishing is allowed.

UPPER LAKE, KILLARNEY

The Upper Lake holds small brown trout and gets a good run of salmon from early in the season to the end of June. Boats are available for hire from:

◆ *Mr John O'Donoghue*, Black Valley, Killarney, Co. Kerry.

LOUGH GUITANE

Lough Guitane lies four miles south-east of Killarney. It holds a big stock of small brown trout and gets a small run of sea trout from July. The fishing is regarded as free, and boats are available locally.

RIVER MAINE
LITTLE RIVER MAINE
BROWN FLESK RIVER
Open Season

Salmon: 17 January to 30 September; *sea trout*: 17 January to 12 October; *brown trout:* 15 February to 12 October.

The River Maine is a medium-sized river with two tributaries, the Brown Flesk and the Little Maine. It flows into Castlemaine Harbour. Much of the river is overgrown. It gets a good run of salmon and sea trout late in the season. It has five draft nets operating at the mouth, including one above Castlemaine. The grilse enter the river in June, and the sea trout run in July.

The Little Maine is primarily a brown trout and sea trout fishery. The Brown Flesk is a spate river and can give good sport for salmon and sea trout after a spate.

Most of the fishing is regarded as free, and enquiries should be made to:

◆ *South-Western Regional Fisheries Board*, 1 Neville's Terrace, Macroom, Co. Cork; telephone (026) 41222.

Shannon Fisheries Region

The Shannon Fisheries Region comprises all the rivers that flow into the sea between Kerry Head, Co. Kerry, and Hag's Head, Co. Clare. The headquarters of the Shannon Regional Fisheries Board is at Thomond Weir, Limerick; telephone (061) 455171.

The Shannon Region consists of a single district, the Limerick District, which comprises Cos. Roscommon and Clare and parts of Cos. Kerry, Limerick, Tipperary, Galway, Offaly, Westmeath, Meath, Sligo, Longford, Leitrim, and Cavan.

The Shannon Region has a wide range of game fishing to offer the angler. In north Kerry it is mainly spring salmon, grilse, and sea trout. Co. Clare mainly offers brown trout possibilities, with occasional salmon and grilse. Castleconnell, the Limerick fisheries and the Mulkear River are prime salmon and grilse fisheries. The Nenagh River and the Suck tributaries have notable brown trout stretches, while the midland lakes – Lough Sheelin, Lough Owel, and Lough Ennell – hold some of the finest stocks of brown trout in the country.

There is an 8 inch size limit on the entire system above Limerick and in the Rivers Fergus and Maigue.

Open Season

Salmon and sea trout: 1 March to 15 September.

The River Feale is the most important salmon and sea trout river in north Kerry. It rises in Co. Cork and flows through Abbeyfeale and Listowel to enter the sea just south of Ballybunnion. The river is tidal almost as far up as Finuge Bridge, and rod-and-line fishing ends about two miles below this bridge. Most of the fishing on the river is controlled by angling clubs. A few stretches are let to rods on a yearly basis by private owners, and there are a couple of short stretches that are regarded as free fishing.

The Feale gets equally good runs of salmon and sea trout. The best of the salmon fishing is from the tide up to Abbeyfeale. There are salmon in the river from opening day on 1 March. The sea trout fishing is best either downstream of Listowel or upstream of Abbeyfeale. The first sea trout enter the river in May, and the fishing lasts to September. All legitimate fishing methods are allowed on the river, with spinning, worm and fly being the most popular for salmon. However, some angling clubs impose their own restrictions. The clubs from which day tickets may be obtained are as follows:

Killocrim-Finuge Angling Club:
- *Mr Dan Joy*, Killocrim, Listowel, Co. Kerry
- *Mr George Gaine*, Greenville, Listowel, Co. Kerry.

North Kerry Anglers' Association:
- *Mr Jack Sheehan*, 23 Church Street, Listowel, Co. Kerry
- *Mr Tom Walsh*, tackle dealer, Upper Church Street, Listowel, Co. Kerry.

Tralee and District Anglers' Association:
- *Mr Arthur Drugan*, 114 St Brendan's Park, Tralee, Co. Kerry
- *Mr Matt Doody*, Colbert's Terrace, Abbeyfeale, Co. Limerick
- *Mr Tim Landers*, Landers Leisure Lines, Courthouse Lane, Tralee, Co. Kerry; telephone (066) 24378
- *Mr Joe O'Keeffe*, Glenview, Kilmorna, Co. Kerry; telephone (068) 45189.

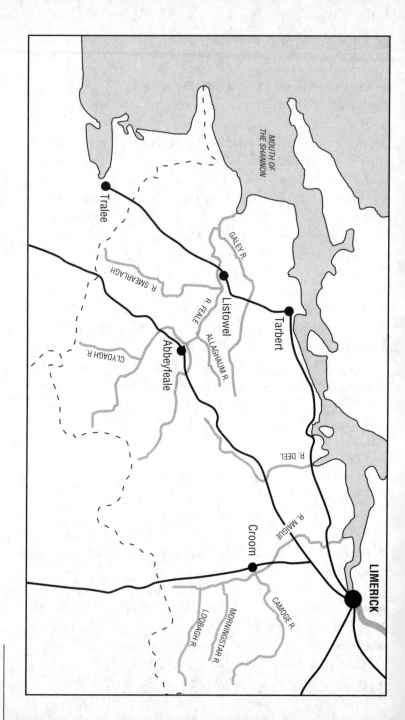

Abbeyfeale Anglers' Association:
◆ *Ryan's Tackle Shop*, New Street, Abbeyfeale, Co. Limerick
◆ *Mr Paddy Sullivan*, Knocknasna Upper, Abbeyfeale, Co. Limerick; telephone (068) 31453.
Brosna-Mountcollins Angling Club:
◆ *Mr Lou Murphy*, Brosna, Co. Kerry; telephone (068) 44148
◆ *Mr Kevin Barry*, Mountcollins, Co. Limerick.

RIVER SMEARLAGH

The River Smearlagh is a tributary of the Feale; it is a spate river that can give good salmon fishing after a flood. The fishing is controlled by North Kerry Anglers' Association (as above).

CLYDAGH RIVER
ALLAGHAUN RIVER
UPPER RIVER FEALE

All these rivers hold sea trout and can give fishing for a short period after a flood.

GALEY RIVER

The Galey River is a tributary of the Feale. It flows through Athea, Co. Limerick, and enters the Feale west of Listowel. It is regarded primarily as a brown trout fishery, and the average size of the trout is about 0.5 lb. Fishing is by permission of the riparian owners.

RIVER DEEL
Open Season

Brown trout: 15 February to 30 September.

A by-law prohibits fishing by any means in certain stretches of the River Deel, particularly near the various weirs in the townlands of Aghalacka, Cloonreask, and Askeaton. It is advisable to check locally before starting to fish.

The Deel rises near Drumina, Co. Cork, and flows north through Co. Limerick to the tide in the Shannon Estuary. Nowadays it only holds brown trout. The river has been drained and the banks are high, and it has other problems associated with arterial drainage works, especially excessive weed growth.

The river holds a fair stock of wild brown trout and in addition is stocked with fry and adult trout by the local angling clubs every season.

Most of the fishing is controlled by the Deel Anglers' Association, which has clubs in Newcastle, Rathkeale, and Askeaton. For permission to fish, contact:

◆ *Mr Matt Scanlan*, tackle shop, Maiden Street, Newcastle, Co. Limerick

◆ *Mr Mike Sheehy*, Bridge Street, Newcastle, Co. Limerick; telephone (069) 62620.

■ RIVER MAIGUE SYSTEM

Open Season
Salmon: 1 February to 30 September;
brown trout: 15 February to 30 September.

The River Maigue rises south of Bruree, Co. Limerick, and flows north through Croom and Adare into the Shannon Estuary. It is a limestone river, as are its tributaries, the Camoge, the Morningstar, and the Loobagh. It was regarded as one of Ireland's premier trout rivers until an arterial drainage scheme began in the 1970s. The scheme destroyed much of the natural character of the river, and the banks are now very high in many places and the tributaries run quite low in summer. Some rehabilitation work has been carried out by the regional fisheries board, and trout stocks have made a come-back in certain areas. Trout range in size from 0.5 lb up to 3 lb. The river has all the fly hatches one associates with a limestone river, including mayfly.

The fishing rights are either privately owned or controlled by angling clubs. With the fishing so reduced as a result of the drainage works, only a limited number of places is available; enquiries should be made to:

◆ *Mr Edmond Costello*, Maigue Anglers' Association, River Farm, Ballycarney, Clarina, Co. Limerick; telephone (061) 355116
◆ *Mrs Eileen McDonagh*, Cooleen House, Bruree, Co. Limerick; telephone (063) 90584
◆ *Recreation Manager*, *Adare Manor Hotel*, Adare, Co. Limerick; telephone (061) 86566.

CAMOGE RIVER

The Camoge River flows west to join the Maigue upstream of Croom. Fishing on the river is strictly confined to fly fishing only. In recent years there has been an improvement in the trout fishing. Enquiries should be made to the secretary of the Camoge Angling Club:

◆ *Mr Dan Quain*, 11 Coshma Avenue, Croom, Co. Limerick; telephone (061) 43672.

MORNINGSTAR RIVER

The Morningstar River suffered badly as a result of the arterial drainage scheme, and it can no longer be recommended as a trout fishery.

LOOBAGH RIVER

The Loobagh River flows west from Kilmallock to join the Maigue. It too suffered badly as a result of the arterial drainage scheme, and much of the fishing was destroyed. There is some fishing left, but the trout are small; enquiries should be made to Kilmallock and District Anglers' Association:

◆ *Mr Raymond Breen*, Riverfeale, Kilmallock, Co. Limerick.

BLEACH LOUGH

Bleach Lough is between Kildimo and Pallaskenry, Co. Limerick. It is stocked annually with brown trout and rainbow trout. Both bank and boat fishing are allowed. Enquiries should be made to:

◆ *Mr Pat Heavenor*, Mount Pleasant, Kildimo, Co. Limerick; telephone (061) 393147.

■ RIVER SHANNON, TRIBUTARIES, AND LAKES

Open Season

Salmon and sea trout: 1 February to 30 September;
brown trout: 15 February to 30 September. (There may be different statutory opening and closing dates for some of the lakes and tributaries on the Shannon system. Various by-laws prohibit fishing for approximately 50 yards downstream of the sluice gates at Killaloe, within 200 yards of the sluices in Ardcloony and Birdhill, and in the tail-race between the power station at Ardnacrusha and the bridge at Garraun.)

The River Shannon is the longest river in Ireland. It rises in Co. Cavan and flows south for 160 miles to Limerick, which is at the top of a 40-mile estuary. It is a great mixed fishery, holding salmon, trout, pike, and coarse fish.

The salmon fishing rights on the Shannon are reserved by the ESB, and a permit is required to fish for salmon on any part of the river or its tributaries.

The brown trout fishing on the Shannon is partly free and partly leased to the Central Fisheries Board and to a number of angling clubs. The fisheries leased to the Central Fisheries Board are all the fisheries, rivers and lakes on the Inny and the Suck systems. The Nenagh River is leased to a local angling club. There is no charge for fishing for brown trout on the other rivers or tributaries of the Shannon.

The main channel can be divided into three sections from a game fisher's point of view: the Castleconnell and Limerick city fisheries, the Meelick fishery, and the Upper Shannon fisheries.

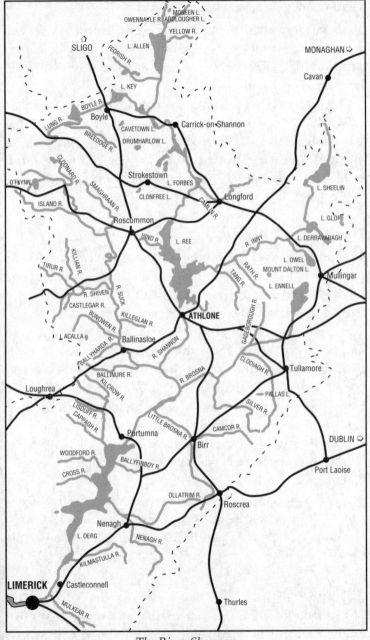

The River Shannon

Castleconnell Fishery

This salmon fishery comprises eight beats, which can accommodate twenty rods. Five beats are let by tender and the remaining three are available on a day ticket basis, and all beats are rotated daily.

This fishery gets a good run of spring salmon and a big run of grilse. The spring fish season peaks in late March and April. The grilse fishing peaks in June. All legitimate fishing methods are allowed except natural shrimp. Applications should be made to:

◆ *Generation Manager, ESB Hydro Group,* Ardnacrusha, Co. Clare; telephone (061) 345588.

Limerick City Fisheries

This stretch of river at Limerick is about six miles long and has five fishing locations. Four of the most famous are the Long Shore, Plassey, Corbally, and the Cut. These fisheries hold varying quantities of spring salmon, grilse, and brown trout. The spring salmon and grilse fishing peak in March and April and in May and June, respectively. During the heavy runs of fish, these areas are very popular fishing locations, and overcrowding often occurs. The banks for the most part are clear and easy to fish, but access to the Long Shore and Corbally is positively difficult. Permits are available from:

◆ *ESB Shop,* Bishopsgate, Limerick; telephone (061) 415599
◆ *Mr Jim Robinson,* tackle shop, Thomond Shopping Centre, Limerick; telephone (061) 414900
◆ *The Angling Centre,* Castle Oaks House Hotel, Castleconnell, Co. Limerick; telephone (061) 377666.

Gillies can be arranged through Mr Jim Robinson or the Castle Oaks Hotel.

Meelick Fishery

The salmon fishing at Meelick on the Shannon is about five miles downstream of Banagher, Co. Offaly. This fishery is heavily fished at the peak of the season. The fishing is in two parts: the right bank or Eyrecourt side and the left bank or Offaly side.

The salmon fishing begins at Meelick around the third week of May, with the peak in the last week of June or early July. Access to the right bank is off the Banagher–Eyrecourt road at Kilnaborris; access to the left bank is from Banagher, via Lusmagh village to Victoria Lough. A boat is necessary to fish this side, and anglers must provide their own. Permits for salmon fishing are available from:

◆ *Electricity Supply Board*, Birr, Co. Offaly; telephone (0509) 20500

◆ *Electricity Supply Board*, Ballinasloe, Co. Galway; telephone (0905) 42340

◆ *Mr Jim Robinson*, fishing tackle shop, Thomond Shopping Centre, Limerick; telephone (061) 414900.

Upper Shannon Fisheries

A by-law prohibits fishing for salmon or trout within 20 yards of the weir wall at Tarmonbarry. The top stretch of the Shannon extends for a distance of about six miles from Ballantra Bridge to just below Battle Bridge near the village of Leitrim. Here the trout fishing is free. The river holds fair stocks of brown trout up to about 2 lb. Roach have spread into this part of the Shannon, and a lot of coarse fishing also takes place in this area. Access to the better trout fishing stretches at this location is quite difficult.

LOUGH DERG

This is the largest lough on the Shannon and stretches for twenty-two miles from Portumna south to Killaloe. It is a great mixed fishery, with salmon, trout, pike, and coarse fish. Public access is good, and the following access points should be noted: Portumna, Terryglass, Kilgarvan, Dromineer, Garrykennedy, Ballina, Killaloe, Tinorana Bay, Scarriff and Mountshannon, Knockaphort and Church Bay.

This was one of the great trout fisheries, though the fishing was mainly concentrated at mayfly time; it is generally agreed that the fishing has dropped off considerably in recent times. The average weight of the trout is 2 lb, and some very large fish are taken every year on both dapped mayfly and the spent gnat. Wet fly fishing is not widely practised. Water clarity has deteriorated, and increasing eutrophication has given rise to an algal growth, especially during the summer months.

Boats and sometimes outboard motors are available for hire from:

- ◆ *Mr J. Bottcher*, Mountshannon, Co. Clare; telephone (0619) 27225
- ◆ *Mr Arthur Monaghan*, Shannon Road, Portumna, Co. Galway
- ◆ *Mr Tony Cunningham*, Dominick Street, Portumna, Co. Galway
- ◆ *Mr Jackie Keane*, Middle Line, Mountshannon, Co. Clare
- ◆ *Mr James Minogue*, Middle Line, Mountshannon, Co. Clare
- ◆ *The Sail Inn*, Dromineer, Co. Tipperary; telephone (067) 24114.

Boats and outboards are also available for hire at both Whitegate and Scarriff.

LOUGH REE

This is the second of the great loughs on the River Shannon. It stretches for sixteen miles from Lanesborough to Athlone.

Access to the lough is reasonably good. There are a number of boat slips and moorings in the vicinity of Lanesborough. There is a boat harbour and boat slip at Elfeet Bay, and similar facilities exist at Barley Harbour. There is a natural slipway and berthage for anglers' boats at Portlick Castle. At Coosan Point there is a car park and access to the lough, and similar facilities exist at Barry More and Hodson's Bay. Gallay Bay has a slipway and moorings. Boats may also be moored at Portrunny Bay, but this is a very exposed area.

Lough Ree is a great wild, mixed fishery that holds a good stock of trout as well as pike and coarse fish. The peak of the trout fishing is from mid-May during the mayfly season. The average weight is probably over 2 lb. Dapping is widely practised, but the trout will also take a Green Drake Mayfly imitation, and the spent gnat fishing is said to be extremely good. The fishing is free.

A limited number of boats are available for hire, and enquiries should be made to:

◆ *SGS Marine*, Ballykeeran, Co. Westmeath; telephone (0902) 85163
◆ *Mr Harry Waterstone,* Griffith Street, Athlone, Co. Westmeath; telephone (0902) 72896
◆ *Mr P. Naughton,* Galey Bay Caravan Park, Knockcrockery, Co. Roscommon; telephone (0903) 7058
◆ *Mr Peter Quigley,* Killinure, Athlone; telephone (0902) 85105.

LOUGH ALLEN

Lough Allen is the first of the three great loughs on the River Shannon. It is eight miles long by three miles wide. The water level is controlled by sluice gates and can fluctuate by as much as eight feet. Lough Allen is noted as a pike fishery, and holds coarse fish too. It holds a good stock of brown trout averaging about 1 lb. There is a small mayfly hatch, but it is thought that the best of the trout fishing is in April, August, and September. Dapping can be very effective in August and September.

Boats are available for hire from:

◆ *Mr Brian McGourty,* Carrick Road, Drumshanbo, Co. Leitrim
◆ *Mr Cyril Reynolds,* Drumshanbo, Co. Leitrim; telephone (078) 41057
◆ *Ms Marian Kane,* Drumshanbo, Co. Leitrim; telephone (078) 41434
◆ *Mrs Eva Mooney,* Drumshanbo, Co. Leitrim; telephone (078) 41013
◆ *Mr R. O'Dwyer,* Lakeside House, Cormongan, Drumshanbo, Co. Leitrim; telephone (078) 41112.

MULKEAR RIVER
Open Season
Salmon: 1 March to 30 September.

No fishing is allowed for fifty yards downstream of the Mill Weir at Ballyclough, and after 31 May between the New Road Bridge at Annacotty and 50 yards above the Annacotty Weir.

The Mulkear River rises north of Tipperary town and flows in a north-westerly direction to the Shannon at Annacotty. It is a spate river. The salmon fishing extends over approximately twenty miles of water, which includes the headwaters of the Mulkear and its tributary, the Newport River. This is primarily a grilse system and gets a small run of spring salmon. The spring salmon fishing peaks in April, and the grilse fishing begins around mid-June.The river is heavily fished and can get overcrowded at the peak of the fishing season.

Permits are available from:

◆ *ESB Shop,* Bishop's Quay, Limerick; telephone (061) 45599
◆ *Mr Jim Robinson,* Tackle Shop, Thomond Shopping Centre, Limerick; telephone (061) 414900
◆ *Angling Centre,* Castle Oaks House Hotel, Castleconnell, Co. Limerick; telephone (061) 377666.

KILMASTULLA RIVER
Open Season
Brown trout: 1 March to 30 September.

The Kilmastulla River empties into the Shannon at Parteen. It is a drained river, with very high banks in places. It holds moderate stocks of trout close to the headwaters and in a short stretch immediately upstream of the Nenagh–Limerick road. Access is difficult.

NENAGH RIVER
Open Season
Brown trout: 1 March to 30 September. A by-law prohibits fishing between the Ballyartella Weir and the upstream face of the Ballyartella Bridge.

The Nenagh River rises in the Silver Mine Mountains, Co. Tipperary, and flows into Lough Derg at Dromineer. It is primarily a brown trout river, with over thirteen miles of trout fishing on the main river and nine miles on its tributary, the Ollatrim River. It holds excellent stocks of trout to about 5 lb and some larger trout in the 6 to 12 lb range.

Access to the river banks is fair. The banks are high, difficult, and overgrown, but it is possible to fish in certain areas. The river has all the usual fly hatches associated with a rich limestone river, including mayfly.

The river gets a run of lake trout, known locally as 'croneen'. These fish tend to run on a flood after mid-July. They are usually fished with worm in a flood or with a fly or spinner late in the evening.

The Nenagh River and the Ollatrim River are leased by the ESB to Ormond Anglers' Association. Permits and enquiries about the fishing should be made to:

◆ *Whelan's Tackle Shop*, Summerhill, Nenagh, Co. Tipperary.

BALLYFINBOY RIVER
This was once a prolific trout river but it has been so seriously damaged by arterial drainage works that it is unlikely to recover as a trout fishery.

❑ LITTLE BROSNA SYSTEM

Open Season
Salmon and brown trout: 1 March to 30 September. There is a 9 inch size limit and a six-trout bag limit. Artificial fly only is permitted from Milltown Bridge to Monastery Bridge, from Brosna Bridge to Sharavogue Bridge, and from Purcell's Drain to Riverstown.

Trout fishing is not permitted upstream of Milltown Bridge, in the interest of conservation, and the fisheries board's permit does not confer a right to fish those stretches of the Little Brosna and Camcor Rivers that flow through Birr Castle demesne.

The Little Brosna and its tributaries, the Camcor and the Bunow River, rise near Roscrea, Co. Tipperary; the river joins the Shannon at Meelick. This is a noted brown trout system and holds fair stocks of salmon in summer in the lower reaches. The average size of the trout is less than 0.5 lb. It has all the fly hatches one associates with a limestone river, including mayfly. The best of the salmon fishing is downstream of Riverstown.

The Camcor joins the Little Brosna at Birr. The indigenous trout stocks are small, but from mid-June it gets a run of 'croneen' from Lough Derg. Access to both rivers is good, mainly from the bridges, and the banks are well serviced with stiles and footbridges.

The river may be fished with a fisheries board permit. This is available from:

◆ *The Fish Farm*, Fanure, Roscrea, Co. Tipperary
◆ *Mr Michael Madden*, Tackle Shop, Main Street, Birr, Co. Offaly
◆ *Mr Michael Davis*, Emmet Street, Birr, Co. Offaly.
  Salmon permits are available from:
◆ *Fisheries Office*, ESB Hydro Group, Ardnacrusha, Co. Clare
◆ *ESB Shop*, Birr, Co. Offaly.

❖ ❖

❏ RIVER BROSNA SYSTEM

Open Season
Salmon and brown trout: 1 March to 30 September.
The River Brosna rises in Lough Ennell, Co. Westmeath, and flows through Kilbeggan, Clara and Ferbane to the Shannon at Shannon Harbour, Co. Offaly. It gets a small run of spring salmon and a fair run of summer fish every season. The best salmon fishing is all downstream of Clonmony Bridge. Access to the river is mainly at the bridges; the banks are fairly good but overgrown in places.

The brown trout fishing can be good early in the season, especially in March, and lasts until the river becomes overgrown with weed around mid-June. There are a number of good trout fishing stretches at Ballingore, Kilbeggan, Clara, Ballycumber, and downstream of Belmont Bridge.

SILVER RIVER (KILCORMAC)
The Silver River joins the Brosna east of Ferbane, Co. Offaly. It flows almost entirely through bogland, and this presents many problems of access for the angler. It holds fair stocks of brown trout in certain areas.

CLODIAGH RIVER
The Clodiagh River flows north through Clonaslee and Rahan to join the River Brosna. It holds some good stocks of trout and gets a good late run of salmon. The best of the brown trout fishing is from Rahan to the junction of the Tullamore River; the best of the salmon fishing is in a stretch downstream of Rahan, and the salmon usually arrive in July if there is enough water to bring them up.

SILVER RIVER (TULLAMORE)
The Tullamore Silver River flows west to join the Clodiagh River downstream of Rahan, Co. Offaly. It holds a good stock of brown trout averaging 6 oz. It can be fished early in the season from its confluence with the Clodiagh upstream. This is a limestone river with a good mayfly hatch. Weed growth becomes a problem after the end of May.

GAGEBOROUGH RIVER
The Gageborough River joins the Brosna a mile downstream of Clara, Co. Offaly. The trout stocks and fishing conditions are much the same as on the Tullamore Silver River. The best of the trout fishing is in the three miles upstream of the confluence.

Salmon permits are available from:
- *ESB Shop*, Athlone, Co. Westmeath
- *ESB Shop*, Tullamore, Co. Offaly

- *ESB Shop*, Birr, Co. Offaly.
  Trout permits are available from:
- *Mr Jim Griffin*, The Tackle Shop, Rahan, Co. Offaly;
  telephone (0506) 55979
- *Mr Joe Finlay*, William Street, Tullamore, Co. Offaly
- *Mr Al Conroy*, Stella Crescent, Tullamore, Co. Offaly
- *Mr J. Rabbitt*, supermarket, Clara, Co. Offaly
- *Mr M. F. Kenny*, River Street, Clara, Co. Offaly
- *Nannery's Grocery Shop*, Kilbeggan, Co. Westmeath.

LOUGH ENNELL
Open Season
Brown trout: 1 March to 12 October. There is a six-trout bag limit and a 300 mm size limit.

Lough Ennell lies two miles south of Mullingar. It is a trout fishery of note and produces some of the finest brown trout in the country. They don't give themselves up easily! The average size is about 2 lb.

The duckfly hatch reaches its peak at the end of April. The lake olives hatch in early May, and there is a good mayfly hatch from mid-May. The lake has good hatches of various species of midges.

Boats are available for hire from:
- *Mr Myles Hope*, Lakeview, Lough Ennell, Mullingar,
  Co. Westmeath; telephone (044) 40807
- *Bloomfield House Hotel*, Mullingar, Co. Westmeath;
  telephone (044) 40894.

There is public access to the lough with good car parking facilities at Ladestown, Butler's Bridge, White Bridge Bay, and Lilliput at the southern end. A fisheries board permit is required to fish the lake.

PALLAS LAKE
Open Season
1 March to 12 October.

Pallas Lake is a small fishery eight miles south-west of Tullamore. It is stocked with brown trout and rainbow trout.

Bank fishing only is permitted. The fishing methods are restricted to artificial fly, and there is a six-trout bag limit and an 11 inch size limit.

A fisheries board permit is all that is required, and this is available from:

- *Mr Sammy Smyth*, tackle shop, Castle Street, Mullingar, Co. Westmeath
- *Mr David O'Malley*, tackle shop, Dominick Street, Mullingar, Co. Westmeath
- *Shannon Regional Fisheries Board*, Tudenham, Mullingar; telephone (044) 48769.

❖ ❖

❏ INNY RIVER SYSTEM

Open Season

Salmon and brown trout: 1 March to 30 September. There is a 250 mm (9.8 inch) size limit for brown trout.

The Inny River rises near Oldcastle, Co. Meath, and drains several of the midland lakes before flowing into Lough Ree. An arterial drainage scheme in the 1960s left the banks high and difficult in many places. At present it is considered a mixed fishery, holding big stocks of coarse fish, pike, and some trout.

TANG RIVER

The Tang River joins the Inny downstream of Ballymahon, Co. Longford. A drainage scheme has left the banks high and difficult to fish. It holds trout up as far as Ballymore, but after June the river runs low and fishing becomes a problem because of weeds.

RATH RIVER

The Rath River joins the Inny upstream of Ballymahon, Co. Longford. It holds a stock of small brown trout averaging 8 inches. It is best fished early in the season, in March and April, and thereafter it runs very low. The banks are overgrown.

A fisheries board permit is required to fish these rivers, available from:

◆ *Mr Sammy Smyth*, tackle shop, Castle Street, Mullingar, Co. Westmeath

◆ *Mr David O'Malley*, tackle shop, Dominick Street, Mullingar, Co. Westmeath.

MOUNT DALTON LAKE
Open Season
1 May to 12 October

Mount Dalton Lake is a small lake in the grounds of Brabazon Hall to the west of Mullingar. The lake is stocked with fingerling brown trout that grow naturally. Boat fishing with artificial fly only is the rule. A fisheries board permit is required to fish the lake. There is a boat for hire from:

◆ *Mrs Catherine Gibson-Brabazon*, Mount Dalton, Mullingar, Co. Westmeath; telephone (044) 55102.

LOUGH DERRAVARAGH
Open Season
Brown trout: 1 March to 12 October. There is a 12 inch size limit for trout.

Lough Derravaragh lies eight miles north of Mullingar, and there is access to it near Multyfarnham or at Collure off the Castlepollard–Mullingar road. The trout stocks have decreased dramatically here in recent years. It is now generally regarded as a pike fishery and holds a small stock of big trout that are usually taken trolling. A fisheries board permit is required. Boats are available for hire from:

◆ *Mr Tom Newman*, Multyfarnham, Co. Westmeath.

LOUGH GLORE
Open Season
1 March to 12 October. There is a 10 inch size limit and a six-trout bag limit.

Lough Glore lies to the north of the Castlepollard–Oldcastle road. It holds a good stock of brown trout, and bank fishing is not possible. The average size of the trout is over 1.5 lb. A fisheries board permit is required. Enquiries about boats for hire should be made to:

◆ *Mr Fergus Dunne*, Chapel Road, Castlepollard, Co. Westmeath.

LOUGH SHEELIN
Open Season
1 March to 12 October. (1 March to 30 April, artificial fly only; 1 May to 15 June, artificial fly, blowline dapping, spinning and trolling are permitted but under oars only; 16 June to 30 September, all legitimate methods.) There is a 12 inch size limit and a six-trout bag limit.

Lough Sheelin is a big, rich limestone lake that holds fair stocks of trout averaging about 2.25 lb. It is stocked annually with brown trout.

In the early season the trout are taken close to the shore. The duckfly hatch occurs at the end of April, and there is a small hatch of lake olives in early May. The mayfly hatch begins around 20 May and continues almost to mid-June. The spent gnat fishing can be especially good and spectacular at this time. After the mayfly the trout tend to feed on perch and roach fly, and the fly fishing picks up again in August with the onset of hatches of sedge. Wet fly fishing can be especially productive to September and into early October.

A boat with outboard motor is a necessity to fish Lough Sheelin. Boats are available for hire from:

◆ *Mr Stephen Reilly*, Finea, Co. Westmeath; telephone (043) 81124
◆ *Sheelin Shamrock Hotel*, Mount Nugent, Co. Cavan; telephone (049) 40113
◆ *Crover House*, Mount Nugent, Co. Cavan; telephone (049) 40206
◆ *Mr Robert Chambers*, Mullaghboy House, Ballyheelan, Kilnaleck, Co. Cavan
◆ *Mr P. Leggett*, Kilnahard, Ballyheelan, Kilnaleck, Co. Cavan
◆ *Ross House*, Mount Nugent, Co. Cavan

- *McTeare's*, Lough Sheelin, Finea, Co. Westmeath; telephone (043) 81311
- *Conleen House*, Mount Nugent, Co. Cavan; telephone (049) 40314
- *Mr Fergus Lynch*, Hollywell Lodge, Ballyheelan, Co. Cavan; telephone (049) 36158
- *Mr Gerry O'Connell*, Eagle View, Fortland, Kilnaleck, Co. Cavan; telephone (049) 36563.

  A fisheries board permit is required, and this is available from:
- *Shannon Regional Fisheries Board*, Kilnahard, Ballyheelan, Co. Cavan; telephone (049) 36144
- *Mr Wesley Harper*, The Caravan, Kilnahard, Ballyheelan, Co. Cavan.

LOUGH OWEL

Open Season

1 March to 12 October. There is a size limit of 12 inches.

Lough Owel is a large, limestone lake of approximately 2,500 acres. It is four miles long and two miles wide and lies two miles north-west of Mullingar. This is a deep lake; it holds a fair stock of wild brown trout averaging 2 lb, and is heavily stocked with brown trout by the fisheries board.

The lake has a good hatch of buzzers and a hatch of mayfly. It is especially noted for its hatch of large sedges, locally known as 'green Peters', which occurs around 17 July and lasts into the first week of August. The fishing at this time can be very good. Dapping the grasshopper can be especially effective in August and September.

Rowing boats are available for hire from:
- *Mr Jack Doolan*, Levington, Mullingar, Co. Westmeath; telephone (044) 42085.

  A fisheries board permit is required, and this is available from:
- *Mr Sammy Smyth*, Castle Street, Mullingar, Co. Westmeath
- *Mr David O'Malley*, Dominick Street, Mullingar, Co. Westmeath

◆ *Mr Jack Doolan*, Levington, Mullingar, Co. Westmeath; telephone (044) 42085.

❖ ❖

CAMLIN RIVER

The trout fishing on the Camlin River in Co. Longford is reputed to be so bad that it cannot be recommended.

YELLOW RIVER

Open Season

Brown trout: 1 March to 30 September.

The Yellow River enters Lough Allen from the east. It is a spate river and holds small brown trout in the lower reaches. The fishing is regarded as free.

OWENNAYLE RIVER

Open Season

Brown trout: 1 March to 30 September.

The Owennayle River is a mountain stream that enters Lough Allen from the north. It is reputed to hold some brown trout, and the average size is 0.5 lb. The fishing is regarded as free.

FEORISH RIVER

Open Season

Brown trout: 1 March to 30 September.

This small river comes down from Lough na Bo and joins the Shannon upstream of Wooden Bridge. It holds brown trout up to 1 lb, and is said to have good hatches of olives, sedges, and mayfly.

MONEEN LOUGH
ARDLOUGHER LOUGH

Open Season

Brown trout: 1 March to 30 September.

These two small lakes are near Dowra, Co. Cavan. They each hold a stock of brown trout averaging 0.5 lb. The fishing is regarded as free.

BOYLE RIVER
Open Season
Brown trout: 1 March to 30 September.
The Boyle River rises in Lough Gara and flows into Lough Key. It holds brown trout averaging 0.5 lb, with some up to 2 lb, and there is said to be a good stock of trout in the vicinity of Boyle.

LOUGH KEY
Open Season
Brown trout: 1 March to 30 September.
Lough Key is just over a mile north-east of Boyle, Co. Roscommon. There is access to the shore, with ample car parking and the possibility of launching a boat at Doon Shore, at Drum Bridge, and from the forest park. Lough Key holds a small stock of big brown trout. Anglers usually only fish there at mayfly time, which generally begins around mid-May. There are boats for hire from:
- *Mr James Egan,* Deer Park, Boyle, Co. Roscommon
- *Mr Thomas Egan,* Deer Park, Boyle, Co. Roscommon
- *Mr P. Walsh,* Rockingham, Boyle, Co. Roscommon.

DRUMHARLOW LAKE
Open Season
Brown trout: 1 March to 30 September.
Drumharlow Lake lies a little over a mile west of Carrick-on-Shannon, Co. Leitrim. It holds a good stock of brown trout with a big average size, probably over 2 lb. They are mainly taken at mayfly time. Access to the lake is difficult. Boats and outboard motors can be hired from:
- *Mr Michael Lynch,* The Bridge, Carrick-on-Shannon, Co. Leitrim; telephone (078) 20034.

CAVETOWN LAKE
Open Season
Brown trout: 1 March to 30 September.

Cavetown Lake lies five miles south of Boyle, Co. Roscommon. Access to it is good, with a road running along the south shore. It holds a fair stock of wild brown trout, and is occasionally stocked by the local angling association. It has a good mayfly hatch, and is heavily fished at that time of year. Enquiries about the fishing should be made to the honorary secretary of Cavetown Anglers' Association:

◆ *Mr Francis Beirne*, Croghan, Co. Roscommon.

LOUGH CANBO
Open Season
Brown trout: 1 March to 30 September.
Lough Canbo is approximately five miles south-west of Carrick-on-Shannon, Co. Leitrim. It holds a good stock of brown trout, averaging 0.5 lb. This lake has reeds all round, and a boat is necessary to fish. The fishing is regarded as free.

LISDALY LAKE
Open Season
Brown trout: 1 March to 30 September.
This small lake lies a few hundred yards north of Lough Canbo. It holds a small stock of trout slightly larger than those in Lough Canbo. The banks are soft, with high reeds, but it is possible to fish from platforms that have been erected for the benefit of coarse fishermen.

CORBALLY LOUGH
Open Season
Brown trout: 1 March to 30 September.
Corbally Lough lies approximately four miles south of Carrick-on-Shannon, Co. Leitrim. It holds a good stock of brown trout, averaging 0.5 lb, with some fish to 1.5 lb or better. It is necessary to obtain the permission of the riparian owners to cross the land to gain access to the fishing.

HIND RIVER
Open Season
Brown trout: 1 March to 30 September.
The Hind River flows through Roscommon into Lough Ree, and the fishing is leased by the ESB to Roscommon Rod and Gun Club. It has a chronic pollution problem and cannot be recommended for trout fishing at the present time.

LUNG RIVER
BREEDOGE RIVER
Both of these rivers have been recently subjected to arterial drainage schemes and they cannot be recommended.

◻ RIVER SUCK SYSTEM

Open Season
Salmon and brown trout: 1 March to 30 September.
The Suck is an extensive system and a tributary of the Shannon, draining large areas of Cos. Galway and Roscommon. The character of the river varies greatly. Upstream of Ballymoe, Co. Galway, there is a lot of streamy, fast-flowing water. From Ballymoe downstream to the confluence it is mainly deep and slow and noted for its coarse fish population. There are a limited number of fast-flowing areas in the vicinity of fords where salmon fishing and occasional trout fishing takes place. The tributaries nearly all hold stocks of brown trout.

Salmon fishing on the River Suck is controlled by the ESB. Permits are available from:
◆ *Electricity Supply Board,* Market Square, Ballinasloe,
Co. Galway.

Brown trout fishing is leased by the ESB to the Central Fisheries Board and is managed by the Shannon Regional Fisheries Board. Permits to fish for brown trout on the River Suck, its tributaries and lakes are available from:
◆ *Mr Pádraig Campbell,* Lough O'Flynn Bar, Ballinlough,
Co. Roscommon

- *Mr John Hunt*, Patrick Street, Castlerea, Co. Roscommon
- *Mr Patrick Keogh*, The Square, Ballinasloe, Co. Galway
- *Mr Tom Kenny*, The Square, Ballygar, Co. Galway
- *Finn's Fishing Tackle*, Main Street, Roscommon.

The river gets a small run of spring salmon and a run of grilse from mid-June. The salmon fishing takes place at five distinct locations along the river. At the time of writing, a number of these fords have been dredged and the salmon fishing has been upset. Up-to-date information on the state of fishing is available from the local Shannon Regional Fisheries Board inspector:

- *Mr Brian Connaughton*, Harbour Road, Ballinasloe,
  Co. Galway; telephone (0905) 42367.

There is about seven miles of brown trout fishing early in the season from Laragh Bridge, which is downstream of Castlerea, Co. Roscommon, all the way up towards the headwaters. The trout range from 0.5 to 0.75 lb. This is an early season fishery, and the growth of instream vegetation becomes a problem after May. It is heavily fished by local anglers, and there is a good mayfly hatch. Information on the fishing is available from the fisheries inspector:

- *Mr John Ryan*, Ballinlough, Co. Roscommon;
  telephone (0907) 40063/40103.

Downstream of Laragh Bridge there is trout fishing immediately upstream of the bridge at Castlecoote, and in the vicinity of the footbridge at Cloondrea, near Mount Talbot. In the Ballinasloe area there is trout fishing at Mellagill Bridge and the Railway Bridge upstream of the town and at Pollboy downstream. There is also a short stretch of trout fishing at Derreen Footbridge upstream of Ballyforan.

LOUGH O'FLYNN
Open Season
Brown trout: 1 March to 12 October. There is a minimum size limit of 10 inches and a six-trout bag limit.

Lough O'Flynn is a limestone lake of approximately 600 acres, a short distance north of Ballinlough, Co. Roscommon. There is good public access to the lake, with a car park and a boat harbour. The trout average about 1 lb. Fishing methods are restricted to fly fishing, dapping, and spinning, with trolling under oars only. The fishery is managed by the Shannon Regional Fisheries Board for the Central Fisheries Board. It has prolific hatches of duckfly, chironomids, lake olive, mayfly, and sedges. Dapping the daddy is popular in August and September. Rowing boats are available for hire from:

◆ *Mr Pádraig Campbell*, Lough O'Flynn Bar, Ballinlough, Co. Roscommon.

A fisheries board permit is required to fish the lake, and this can be obtained from:

◆ *Mr Pádraig Campbell*, as above.

CLOONARD RIVER
Open Season
Brown trout: 1 March to 30 September.

The Cloonard River drains Lough Glinn and joins the Suck at Castlerea. It holds a fair stock of trout up to about 0.5 lb. It is a drained river and fishes best either early in the season, in March and April, or in September if there is sufficient water. The best of the fishing is from Clonree downstream to the confluence.

Regulations regarding fishing permits are the same as for the River Suck.

ISLAND RIVER
Open Season
Open season and fishing permits are the same as for the River Suck and its tributaries.

The Island River flows west to the Suck at Ballymoe, Co. Galway. It is a limestone river, and quite deep and slow-flowing in places. It tends to weed up in summer. The best of the trout fishing is early in the season, and it holds plenty of trout up to 1.5 lb or better. Early in the season it can be fished from Island Bridge to Buchalla Bridge, and there is a good stretch at Ballymoe.

This river has no stiles or footbridges, and access is relatively difficult. It has all the usual fly hatches one associates with a limestone river, including mayfly. Up-to-date information on the fishing is available from the fishery inspector:

◆ *Mr John Ryan,* Ballinlough, Co. Roscommon;
   telephone (0907) 40063/40103.

Permits and local information are available from fishing tackle shops in Roscommon, Castlerea, and Ballinlough.

SMAGHRAAN RIVER
Open Season
Open season and fishing permits are the same as for the River Suck .
The Smaghraan River holds a small stock of trout upstream of its confluence with the River Suck.

☐ RIVER SHIVEN SYSTEM

Open Season
Brown trout: 1 March to 30 September.
The Shiven drains into the River Suck. It is a limestone river, rich in fly life, and was once regarded as one of the prime trout fisheries in the country. It also runs low in summer because of a drainage scheme. The best of the trout fishing is from early in the season to about mid-June. The average size of the trout is said to be approximately 0.75 lb. The best of the mayfly hatch is from Rookhill downstream. Stretches that are very worth while are in the vicinity of Tryhill and Ilandcave Bridges, and also at Nolan's Fort. Information on the fishing is available from:

◆ *Mr Tom Kenny,* The Square, Ballygar, Co. Galway.

These rivers are managed by the Shannon Regional Fisheries Board, and permits are available from:

- *Mr Patrick Keogh*, The Square, Ballinasloe, Co. Galway
- *Mr Tom Kenny*, The Square, Ballygar, Co. Galway.

CASTLEGAR RIVER, NORTH
CASTLEGAR RIVER, SOUTH

The Castlegar Rivers hold trout averaging 0.75 lb and some bigger fish. The best of the fishing is from early April to about mid-May. Permits are available from:

- *Mr Pádraig Campbell*, Lough O'Flynn Bar, Ballinlough, Co. Roscommon
- *Mr John Hunt*, Patrick Street, Castlerea, Co. Roscommon
- *Mr Patrick Keogh*, The Square, Ballinasloe, Co. Galway
- *Mr Tom Kenny*, The Square, Ballygar, Co. Galway
- *Finn's Fishing Tackle*, Main Street, Roscommon.

TIRUR RIVER

The Tirur River is another early season trout stream. The best stocks are half a mile upstream of Tirur Bridge and down as far as the confluence.

Permits are available from:

- *Mr Pádraig Campbell*, Lough O'Flynn Bar, Ballinlough, Co. Roscommon
- *Mr John Hunt*, Patrick Street, Castlerea, Co. Roscommon
- *Mr Patrick Keogh*, The Square, Ballinasloe, Co. Galway
- *Mr Tom Kenny*, The Square, Ballygar, Co. Galway
- *Finn's Fishing Tackle*, Main Street, Roscommon.

KILLIAN RIVER

The Killian River is reported to have an excellent mayfly hatch. Bank access is now good. The trout average 0.5 lb, and the river can be fished at various bridges downstream from Kentstown Bridge. Permits are available from:

- *Mr Pádraig Campbell*, Lough O'Flynn Bar, Ballinlough,

Co. Roscommon
- *Mr John Hunt*, Patrick Street, Castlerea, Co. Roscommon
- *Mr Patrick Keogh*, The Square, Ballinasloe, Co. Galway
- *Mr Tom Kenny*, The Square, Ballygar, Co. Galway
- *Finn's Fishing Tackle*, Main Street, Roscommon.

★ ★

KILLEGLAN RIVER

The Killeglan River joins the Suck north of Ballinasloe. It is a spring-fed stream and very rich in insect life. It holds a small stock of 0.5 lb brown trout with occasionally better trout, and it fishes best in springtime. Permits are available from:

- *Mr Pádraig Campbell*, Lough O'Flynn Bar, Ballinlough, Co. Roscommon
- *Mr John Hunt*, Patrick Street, Castlerea, Co. Roscommon
- *Mr Patrick Keogh*, The Square, Ballinasloe, Co. Galway
- *Mr Tom Kenny*, The Square, Ballygar, Co. Galway
- *Finn's Fishing Tackle*, Main Street, Roscommon.

BUNOWEN RIVER

Open Season

Brown trout: 1 March to 30 September.

The Bunowen River flows through Clonbrock and Ahascragh to join the Suck north of Ballinasloe, Co. Galway. It is a medium-sized river and is regarded as potentially one of the finest brown trout rivers in the country, although stocks have declined in recent times. The average size is 0.75 lb.

The best fishing stretches are from half a mile upstream of Clonpee Bridge downstream for about three miles, a stretch downstream of Ahascragh Bridge, and a stretch of about two miles from Sonnagh downstream past Killure Castle. The river has excellent hatches of all the usual flies one expects to find on a limestone river, including mayfly. It is heavily fished early in the season.

Permit requirements are the same as for the River Suck.

BALLYHARDA RIVER

This small river joins the Suck a short distance upstream of Ballinasloe, Co. Galway. It flows east from Kilconnell, and has trout averaging 0.5 lb in the last four miles. Access is difficult and mainly at the bridges.

BALLINURE RIVER

The Ballinure River joins the Suck downstream of Correen Ford. It is a limestone river and holds moderate stocks of 0.75 lb trout. Access is difficult and mainly at the bridges.

LOUGH ACALLA

Open Season

Trout: 1 May to 31 October. There is an 11 inch minimum size limit and a four-trout bag limit.

Lough Acalla is a small lake, 30 acres in area, two miles north of Kilconnell, Co. Galway. The lake is stocked with rainbow trout. Artificial fly only is permitted. More than half the banks are clear, and wading is possible. It is a lough that tends to weed heavily in summer. There is a car park by the lake shore.

Lough Acalla is managed by the Shannon Regional Fisheries Board. Permits are available at fishing tackle shops in Ballinasloe.

CLONFREE LOUGH

Clonfree Lough is two miles south-west of Strokestown, Co. Roscommon. It holds a good stock of wild brown trout said to average about 1.5 lb. Access to the lake is difficult. Most of the banks are heavily reeded, and a boat and outboard motor is necessary for fishing here. These are sometimes available for hire, and enquiries can be made locally. The fishing is regarded as free.

LOUGH CREEVIN

This small lough lies about a mile north of the Roscommon–Ballymoe road. The trout average 0.75 lb. It can only be fished from the bank, and the banks are soft and unfishable in certain areas, but at least half the lough is fishable from the shore. The fishing is regarded as free.

LOUGH FERGUS
Lough Fergus lies to the north of the Roscommon–Ballymoe road. It holds a medium stock of brown trout averaging 0.75 lb. The banks are soft, with high reeds, and it is impossible to fish from the shore. The fishing is regarded as free.

❖❖❖❖❖❖❖❖❖❖❖❖❖❖❖❖❖❖❖❖❖❖❖❖❖❖❖❖❖❖❖❖❖❖

KILCROW RIVER
Open Season
Brown trout: 15 February to 30 September.
The Kilcrow River flows through Killimor, Co. Galway, into the top of Lough Derg. It holds a stock of trout averaging about 1 lb. The best of the fishing is from Oxford Bridge downstream. The fishing is regarded as free. Up-to-date information is available from:
◆ *Mr Brian Connaughton*, Harbour Road, Ballinasloe,
   Co. Galway; telephone (0905) 42367
who can also provide information on the Lisduff River, Cappagh River, and Woodford River below.

LISDUFF RIVER
Open Season
Brown trout: 15 February to 30 September.
The Lisduff River joins the Killimor River from the west. It can provide good early season wet fly fishing from Gortymadden downstream.

CAPPAGH RIVER
Open Season
Open season and permission are the same as for the Kilcrow River above.
The Cappagh River flows into the Killimor River, less than a mile up from Lough Derg. The trout average 1 lb. The best of the fishing is between Duniry Bridge and Cappagh Bridge.

WOODFORD RIVER
Open Season
Open season and permission are the same as for the Kilcrow River.

The Woodford River holds a moderate stock of brown trout. It is very difficult to fish with anything except a worm, as it is quite overgrown.

CROSS RIVER
Open Season
Brown trout: 1 March to 30 September.

This is a limestone river that enters the Shannon downstream of Athlone, and holds trout ranging from 0.5 to 0.75 lb. The fishing is regarded as free. Information on the fishing is available from:

◆ *Mr Niall O'Shea*, The Mill Bar, Tuam Road, Athlone, Co. Westmeath; telephone (0902) 92927.

BREENSFORD RIVER
Open Season
Brown trout: 1 March to 30 September.

The Breensford River, also known as the Ballykeeran River, flows into Killinure Lough north of Athlone. The trout are said to average 0.75 lb, and the river is fishable only early in the season. It is sometimes stocked by the local angling association. The fishing is regarded as free.

BUNRATTY RIVER
Open season
Salmon and sea trout: 1 February to 30 September;
brown trout: 15 February to 30 September.

The Bunratty River enters the Shannon Estuary at Bunratty Castle. It holds a small stock of brown trout averaging 0.5 lb. It gets a run of grilse and a run of sea trout in early June. It is mainly fished for its sea trout. The banks are good.

The fishing is regarded as free. Fishing is prohibited between the Mill Weir at Sixmilebridge and 45 yards above the Road Bridge adjoining Main Street.

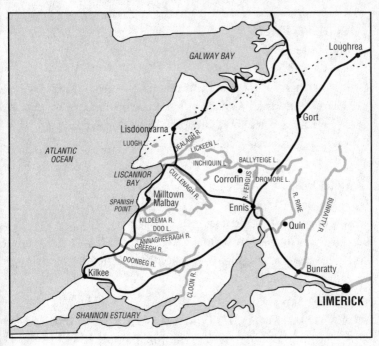

RIVER RINE
Open Season
Salmon and sea trout: 1 February to 30 September;
brown trout: 15 February to 30 September.

The River Rine rises in Co. Clare and flows through Quin to the Shannon Estuary. It is a clear-flowing river and is partly overgrown. It gets a small run of grilse and sea trout in July; it also holds a stock of resident brown trout averaging 0.5 lb, and there are plentiful fly hatches. A gillie can be arranged through:

◆ *Recreation Manager, Dromoland Castle Hotel*,
   Newmarket-on-Fergus, Co. Clare; telephone (061) 71144

◆ *Mr Dennis Exton*, Keevagh, Quin, Co. Clare;
   telephone (065) 25879.

Part of the river is free, but those parts that flow through the grounds of Dromoland Castle Hotel are reserved, and fishing should be arranged through the hotel.

LOUGH ATORICK
Open Season
15 February to 30 September.
Lough Atorick is in the mountains north-east of Flagmount, Co. Clare. It holds a big stock of trout up to 10 inches. Access is good, and there is a slipway where a boat can be launched. The fishing is regarded as free.

LOUGH EA
Open Season
15 February to 30 September.
Lough Ea is in the mountains above Feakle. It is a mountain lake with trout averaging 0.5 lb. Access is difficult. The fishing is regarded as free.

MUCKANAGH LOUGH (TULLYMACKEN LOUGH)
This shallow lake of 180 acres holds a small stock of good brown trout. The banks are soft and unfishable. The fishing is regarded as free. A boat can be arranged for hire through:
- *Mr Michael Cleary*, Corrofin, Co. Clare;
  telephone (065) 27675.

■ RIVER FERGUS SYSTEM

Open Season
Salmon: 1 February to 30 September;
brown trout: 15 February to 30 September.
The River Fergus rises north-west of Corrofin, Co. Clare, and enters the Shannon Estuary at Newmarket-on-Fergus. It is a limestone river with several interconnected lakes along its course, and it holds a good stock of brown trout. It is also a noted salmon fishery.

The upper reaches fish best for brown trout in high water, and the lower river fishes best when the water drops. Some stretches are quite inaccessible because of overgrown or high banks. The trout average 0.75 lb. The river has good hatches of all the usual flies one associates with a limestone river, including some mayfly, and it is noted for giving good dry fly fishing on summer evenings.

The Fergus gets a good run of spring salmon and a run of grilse. The spring fishing is best in February or March in the vicinity of Ennis and downstream. The grilse enter the river in mid-June, and it is possible to catch one at any time from then to the end of September. Spinning and worming are the most suitable salmon fishing methods on the river. The fishing is regarded as free.

LOUGH CULLAUN (MONANAGH LAKE)
This lake lies off the Corrofin–Tobber road and holds a small stock of big trout. They are usually taken trolling. Boats can be arranged through:
◆ *Mr Michael Cleary*, Corrofin, Co. Clare;
   telephone (065) 27675.
   The fishing is regarded as free.

INCHIQUIN LOUGH
Open Season
15 February to 12 October.
This 260-acre lake lies near Corrofin, Co. Clare. It holds an excellent stock of wild brown trout averaging 1 lb, with many fish to 3 lb. It fishes well early in the season, but the fishing can be difficult in summer. The water runs low in summer and part of the lake becomes weeded. September fishing can be very good.

There is good access, with a car park and a boat jetty. Boats can be hired at:
◆ *Burke's Shop*, Main Street, Corrofin, Co. Clare;
   telephone (065) 27677.
   The fishing is free.

BALLYTEIGE LOUGH
Open Season

15 February to 12 October.

This is a rich limestone lough one mile north-east of Ruane, Co. Clare. Access is difficult and involves a half-mile walk. The lake holds a small stock of big trout. The best of the fishing is in March and April or in September. A boat is necessary to fish this lake, and arrangements can be made through:

◆ *Mr Michael Cleary*, Corrofin, Co. Clare;
   telephone (065) 27675.
   The fishing is regarded as free.

DROMORE LOUGH
BALLYLINE LOUGH
Open Season

15 February to 12 October.

These lakes lie six miles east of Corrofin, Co. Clare, and are surrounded by forest. Dromore Lake is a rich limestone lake with a small stock of big trout. It fishes best in low water in March, April, May, and September. A boat is necessary for fishing here and can be arranged through:

◆ *Mr Michael Cleary*, Corrofin, Co. Clare;
   telephone (065) 27675.

Ballyline Lake is accessible only by boat from Dromore Lake. The trout stocks and fishing seasons are the same as for Dromore, and this lake also holds occasional salmon at the river mouth. The fishing is regarded as free.

GORTAGANNIVE LOUGH
GORTAGANNIVE RESERVOIR
Open Season

1 March to 30 September.

These two small waters lie about five miles from Ennis, Co. Clare, on the Milltown Malbay road. Access to each of them is good, and it is bank fishing only. The lakes are stocked with brown trout. For further information on the fishing, contact the secretary of Kilmailey Anglers' Association:

◆ *Mr Noel Mungovan*, Kilmailey, Co. Clare.

LOUGH NAMINNA

Open Season

Brown trout: 1 March to 30 September.

This 45-acre lake is about twelve miles from Ennis, Co. Clare. It holds a big stock of small free-rising brown trout and is stocked annually with trout averaging 1 lb. There is a boat available, and access is good. For information on the fishing, contact the secretary of Kilmailey Anglers' Association:

◆ *Mr Noel Mungovan*, Kilmailey, Co. Clare.

CLOONSNEAGHTA LOUGH

Open Season

Brown trout: 1 March to 30 September.

This 30-acre lake has been converted into a reservoir and is almost entirely dependent on stocked trout. The average weight of the trout is about 0.75 lb, and the best fishing is in April and May. It is bank fishing only, and access to the lake shore is good. The fishing is regarded as free.

GORTGLASS LOUGH

Open Season

Brown trout: 1 March to 30 September.

This 80-acre lough is by the road three miles from Killadysert, Co. Clare. It holds a small stock of wild brown trout and is stocked annually; the average size of the trout is about 1 lb. The lake can be fished from the bank. For information on boats for hire, contact:

◆ *Mr Michael Cleary*, Corrofin, Co. Clare;
    telephone (065) 27675.
    The fishing is regarded as free.

CLOON RIVER
Open Season
1 March to 30 September.

This small river enters the north-east corner of Clonderalaw Bay about two miles north-west of Labasheeda, Co. Clare. It gets a run of sea trout in June and July. It is fishable from the tide up to a bridge known as the New Bridge, a distance of about two miles. The banks are very overgrown and difficult to fish. The fishing is regarded as free.

KNOCKERRA LOUGH
Open Season
1 March to 30 September.

This 50-acre lake is to the north-east of Kilrush. It holds a fair stock of small wild brown trout and fishes best in April and May. It can be fished from the bank, and the fishing is regarded as free.

KILKEE RESERVOIR
Open Season
1 March to 30 September.

This is a 10-acre reservoir about a mile from Kilkee, Co. Clare, on the Lehinch road. It is stocked annually with brown trout and rainbow trout. For information on the fishing, contact:

◆ *Mr Manuel di Lucia,* The Restaurant, Corbally, Kilkee, Co. Clare; telephone (065) 56211.

LOUGH ACHRYANE
Open Season
1 March to 30 September.

This is a 30-acre lake off the Ennis–Kilrush road, with bank fishing. It holds small but wild brown trout. The banks are clear, and the fishing is regarded as free.

KNOCKALOUGH LOUGH

Open Season

1 March to 30 September.

This lake lies off the Ennis–Kilrush road. It holds a good stock of brown trout averaging 0.5 lb. It can be fished from the bank; a boat should be used to get to the best fishing areas, but no boat is available for hire. The fishing is regarded as free.

DOONBEG RIVER

Open Season

1 March to 30 September.

The Doonbeg River rises in Liscasey, Co. Clare, and flows through Corraclare and Doonbeg to the sea. It gets a small run of spring salmon and a medium run of grilse. It also gets a run of sea trout from June. The early sea trout range from 2 to 5 lb, and the big run of finnock arrives in July. There have been major bank improvements along this river recently, and bank access is now good. The fishing is regarded as free.

CREEGH RIVER

This little river rises east of Cahermurphy and flows west to the sea. It gets a small run of grilse in mid-June and can fish on a spate up to September. It also gets a run of sea trout. The brown trout average about 0.5 lb. The banks are clear and easy to fish. It is regarded as free fishing.

DOO LOUGH

Open Season

1 March to 30 September.

Doo Lough is a lake of 220 acres. It holds a big stock of small brown trout to about 0.5 lb. The banks are clear, and access is good along the south shore. The fishing is regarded as free.

LOUGH DONNELL, ANNAGHEERAGH RIVER
Open Season

1 March to 30 September.

Access to Lough Donnell is via a secondary road on the north bank and then south along the Co. Clare coast. There is a car park. The inflowing river can give good sea trout fishing at dusk for about one mile upstream from Lough Donnell in June and July. The rest of the river can give fair to good sea trout fishing up as far as Moyglass Bridge. The fishing is regarded as free.

KILDEEMEA RIVER
Open Season

1 March to 30 September.

This is a spate river that enters the sea south of Spanish Point, Co. Clare. It gets a run of grilse and sea trout. The best of the fishing is in June and July, when water conditions are right. The fishing is regarded as free.

ROCKMOUNT LAKE (LOUGH KEAGH)
Open Season

1 March to 30 September.

This is a remote hill lough that holds a fair stock of wild brown trout up to 1.5 lb. It is also stocked with trout averaging 1 lb. Access is reasonably good, and the fishing is done from the banks. For further information on the fishing, contact the secretary of Milltown Malbay Angling Club:

◆ *Mr Martin O'Brien*, Clonbony, Milltown Malbay, Co. Clare.

AILLBRACK LOUGH
Open Season

1 March to 30 September.

This is a 20-acre lake stocked with brown trout that average 1 lb. It is bank fishing only, and the access is reasonably good. For further information, contact the secretary of Milltown Malbay Angling Club:

◆ *Mr Martin O'Brien*, Clonbony, Milltown Malbay, Co. Clare.

MORGAN'S LAKE, CARTHY'S LAKE
Open Season
1 March to 30 September.
These two lakes lie within a short distance of Inagh, Co. Clare.
Both hold good stocks of wild brown trout averaging 0.5 lb.
The fishing is regarded as free.

LOUGH CAUM
Open Season
1 March to 30 September. There is a bag limit of four trout.
Lough Caum is a 45-acre lake two miles west of Inagh, Co.
Clare, stocked regularly with brown and rainbow trout. It is
boat fishing only. Boats are available for hire. Enquiries about
the fishing should be made to:
◆ *Mr James Allard*, Beech Park, Ennis, Co. Clare;
   telephone (065) 24367.

LICKEEN LOUGH
Open Season
1 March to 30 September.
This is a lake of approximately 200 acres two miles south of
Kilfenora, Co. Clare. It holds a good stock of brown trout
averaging 0.5 lb. It is stocked annually with rainbow trout
averaging 1 lb. Boats are available for hire. For information on
the fishing, contact the secretary of Lickeen Trout Angling
Association:
◆ *Mr John Vaughan*, Lickeen, Kilfenora, Co. Clare;
   telephone (065) 71069.

DEALAGH RIVER
Open Season
1 March to 30 September.
The Dealagh River flows into the sea at Liscannor, Co. Clare. It
is a spate river and gets a run of grilse and sea trout in June
and July. The best sea trout fishing is between dusk and dawn.
The fishing is regarded as free.

Western Fisheries Region

The Western Fisheries Region comprises all the inland river systems on the Atlantic coast from Pidgeon Point near Westport, Co. Mayo, to Hag's Head, Co. Clare. The region is divided into the Ballynakill, Connemara and Galway Districts.

The region is characterised by three distinctive features. To the east there are the limestone rivers, primarily trout waters but some also holding spring salmon and grilse. Dividing the region in half are Lough Corrib, Lough Mask, and Lough Carra, devoted almost entirely to brown trout, although Lough Corrib has salmon as well. To the west there are the Connemara and Ballynakill areas, noted for their salmon and sea trout fisheries. (A serious decline in the sea trout stocks occurred around 1989, and since then a virtual collapse of adult sea trout populations has taken place.) The Connemara area is also noted for its grilse runs, which begin in early June and give good sport through the summer months to the end of the season.

GALWAY DISTRICT

The Galway Fisheries District comprises parts of Cos. Clare, Galway, and Mayo, and embraces all rivers flowing into the sea between Hag's Head, Co. Clare, and the point south-east of Cashla coastguard station on the eastern shore of Cashla Bay, Co. Galway.

LUOGH LOUGH

Open Season

Brown trout: 15 February to 12 October.

This lake lies near the Cliffs of Moher, Co. Clare. It holds a stock of brown trout and is stocked annually with rainbow trout. Access is good, and it is bank fishing only. The fishing is regarded as free.

AILLE RIVER

Open Season

Brown trout: 15 February to 12 October.

The Aille River flows through Lisdoonvarna, Co. Clare, and enters the sea at Doolin. It holds brown trout up to 1 lb, and gets a small run of salmon in late June. The best fishing is between Broadford and Lisdoonvarna, and the river fishes best for salmon after a flood. In drought conditions the river runs dry near Doolin. Access along the banks is difficult, and spinning and worm fishing are the most productive methods. The fishing is regarded as free.

DUNKELLIN RIVER

Open Season

Salmon: 1 February to 30 September;

brown trout: 17 March to 15 September. There is a 9 inch statutory size limit for trout on the Dunkellin River and Lough Rea.

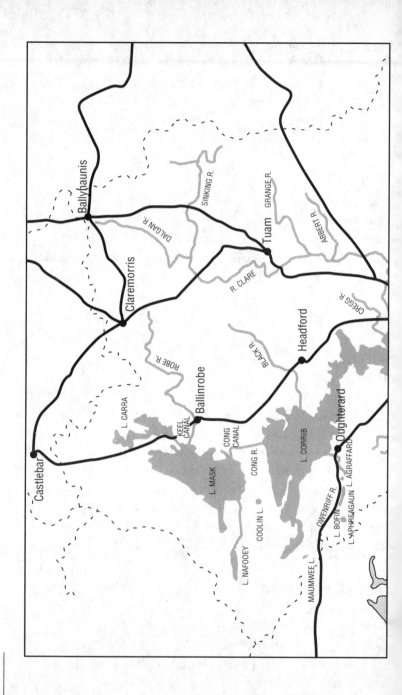

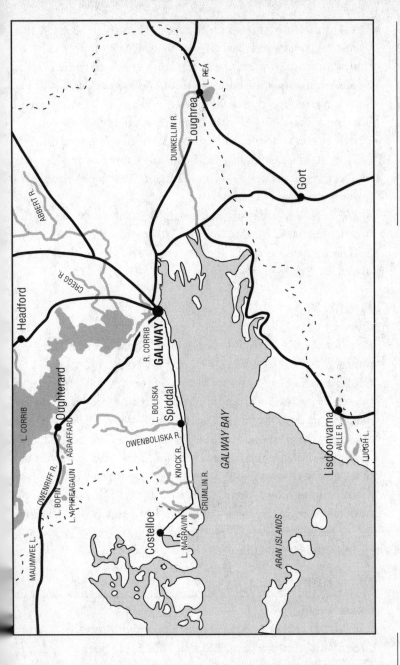

The Dunkellin drains Lough Ree into Galway Bay. It is a limestone river, and part of it runs dry in summer. It holds salmon and sea trout and has a fair stock of brown trout to 2.5 or 3 lb. Once famous for both sea trout and salmon, and grilse in summer, it too has diminishing sea trout runs and less salmon of late, but grilse are still fairly plentiful, especially in September. Dry fly for brown trout can be excellent from July onwards.

The regional fisheries board controls fishing over 645 yards of the north bank in the townland of Stradbally East. Day permits are available from:

◆ *Western Regional Fisheries Board*, Earl's Island, Galway; telephone (091) 63118.

The ownership of fishing rights on the rest of the river is uncertain.

LOUGH REA
Open Season
Brown trout: 17 March to 15 September. There is an 11 inch minimum size limit and a six-trout daily bag limit.

Lough Rea is beside the town of Loughrea, Co. Galway. It is managed by the local angling club. Fishing methods are fly fishing and dapping only. This is a well-stocked lake, and the average size is about 1.25 lb. There is excellent wet fly and 'buzzer' fishing on the lake in April and May, and wet fly in the other months is also good. Access is good, with two boat jetties.

Information and permission to fish the lake are available from the honorary secretary of Lough Rea Anglers' Association:

◆ *Mr Michael Sweeney*, West Bridge, Loughrea, Co. Galway; telephone (091) 41552.

■ CORRIB SYSTEM

Open Season
Salmon: 1 February to 30 September; *sea trout:* 1 June to 30 September; *brown trout:* 1 March to 30 September.

The Corrib is a system of large and small loughs with many rivers and streams. It is a great fishery, holding some sea trout, salmon and grisle, brown trout, and coarse fish. The system can be divided into three categories: (a) the great loughs of Lough Corrib, Lough Mask, and Lough Carra, (b) the river systems of interest to game anglers such as the Corrib River, the Claregalway River, the Cong Canal, the Robe River, etc., and (c) the smaller lakes on the mountainous north and west shores of Lough Corrib and Lough Mask.

RIVER CORRIB

The River Corrib drains Lough Corrib and all its tributaries, including Lough Mask and Lough Carra, into Galway Bay. It is owned and managed by the Central Fisheries Board.

The fishery is divided into four distinct angling sections. The first section reaches from the Friar's Cut and beyond the mouth of the old river in Lough Corrib to the Weir in Galway. This water holds salmon, coarse fish, and brown trout. Every year anglers enjoy salmon and trout fishing in these stretches. Most of the fish are caught by trolling spoon baits or by 'shrimping', but fly fishing is excellent for taking trout at certain times.

Downstream is the famous Galway Weir salmon fishery. It takes a maximum of six rods, and is equally good for spring salmon and grilse. The best months are from April to mid-July and again in September.

The third section is the New Beat, which extends downstream from the Salmon Weir Bridge to the fish traps. It can only be fished by wading. Some sea trout frequent this beat at times.

The lower reach, from McDonagh's Turbine to the estuary at Nimmo's Pier, is bank fishing only and is reserved for local anglers. Part of the fishery used to get late runs of sea trout, but the species has become scarce of late.

Applications for fishing between the Weir and Nimmo's Pier should be made to:

◆ *Fishery Manager*, Galway Fishery, Nun's Island, Galway; telephone (091) 62388.

LOUGH CORRIB
Open Season
Salmon: 1 February to 30 September; *brown trout:* 15 February to 30 September; *sea trout:* 1 June to 30 September. There is a size limit of 12 inches.

Lough Corrib holds salmon, char, brown trout, and coarse fish. It stretches from the Friar's Cut north of Galway to Maum Bridge, a distance of about thirty miles. The trout fishing season begins on 15 February, and the first trout are usually taken on trolled baits. Fly fishing begins in March with the first hatches of duckfly. Lake olives hatch in mid-April; the first mayfly hatch begins around the middle of May, and towards the end of the month is the high point of the trout season. Dapping the natural mayfly is by far the most successful method. From mid-June, fishing becomes difficult, but by mid-August, dapping the natural daddy long-legs is a very successful method of catching trout. Grilse often provide good sport to both wet fly and the mayfly dapping at the end of May and over the first week of June.

There are big runs of spring salmon and grilse, and these fish are taken mainly by trolling.

Access to Lough Corrib is relatively good. There are numerous car parks, public quays, and slipways. Information on angling is available from the regional fisheries board, which has for sale a detailed angling guide and map of Lough Corrib.

Boats, boatmen and gillies are available for hire all round the lake:

- *Mr Alan Broderick,* Annaghdown Lodge, Annaghdown, Claregalway, Co. Galway; telephone (091) 91653
- *Lal Faherty's Angling Centre,* Portacarron, Oughterard, Co. Galway; telephone (091) 82121
- *Mr Roy Pierce,* Gillie Angling, Grasshopper Cottage, Dooras, Cornamona, Maum, Co. Galway; telephone (092) 48165
- *Cloonabinna House Hotel,* Cloonabinna, Moycullen, Co. Galway; telephone (091) 85555

- *Mr Mike Holian,* The Derries, Cross, Cong, Co. Mayo;
  telephone (092) 46385
- *Glann House,* Glann, Oughterard, Co. Galway;
  telephone (091) 82127
- *Angler's Rest Hotel,* Headford, Co. Galway;
  telephone (093) 35528
- *Ballindiff Bay Lodge,* Luimnagh, Corrandulla, Co. Galway;
  telephone (091) 91195
- *Knockferry Lodge,* Knockferry, Rosscahill, Co. Galway;
  telephone (091) 80122
- *The Corrib Hotel,* Oughterard, Co. Galway;
  telephone (091) 82329
- *Corrib Wave House,* Portacarron, Oughterard, Co. Galway;
  telephone (091) 82147
- *Ross Lake House Hotel,* Rosscahill, Co. Galway;
  telephone (091) 80184
- *The Boat Inn,* The Square, Oughterard, Co. Galway;
  telephone (091) 82194
- *'Westford',* 13 Oldfield, Kingston, Galway;
  telephone (091) 26959
- *Connemara Gateway Hotel,* Oughterard, Co. Galway;
  telephone (091) 82328
- *Currarevagh House,* Oughterard, Co. Galway;
  telephone (091) 82312
- *Egan's Lake House,* Oughterard, Co. Galway;
  telephone (091) 82272
- *Sweeney's Oughterard House,* Oughterard, Co. Galway;
  telephone (091) 82207
- *Ashford Castle,* Cong, Co. Mayo; telephone (092) 46003
- *Carmel and Frank Lydon,* Cong, Co. Mayo;
  telephone (092) 46053
- *Mrs P. O'Sullivan,* Oakland House, Cornamona, Maum,
  Co. Galway; telephone (092) 48007
- *Mr Roger Beale,* Dooneish, Oughterard, Co. Galway;
  telephone (091) 82419.

Open Season

Salmon: 1 February to 30 September;

trout: 1 March to 30 September.

The Clare River rises north of Ballyhaunis, Co. Mayo, and flows south through Milltown, Tuam and Claregalway to enter Lough Corrib. Its upper reaches are known as the Dalgan River. It is mainly a limestone river, with excellent brown trout fishing, and it also holds good stocks of spring salmon and grilse in season. Spring salmon run from early February, and grilse begin running in late May.

Brown trout fishing here is regarded as first class; the resident brown trout are said to average 2 lb. The river gets big runs of trout from Lough Corrib in late June and July.

The fishing rights on the river are controlled by various fishing interests. The Buckley fishery is upstream from Lough Corrib. It is mainly a salmon fishery, though brown trout can be taken higher up. For information on the fishing, contact:

◆ *Buckley Fishery,* Spiddal House, Spiddal, Co. Galway; telephone (091) 83393.

Corrofin Fishing Association has a number of fishing stretches on the river. This is mainly a brown trout fishery, and the fishing is said to be very good. Enquiries should be made to:

◆ *Mr Ned Cusack,* Ballinahulla, Moycullen, Co. Galway; telephone (091) 85257.

St Colman's Angling Club has good salmon and grilse fishing as well as good brown trout fishing on the river. Enquiries about the fishing there should be made to the secretary:

◆ *Mr Patrick Balfe,* Corrofin, Cummer, Co. Galway.

Tuam and District Anglers' Association has extensive fishing rights on the river. This water offers some excellent spring salmon fishing from mid-April and grilse fishing in June and July. It also has very good brown trout fishing. Enquiries about the fishing should be made to:

◆ *Mr Declan Martin*, Tuam and District Anglers' Association, Weir Road, Tuam, Co. Galway

◆ *Mr Sonny Martyn*, Esso Station, Galway Road, Tuam, Co. Galway; telephone (093) 24151.

The riparian owners have the remainder of the fishery rights, and much of the fishing is as good as on the other stretches.

DALGAN RIVER

The Dalgan River is an extension of the Clare River. Once an excellent salmon and trout river, it suffered badly from pollution for many years but is beginning to improve of late.

ABBERT RIVER

The Abbert River flows west from Monivea, Co. Galway, through Abbeyknockmoy to join the Clare River at Anbally. Most of this river is too shallow to hold fish, though there are some trout stocks in a couple of deeper sections. The best time for trout is April and again in September. Hatches of olives in spring are excellent. Enquiries about the fishing should be made to Tuam Anglers' Association:

◆ *Mr Sonny Martyn*, Esso Station, Galway Road, Tuam, Co. Galway; telephone (093) 24151.

GRANGE RIVER

The Grange River flows west to join the Clare River south of Tuam. This is a river that was badly affected by an arterial drainage scheme, but some of it has recovered, especially upstream of Grange Bridge. It holds brown trout to 3 lb and can fish well early in the season or in high water in August and September for brown trout. It gets a small run of late-running summer salmon from Lough Corrib. The fishing is by permission of the riparian owners. Tuam and District Anglers' Association has some fishing here also.

SINKING RIVER

The Sinking River flows through Dunmore, Co. Galway, and joins the Clare River below Dalgan Bridge. It holds fair stocks of brown trout in certain areas, and it also has some grilse from May onwards. The river has good hatches of olives and some mayfly.

❖ ❖

CREGG RIVER
Open Season
Salmon: 1 February to 30 September;
trout: 1 March to 30 September.

For half a mile above Cregg Mill House is good nursery water for trout, and angling is not encouraged here, as stocking with fry is frequently carried out by the fisheries board. Downstream is too weedy to fish in summer, even though there are some large trout in certain areas.

BLACK RIVER
Open Season
Salmon: 1 February to 30 September;
brown trout: 1 March to 30 September.

This is a rich limestone river but was so severely damaged by a drainage scheme that it now runs very low in summer. It offers some prospects for trout wet fly fishing in March and April, and hatches of olives bring on rises of trout during these months. Later in the season the blue-winged olive gives some late evening fishing with dry fly.

Part of the fishing is free and part of it is controlled by the fisheries board. A permit can be obtained from:

◆ *Western Regional Fisheries Board,* Weir Lodge, Earl's Island, Galway; telephone (091) 63118.

CONG RIVER
Open Season
Salmon: 1 February to 30 September;
brown trout: 1 March to 30 September.

The Cong River rises in Cong, Co. Mayo, and flows into Lough Corrib. It is about one mile long. The river gets an excellent run of spring salmon. The peak of the fishing is in April, and the grilse come in May and June. The river also holds a good stock of big brown trout. It has good hatches of all the usual flies found on a limestone river.

Some of the river can be fished from the bank; in other places it is possible to wade, but care must be exercised, and because of the width of the river, much of it is better fished from a boat. Gillies are available locally.

The fishing is regarded as free, but there is a small charge made by Ashford Castle for admission to the castle grounds.

MAUMWEE LOUGH
TANAGH LOUGH
LOUGHAUNIERIN

These three loughs are in the bog and lie between Maum Cross and Maum Bay on the north-western tip of Lough Corrib. They all hold brown trout. Tanagh Lough needs a boat to fish from, because of excessive shore weed, but the other two have some clear shores from which to fly-fish. Enquiries about some of the fishing should be made to:

◆ *Mr H. D. Hodgson,* Currarevagh House, Oughterard,
   Co. Galway; telephone (091) 82313.

LOUGHANILLAUN

Loughanillaun lies between Maum Cross and Lough Corrib. The fishing is private.

Open Season

Salmon: 1 February to 30 September;

brown trout: 1 March to 30 September.

The Owenriff River rises south of Maum Cross and flows through Oughterard into Lough Corrib. The river receives runs of salmon and grilse, depending entirely on floods to take them up. The first good run occurs with a flood in late May or early June.

Some of the fishing is leased by the local angling club. All angling for trout and salmon is regarded as free for approximately one mile up from Lough Corrib. Upstream of the main waterfall, private rights are claimed on most of the waters, including those of the O'Flaherty estates.

LOUGH AGRAFFARD
LOUGH BOFIN
LOUGH APHREAGAUN
LOUGH CROMLEC

This group of loughs is at the top of the Owenriff River and lies to the south of the Oughterard–Maum Cross road. They all hold brown trout, and the lower two on the system, Lough Agraffard and Lough Bofin, hold salmon. They are acid lakes, and the average size of the trout is probably around 0.5 lb. Enquiries about the fishing on Lough Aphreagaun should be made to:

◆ *Screeb House*, Screeb, Camus, Co. Galway;
   telephone (091) 74110

and for fishing on Lough Agraffard to:

◆ *Mr David Morton Jack*, Otter House, Addington,
   Oxford OX5 2R6, England.

❖ ❖

CONG CANAL

Open Season

Brown trout: 1 March to 30 September.

The Cong Canal was intended to link Lough Mask with Lough Corrib. It extends from Ballinchalla Bay on Lough Mask towards Cong. It is regarded as a good brown trout fishery, and the average weight of the trout is probably 2 lb. It has all the usual hatches associated with a limestone river. Trout angling is best between Lough Mask and Cahernagawer Bridge on the Cong–Ballinrobe road, and is particularly good for dry fly at the outlet from the lake in June, July, and August, giving up trout to 6 lb.

The fishing is regarded as free, but where it is necessary to cross private lands, anglers should consult the riparian owner.

LETTERCRAFFROE LOUGH

Lettercraffroe Lough lies to the west of the Oughterard–Costelloe road. There is a forest road almost to the shore, and the lake is almost entirely surrounded by pine woods. It holds a stock of small brown trout averaging about 0.5 lb. It is possible to fish from the shore in places. Enquiries about the fishing should be made to:

◆ *Costelloe and Fermoyle Fisheries Company*, Bridge Cottage, Costelloe, Co. Galway; telephone (091) 72196.

☐ LOUGH MASK

Open Season

Brown trout: 1 March to 30 September. There is a 12 inch statutory brown trout size limit on Lough Mask.

Lough Mask is a large limestone lake of 20,000 acres, ten miles long and four miles wide. The average size of the trout here is probably in the region of 1.5 lb, and 3 to 6 lb trout are not uncommon on wet fly. It holds a big stock of ferox trout to over 20 lb.

Wet fly fishing from April and dapping the mayfly in late May and June are very productive. There are good hatches of chironomids from early April, and later in the month lake olives appear and continue into May. Mayfly dominates the fishing from mid-May to late June. At this time there is good buzzer fishing at night in many of the bays along the eastern shore. Fishing slows down in July but picks up again with wet fly and dapping in August and September. Trolling spoon baits will take large ferox throughout the season.

Access to the lough is good, with numerous safe mooring places and slipways around the shore. The fishing is free.

A number of boats and boatmen are available for hire:

◆ *Mr Bryan Joyce,* Derrypark Lodge, Toormakeady, Co. Mayo; telephone (092) 44081

◆ *Mr Pádraic Heneghan,* Toormakeady, Co. Mayo; telephone (092) 44028

◆ *Mr David Hall,* Cahir, Ballinrobe, Co. Mayo; telephone (092) 41389

◆ *Mr Joe Cusack,* Cushlough, Ballinrobe, Co. Mayo; telephone (092) 41180

◆ *Mr John Sheridan,* Cushlough, Ballinrobe, Co. Mayo; telephone (092) 41148

◆ *Mr Robbie O'Grady,* Cushlough, Ballinrobe, Co. Mayo; telephone (092) 41142

◆ *Mr Peter Roberts,* Kilkeeran, Partry, Co. Mayo; telephone (092) 43046

◆ *Mr Ciarán Bourke,* Clonbur, Co. Galway; telephone (092) 46175

◆ *Mr Jimmy O'Donnell,* Clonbur, Co. Galway; telephone (092) 46157.

The regional fisheries board has a development and information centre at Cushlough on the eastern shore:

◆ *Western Regional Fisheries Board,* Cushlough, Ballinrobe, Co. Mayo; telephone (092) 41562.

Information is also available from:

◆ *Angling Officer, Western Regional Fisheries Board,* Weir Lodge, Earl's Island, Galway; telephone (091) 63118.

The Western Regional fisheries board has for sale a detailed angling guide and map of Lough Mask.

ROBE RIVER
Open Season
Brown trout: 1 March to 30 September.

The Robe River rises near Ballyhaunis, Co. Mayo, and flows past Claremorris, Hollymount and Ballinrobe to enter Lough Mask. It is a rich limestone river, which underwent an arterial drainage scheme in the 1980s but has recovered partially from dredging, and rehabilitation works have been carried out by the fisheries board.

The river holds a moderate stock of wild brown trout. It has all the usual hatches, including mayfly, that one associates with a rich limestone river. The banks are well developed, and stiles and footbridges have been erected by the fisheries board throughout the length of the river. It should be noted that some parts of the river suffer badly from an algal problem in summer. The fishing is free. Enquiries should be made to:

◆ *Western Regional Fisheries Board,* Cushlough, Ballinrobe, Co. Mayo; telephone (092) 41562
◆ *Western Regional Fisheries Board,* Weir Lodge, Earl's Island, Galway; telephone (091) 63118.
   Angling maps are available from the board.

KEEL CANAL
Open Season
Brown trout: 1 March to 30 September.

The Keel Canal is a mile long and joins Lough Carra and Lough Mask. The water is clear, and it holds big brown trout. It has prolific hatches of all the usual flies one associates with a limestone river, including mayfly. Access is good from Keel Bridge, with stiles and footbridges provided by the fisheries board. This water runs low in summer and can become virtually unfishable. The fishing is free.

LOUGH NAFOOEY

Open Season

15 February to 30 September.

Lough Nafooey lies in a deep valley to the west of Lough Mask. It holds a small stock of brown trout. The fishing is free.

COOLIN LOUGH

Open Season

1 March to 30 September.

Coolin Lough lies about two miles west of Clonbur, Co. Galway. It holds a small stock of big brown trout, and the average weight is probably in the region of 1.5 lb. It has the reputation of being a very difficult trout fishery, and it can be fished from its shores. The fishing is free.

LOUGH CARRA

Open Season

1 March to 30 September.

Lough Carra is 4,000 acres in area. It lies to the north-east of Lough Mask and is a good brown trout lough. The average size of the wild trout is in the region of 2 lb. This lake is heavily fished, especially at mayfly time. Public access to the lough is good; the main access points are at Brownstown, Moorhall, and Castleburke. The fishing is free.

There are good hatches of duckfly in late March, and the lake olives appear in April. The lough gets a big mayfly hatch, which begins in late April, peaks by 12 May, and tapers off by the end of May. Hatches of mayfly can be found on days in July, August, and September. During August and September the lake olives, murroughs and small sedges are plentiful, and dapping or artificial flies can produce a result.

Boats can be hired from:

◆ *Mrs J. Flannelly*, Keel Bridge, Partry, Co. Mayo;
   telephone (092) 41706

- *Mr Peter Roberts*, Kilkeeran, Partry, Co. Mayo;
  telephone (092) 43046
- *Mr Robbie O'Grady*, Cushlough, Ballinrobe, Co. Mayo;
  telephone (092) 41142.

The regional fisheries board has for sale a detailed angling guide and map of the lake. Information is available from:

- *Western Regional Fisheries Board*, Cushlough, Ballinrobe, Co. Mayo; telephone (092) 41562.
- *Western Regional Fisheries Board*, Weir Lodge, Earl's Island, Galway; telephone (091) 63118.

❖ ❖

■ OWENBOLISKA SYSTEM (SPIDDAL)

Open Season

Salmon: 1 February to 30 September; *sea trout:* 1 June to
30 September; *brown trout:* 15 February to 12 October.

The Spiddal River drains at least twelve loughs to the sea and is about four miles long. It gets a small run of grilse in June and July and a run of sea trout in the same period.

Part of the river is leased to the local angling club, and efforts to conserve stocks are in progress. The club has carried out restocking in recent times, and some development work on streams in the catchment area is in progress.

BOLISKA LOUGH

Boliska Lough is north of Spiddal. This is a big lough with good access to the shore. It is shallow and holds a resident stock of brown trout averaging 0.5 lb. It gets a run of salmon and sea trout from early July. There is access to the shore. For fishing, enquire locally.

Eleven other loughs on the system hold brown trout, some sea trout, and occasional salmon and some grilse. Some of the loughs are privately owned.

CRUMLIN FISHERY
Open Season
Salmon: 1 February to 30 September; *sea trout:* 1 February to 12 October; *brown trout:* 15 February to 12 October.

The Crumlin fishery consists of the short Crumlin River and over twenty loughs in the hinterland of Inveran and east towards Moycullen. The Crumlin system itself gets a small run of sea trout and grilse. A number of the lakes are let in conjunction with Crumlin Lodge, and boats are available. All these lakes hold small brown trout, but some of them are quite inaccessible. One of the lakes is stocked with sea-reared rainbows from 2 to 3 lb, and day tickets and boats are available from:

◆ *Crumlin Lodge Fisheries,* Inveran, Co. Galway; telephone (091) 93105.

LOUGH OUGHTERAGLANNA
Open Season
Salmon: 1 February to 30 September; *sea trout:* 1 February to 12 October; *brown trout:* 15 February to 12 October.

This small lough is approximately two miles east of the Costelloe–Ballynahown road. There is a bog road to the shore. The lake holds a stock of medium-sized brown trout with an average weight of about 0.75 lb. The fishing is regarded as free.

LOUGH NAGRAVIN
LOUGHAUNEVNEEN
LOUGH NAHOGA
LOUGH NASKANNIVA
Open Season
Salmon: 1 February to 30 September; *sea trout:* 1 February to 12 October; *brown trout:* 15 February to 12 October.

Lough Nagravin (Ballynahown Lough) is south-west of the junction of the Costelloe and Rossaveel roads. It holds a good stock of brown trout that are reported to be quite free-rising and to give good sport. It also gets a small run of salmon. Boats are available for hire.

Loughaunevneen and Lough Nahoga hold small brown trout. They can only be fished from the bank.

Lough Naskanniva holds brown trout and occasional sea trout. There is one boat for hire.

Enquiries about the fishing on all these loughs should be made to:

◆ *Mr M. Bolustrim*, Ballynahown, Co. Galway

who manages some of the waters in this area for the owners.

CONNEMARA DISTRICT

The Connemara Fisheries District comprises part of west Co. Galway and embraces all rivers flowing into the sea from south-east of Cashel coastguard station on the eastern shore of Cashla Bay and Slyne Head.

ROSSAVEEL LOUGH

Rossaveel Lough is near the village of the same name. It holds small brown trout, which are seldom fished for. Permission to fish is not usually required.

COSTELLOE FISHERY
Open Season
Salmon: 1 February to 30 September; *sea trout:* 1 June to 30 September; *brown trout:* 1 February to 12 October.

The Costelloe fishery and the Cashla River (Costelloe River) are near Costelloe, Co. Galway. This is a three-and-a-half mile river that drains a quite large watershed, consisting of a chain of at least twenty-two lakes. The river is a typical moorland river. It is divided into four beats, with two rods per beat. The Costelloe fishery was regarded as a prime sea trout fishery that also gets a run of grilse.

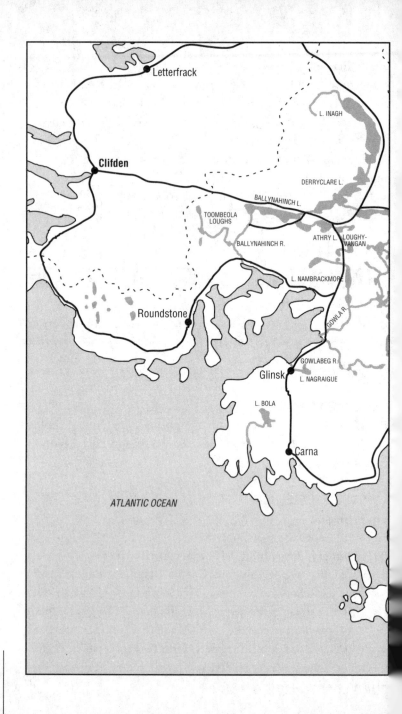

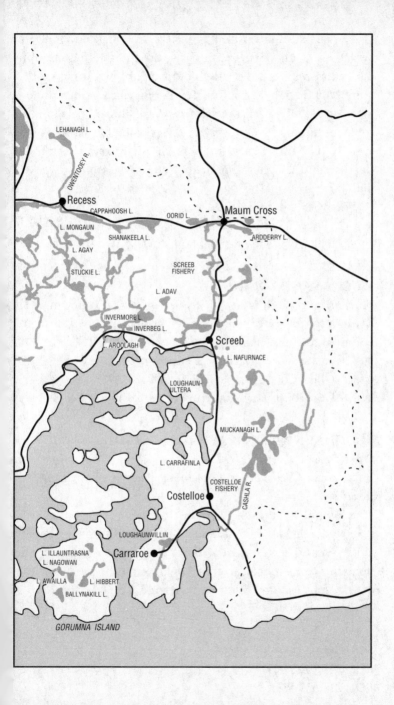

LEHANAGH L.

OWENTOOEY R.

Recess

CAPPAHOOSH L.

OORID L.

Maum Cross

ARDDERRY L.

L. MONGAUN

SHANAKEELA L.

L. AGAY

SCREEB
FISHERY

STUCKIE L.

L. ADAV

INVERMORE L.

INVERBEG L.

L. AROOLAGH

Screeb

L. NAFURNACE

LOUGHAUN-
ULTERA

MUCKANAGH L.

L. CARRAFINLA

COSTELLOE
FISHERY

CASHLA R.

Costelloe

LOUGHAUNWILLIN

Carraroe

L. ILLAUNTRASNA

L. NAGOWAN

L. AWAILLA   L. HIBBERT

BALLYNAKILL L.

GORUMNA ISLAND

The peak of the sea trout season is around 12 July, but the bigger sea trout arrive earlier. Grilse arrive in the system from the end of May. All the lakes hold small brown trout; quite a number of them hold sea trout, except for the higher and more inaccessible lakes. All the sea trout lakes have boats, and in some instances it is necessary to take a gillie on the lakes that are divided into beats, such as Glenicmurrin, Fermoyle, Carrick, and Clogher. One lake, Lough Naskeha, is stocked with rainbow trout.

Enquiries should be made to:

◆ *Costelloe and Fermoyle Fisheries Company*, Bridge Cottage, Costelloe, Co. Galway; telephone (091) 72196.

MUCKANAGH LOUGH

Muckanagh Lough is near Kinvarra school in Connemara. It holds a big stock of small brown trout and has sea trout. Enquiries about the fishing should be made to:

◆ *Costelloe and Fermoyle Fisheries Company*, Bridge Cottage, Costelloe, Co. Galway; telephone (091) 72196

◆ *Mr Peter Walsh*, Glenicmurrin Lodge, Costelloe, Co. Galway.

LOUGHAUNWILLIN (CARRAROE LOUGH)
Open Season
Brown trout: 1 February to 12 October. There is a bag limit of three trout per day.

This lough lies north of Carraroe. It holds a big stock of wild trout averaging about 6 oz, and is stocked with trout averaging 1.5 lb. Enquiries about the fishing should be made to the honorary secretary of Carraroe Angling Club:

◆ *Mr Frank Barrett*, Bóthar Buí, Carraroe, Co. Galway; telephone (091) 95228.

LOUGH ILLAUNTRASNA
LOUGH NAGOWAN
LOUGH AWAILLA

LOUGH HIBBERT
BALLYNAKILL LOUGH
Open Season

Brown trout: 1 February to 12 October; *sea trout:* 1 June to
30 September.

These five loughs are on Gorumna Island in south Connemara.
The first four hold small brown trout with an occasional sea
trout. Ballynakill Lough lies to the south-west of Gorumna
Island. It holds brown trout averaging 1 lb. Fishing is from the
shore. Enquiries about the fishing should be made to:

◆ *Fiontar na nOileán,* Tír an Fhia, Leitir Móir, Co. Galway;
telephone (091) 81351.

LOUGH CARRAFINLA
LOUGH HAWNAGHANEEKYNE
LOUGH VAURATRUFFIUN
LOUGH AUNWEENY
LOUGH NAMROUGHANIA
Open Season

Salmon: 1 February to 30 September; *sea trout:* 1 June to
30 September; *brown trout:* 1 February to 12 October.

These loughs are all part of the Lettermucka fishery. Lough
Carrafinla holds sea trout from July, and there is a boat for
hire. Enquiries about the fishing should be made to:

◆ *Mr P. Berridge,* Furnace Lodge, Camus, Co. Galway.

The other four loughs are let to Rosmuck Anglers'
Association, and the fishing is reserved for its members.

FURNACE FISHERY
Open Season

Salmon: 1 February to 30 September; *sea trout:* 1 June to
30 September; *brown trout:* 1 February to 12 October.

The Furnace fishery consists of Lough Nafurnace and
Loughnagarrivhan. These two lakes are to the east of the
Screeb–Costelloe road. They get a run of sea trout and
occasional salmon from July. The fishing is usually let in

conjunction with a fishing lodge. There are boats available on each lough. Enquiries about the fishing should be made to:

◆ *Mr P. Berridge*, Furnace Lodge, Camus, Co. Galway.

CAMUS LOUGHS (LOUGHAUNULTERA)
Open Season
Brown trout: 1 February to 12 October.

Loughaunultera is a series of interconnected loughs lying to the west of the Screeb–Costelloe road. Access to them is rather difficult. The loughs have a reputation for holding big numbers of small brown trout with an average size of about 0.5 lb. They can be free-rising. The season runs from 1 March to 12 October. Enquiries about the fishing should be made to:

◆ *Screeb Fishery*, Screeb, Camus, Co. Galway;
   telephone (091) 74110.

SCREEB FISHERY
Open Season
Salmon: 1 February to 30 September; *sea trout:* 1 June to 30 September; *brown trout:* 1 February to 12 October.

The Screeb fishery is six miles south of Maum Cross, Co. Galway, at the head of Camus Bay. It consists of an interconnected series of loughs and a short river. In addition to the river and the loughs there are five relatively productive bank beats or stands at the outflow or inflow of some loughs.

This is a salmon and sea trout fishery, with the salmon fishing predominating on the bank beats. It gets a small run of spring fish in April, and these are usually taken at the Salmon Pool. The grilse run from about 20 June and peak in July, and some fresh fish continue running for the rest of the season. The various fishing stands along the fishery are the Butt of Aasleam, the Lady Pool, the Salmon Pool, Derrywonniff Butt, Glencoh Butt, and the Road Pool.

Enquiries about the fishing should be made to:

◆ *Screeb House*, Camus, Co. Galway; telephone (091) 74110.

LOUGH ADAV

Lough Adav lies to the north of Screeb power house, and getting to it involves a long walk. The lough holds a good stock of brown trout, and the average size is probably 0.75 lb. It is reported to hold fish to 2 lb or better. Enquiries about the fishing should be made to:

◆ *Screeb Fishery*, Screeb, Camus, Co. Galway;
   telephone (091) 74110.

ARDDERRY LOUGH

Ardderry Lough is at the top of the Screeb system. It is a shallow lough that holds small brown trout and occasional sea trout and salmon late in the season. Enquiries about the fishing should be made to:

◆ *Mr H. D. Hodgson*, Currarevagh House, Oughterard,
   Co. Galway; telephone (091) 82313.

LOUGH AROOLAGH (ROSMUCK LOUGH)
Open Season
Brown trout: 1 February to 12 October.

Lough Aroolagh is a brown trout lake two-and-a-half miles west of Screeb. It holds a big stock of brown trout averaging 0.5 lb. There is a boat available, and fly fishing and dapping are the favoured methods. Enquiries about the fishing should be made to:

◆ *Tí Clarke*, Rosmuck, Co. Galway
◆ *Mr Paddy Nee*, Turloch, Rosmuck, Co. Galway.

INVERBEG FISHERY
Open Season
Salmon: 1 February to 30 September; *sea trout:* 1 June to 30 September; *brown trout:* 1 February to 12 October.

The Inverbeg fishery consists of four loughs. This is a private fishery, and rods are not usually let.

INVERMORE FISHERY
Open Season

Salmon: 1 February to 30 September; *sea trout:* 1 June to
30 September; *brown trout:* 1 February to 12 October.

The Invermore fishery consists of a short river and twelve
interconnected lakes. The river is about half a mile long and
drains into Kilkieran Bay. It holds salmon from early June, and
sea trout begin running about mid-June. There are six pools on
the river.

Once the Invermore Loughs were among the best-known
sea trout loughs in Connemara. Some of the better known
include Invermore, Currel, Luggeen, Owengarve Lough, and
Cuskeamatinny. Boats are available for hire on all these loughs.
Enquiries about the fishing should be made to:

◆ *Mrs Margaret McDonagh,* Glenview, Cashel, Co. Galway;
   telephone (095) 31054.

LOUGH AGAY
LOUGH MONGAUN

These two loughs lie off the Maum Cross–Recess road. Each of
them holds brown trout, with an average weight of 0.5 lb, and
in a wet season they may get a run of sea trout. Both can be
fished from the bank. Permission to fish is not usually required.

STUCKIE LOUGH

This is a small lake about half a mile north of Lough Curreel. It
holds a stock of brown trout and can be fished from the bank.
Permission to fish is not usually required.

LOUGH NAMBRACKMORE

Lough Nambrackmore is about one-and-a-half miles east of the
Recess–Carna road. There are only brown trout in this lough,
and they tend to be on the small side, with occasional fish to
over 1 lb. Bank fishing only.

GOWLABEG RIVER

Open Season

Salmon: 1 February to 30 September; *sea trout:* 1 June to
30 September; *brown trout:* 1 February to 12 October.

The Gowlabeg River flows north-west into Bertraghboy Bay. It
gets a small run of sea trout from July, and there are a few
holding pools where trout rest on their way to the loughs
upstream. Enquiries about the fishing should be made to:

◆ *Cashel House Hotel*, Cashel, Co. Galway;
   telephone (095) 31001.

GOWLA FISHERY

Open Season

Salmon: 1 February to 30 September; *sea trout:* 1 June to
30 September; *brown trout:* 1 February to 12 October.

The Gowla fishery consists of the Gowla River and an
interconnected series of about twelve loughs. The Gowla River
is about three miles long. It is mainly a sea trout fishery but has
some salmon. The river is divided into four beats.

The most famous of the loughs are Gowla Lough itself,
which has three boats, followed by Mannion's Lough,
Redman's Lough, White's Lough, and Lough Annillaun, each
of which have one boat.

The larger sea trout come in June, evening fishing is good in
July and August, and the better fishing reverts to the daytime
in September and October. Enquiries about the fishing should
be made to:

◆ *The Zetland Hotel*, Cashel, Co. Galway;
   telephone (095) 31111.

CARNA LOUGHS

Open Season

Salmon: 1 February to 30 September; *sea trout:* 1 June to
30 September; *brown trout:* 1 February to 12 October.

The Carna Loughs are a group of lakes in the Carna-Kilkieran district of south Connemara. They all hold brown trout and occasional sea trout. The sea trout run from mid-June, and fishing lasts from then until the end of September or early October, depending on the weather. Carna Anglers' Association control some or all of the fishing on Lough Keeraun, Lough Truskan, Lough Sheedagh, and Lough Skannive; enquiries about the fishing should be made to:

◆ *Mr D. E. Brown*, Carna, Co. Galway;
  telephone (095) 32296/32201.

LOUGH ALIVEE
Lough Alivee is east of the Glinsk–Carna road. It is a small lough and holds a good stock of brown trout averaging about 0.5 lb. It is bank fishing only. Permission to fish is not usually required.

LOUGH BOLA
The fishing is not let on this lake.

LOUGH NAGRAIGUE
Lough Nagraigue is east of Glinsk school. It holds a good stock of brown trout averaging 0.5 lb and is fished from the shore. Permission to fish is not usually required.

LOUGH NANEEVE
Lough Naneeve lies east of Glinsk. It holds a big stock of small brown trout. Permission to fish is not usually required.

LOUGH APHEEBERA
LOUGH AWEE
Both of these lakes are on the Gowlabeg system. They involve a long walk. Each of them holds brown trout and can be fished from the shore. The average size of the trout is said to be between 0.5 lb and 0.75 lb. They rise well to the fly. Permission to fish is not usually required.

OWENMORE RIVER SYSTEM (BALLYNAHINCH RIVER)

Open Season

Salmon: 1 February to 30 September; *sea trout:* 1 June to 30 September; *brown trout*: 1 February to 12 October.

The Ballynahinch system drains a large catchment area in west Connemara. Its most northerly point is the top of the Inagh Valley, and another branch of it flows from Maum Cross in the east. There are eight separate fisheries on the Ballynahinch system; a number of them are private fisheries. The fisheries listed below are available for letting, either on a day ticket or weekly, to visiting anglers.

The first spring salmon run through in February and March, and fish begin resting in the pools in April. The fishery gets a big run of grilse, beginning in late May or early June, with the peak in late June and early July. There is a further small run of summer and autumn fish into the river in September.

The first sea trout begin running in late June, and early July and August see extremely good fishing. The season for daytime fishing is from July to October. There is good night fishing at various points along the Ballynahinch system, and a feature of the fishery is that that sea trout are taken during daylight hours as well.

Ballynahinch Castle Fishery

The Ballynahinch Castle fishery consists of approximately two-and-a-half miles of river and two lakes. There is another short stretch of river further upstream that is developed and used as a salmon beat. The fishery is the first at the bottom of the Ballynahinch system, stretching up from Toombeola Bridge. It is divided into eight salmon beats and four sea trout beats. It is let by the beat, and beats are rotated daily; the tenant for the day may take one guest on the beat. Gillies are available by prior arrangement.

Lower Ballynahinch Lake is a sea trout fishery, and two boats are available. The Church Lake is stocked with brown trout and fished from the bank or a boat.

Enquiries about the fishing should be made to:

◆ *Ballynahinch Castle Hotel*, Ballinafad, Co. Galway; telephone (095) 31006.

Lough Inagh Fishery

The Lough Inagh fishery consists of fishing on Lough Inagh and Derryclare Lough as well as fishing on the outflowing rivers from each of these loughs. There are six bank beats at the Lough Inagh fishery in addition to the lough fishing. The beats are rotated daily between the Inagh Valley Inn and Lough Inagh Lodge Hotel.

The spring salmon fishing begins here in early March and peaks in May. The fish average 10 lb, and fish up to 25 lb have been taken. The grilse come in June and are taken from the bank or from a boat on the loughs up to the end of September. There are six named bank beats: Corloo, the Trout Pool, Derryclare Butts, Glendalough Butts, Pine Island, and Green Point.

Boats are available on both Derryclare Lough and Lough Inagh, and gillies can be arranged by booking in advance. Enquiries about the fishing should be made to:

◆ *Ms Della McAuley*, Inagh Valley Inn, Recess, Co. Galway; telephone (095) 34608
◆ *Lough Inagh Lodge Hotel*, Recess, Co. Galway; telephone (095) 34706.

Upper Ballynahinch Fishery

The Upper Ballynahinch fishery consists of river fishing on two rivers and on a number of loughs. The fishery is near Recess, Co. Galway. It comprises part of the Owentooey River and part of the Recess River, as well as Oorid Lough, Shanakeela Lough, Derryneen Lough, and Cappahoosh Lough. It is mainly a sea trout fishery but is understood to produce a fair number of salmon and grilse as well. The best of the fishing is after the first spate in July, and the fishing can then continue when conditions are right to the end of September and into October for sea trout.

Enquiries about the fishing should be made to:

◆ *Mrs Iris Joyce*, Tullaboy House, Maum Cross, Recess, Co. Galway; telephone (091) 82305

◆ *Mr Leslie Lyons*, Tullaboy, Maum Cross, Recess, Co. Galway; telephone (091) 82462.

Athry Fishery

The Athry fishery is at the top of a tributary of the Ballynahinch system near Athry Crossroads. These lakes get sea trout from July and hold occasional salmon as well. There are brown trout here to about 1 lb. Boats are available for hire.

Enquiries about the fishing should be made to:

◆ *The Zetland Hotel*, Cashel, Co. Galway; telephone (095) 21010.

LOUGHYVANGAN

Loughyvangan lies to the south-east of the Carna–Clifden road. This is a brown trout fishery only, with the fish running from about 0.5 to 2 lb. It is fished only from the bank. Cashel Anglers' Association fish the lake, and enquiries about the fishing should be made locally.

TOOMBEOLA LOUGHS (ANGLER'S RETURN FISHERY)

This fishery comprises a number of interconnecting lakes draining into the Ballynahinch River near Toombeola Bridge. It is mainly a brown trout fishery, with sea trout in some of the lower loughs late in the season. The trout average 0.5 lb, with some up to 2 lb. Boats are not available, but nearly all the lakes can be fished from the shore. Enquiries should be made to:

◆ *Miss L. Prynne*, The Angler's Return, Ballinafad, Co. Galway; telephone (095) 31091.

ROUNDSTONE LAKES

Open Season

Brown trout: 15 February to 12 October.

Roundstone Anglers' Association has fishing on a number of lakes in the vicinity of Roundstone. Lough Scannive is a really good brown trout fishery and holds some sea trout late in the season. The brown trout average 1 lb. Lough Naweelaun has trout averaging 0.5 lb with occasional trout to 2 lb. Lough Nasoodery has trout ranging from 0.5 to 2 lb. Lough Rannaghaun has brown trout only but they are relatively plentiful, with very few fish better than 0.5 lb. Lough Bollard holds small trout coming at about three to the pound, and Lough Nalowney holds nice brown trout averaging 0.5 lb with some up to 1.25 lb.

Information is available from:

◆ *Roundstone Anglers' Association*, Roundstone, Co. Galway.

BALLYNAKILL DISTRICT

The Ballynakill Fisheries District comprises parts of Cos. Galway and Mayo and embraces all rivers flowing into the sea between Slyne Head, Co. Galway, and Pidgeon Point, Westport, Co. Mayo.

DOOHULLA FISHERY

Open Season

Salmon: 1 February to 30 September; *sea trout:* 1 June to 30 September; *brown trout:* 15 February to 12 October

The Doohulla fishery consists of at least half a dozen lakes that hold sea trout and salmon. There are boats for hire. Enquiries about the fishing should be made to:

◆ *Mr Tinney*, Ballyconneely, Co. Galway; telephone (095) 23529.

Carrick Lake is best for brown trout, and its shores are suitable for fly fishing. The Carra Bridge pool on the Doohulla River is best for salmon.

BALLINABOY RIVER

Open Season

Salmon: 1 February to 30 September; *sea trout:* 1 June to
30 September; *brown trout:* 15 February to 12 October

The Ballinaboy River flows into the sea south of Clifden. It gets
a run of sea trout from July, and there are at least a dozen
loughs on the system that are more frequently fished than the
river. Enquiries about the fishing should be made to:

◆ *Col. A. Morris,* Ballinaboy House, Clifden, Co. Galway.

DERRYHORRAUN RIVER

Open Season

Salmon: 1 February to 30 September; *sea trout:* 1 June to
30 September; *brown trout:* 15 February to 12 October.

This is a small river that drains a series of loughs into the Salt
Lake at Clifden. It gets a run of sea trout and a small run of
salmon, but the fish usually run straight through to the loughs.
Permits or day tickets are available from:

◆ *Mr Percy Stanley,* Clifden, Co. Galway;
   telephone (095) 21039.

OWENGLIN RIVER (CLIFDEN)

Open Season

Salmon: 1 February to 30 September; *sea trout:* 1 June to
30 September; *brown trout:* 15 February to 12 October.

No fishing is permitted between the Ardbear New Bridge
and the Ardbear Old Bridge on or after 15 May.

This is a spate river with three waterfalls, and it can provide
some good grilse fishing when the water is right. The first run
of grilse arrives with the first flood in June; fish continue to run
on every flood through the season. The average size of the
grilse tends to be very small.

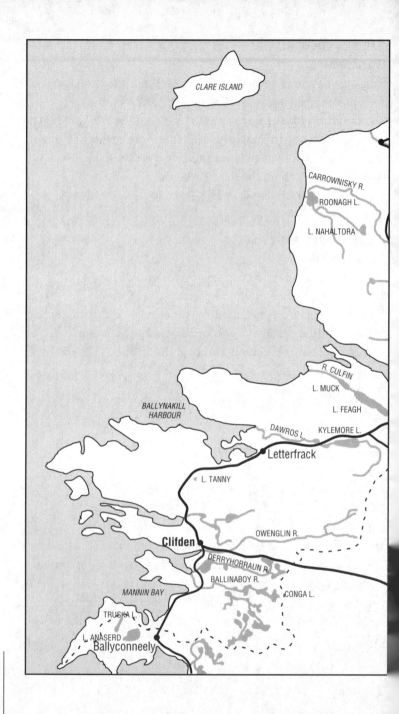

CLARE ISLAND

CARROWNISKY R.

ROONAGH L.

L. NAHALTORA

R. CULFIN

L. MUCK

L. FEAGH

BALLYNAKILL
HARBOUR

DAWROS L.

KYLEMORE L.

Letterfrack

L. TANNY

OWENGLIN R.

Clifden

DERRYHORRAUN R.

BALLINABOY R.

CONGA L.

MANNIN BAY

TRUSKA L.

L. ANASERD

Ballyconneely

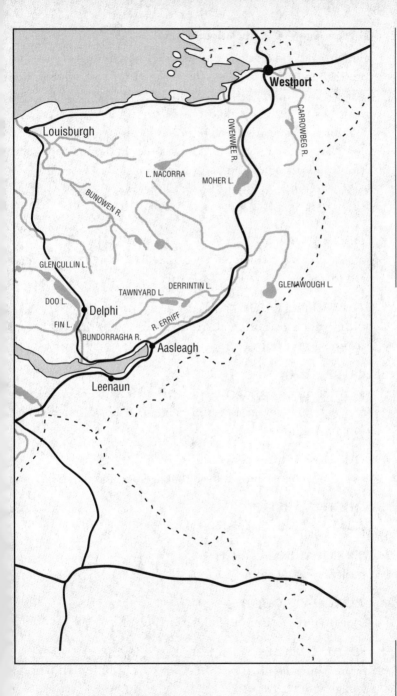

Clifden Anglers' Association has the fishing on many lakes in the Clifden area, including the Owenglin River system, the Derryhorraun River system, and the Ballynaboy system. The majority of the loughs hold brown trout, but some have sea trout and occasional salmon. Day tickets are available on all of them, and boats may be hired on some. Enquiries about the fishing and permits should be made to:

◆ *Mr Noel Kirby*, Westport Road, Clifden, Co. Galway
◆ *Mr Percy Stanley*, Clifden, Co. Galway.

LOUGH TANNEY

holds a small stock of good trout up to 2.5 lb, but they are very hard to tempt.

COURHOOR LOUGH

holds a big stock of small trout up to 0.5 lb. It also holds occasional sea trout.

LOUGH AUNA

has trout of a good average size, probably over 0.5 lb, and some say the average is getting bigger. A boat is sometimes available for hire.

LOUGH ANIMMA

has a good stock of brown trout that average about 0.75 lb.

LOUGH NAHILLION

holds a big stock of small trout coming at three to the pound.

DERRYWAKING LOUGH

usually holds sea trout.

CROAGHAT LOUGH

is one of the best sea trout loughs in the area.

ISLAND LOUGH

is sometimes stocked with fish up to 2.5 lb; its wild stock average about 0.5 lb.

DERRYLEA LOUGH

holds an excellent stock of brown trout averaging 0.5 lb and is sometimes stocked. It is nearly a mile long. There is usually a boat available for hire.

GOULANE LOUGH

holds brown trout up to 1 lb and there is usually a boat for hire.

LOUGH FADDA

holds a good stock of brown trout up to 1 lb and occasionally bigger.

BOOLAGARE LOUGH

has a good stock of brown trout averaging 0.5 lb.

DRY LOUGH

holds a small stock of good-sized brown trout.

BALLYBAWN LOUGH

holds a good stock of brown trout averaging 0.5 lb, with some better ones.

LOUGH BEAGHCAUNEEN

gets a good run of sea trout from early July and holds occasional salmon. There is a boat for hire.

CONGA LOUGH

holds small brown trout and occasional sea trout.

LOUGH NAGAP

holds a small stock of brown trout up to about 0.75 lb.

EMLAGHNABEHY

holds a small stock of good brown trout up to 3 lb, but they don't come easy.

LOUGH NACORRUSAUN

holds a good stock of brown trout averaging 0.75 lb.

LOUGH ANASERD

holds an excellent stock of trout averaging 0.75 lb.

TRUSKA LOUGH

holds trout averaging 1 lb.

DAWROS SYSTEM
Open Season

Salmon: 1 February to 30 September; *sea trout:* 1 June to
30 September; *brown trout:* 15 February to 12 October.

The Dawros system consists of a four-mile length of river and three loughs. The river drains into Ballynakill Harbour. It gets runs of spring salmon, sea trout, and grilse. Access is good, and the banks have been cleared in recent years. Enquiries about the fishing should be made to:

◆ *Mrs W. Aspell,* Kylemore, Co. Galway; telephone (095) 41145
◆ *Renvyle House Hotel,* Renvyle, Co. Galway.

The three loughs on the system are the Abbey Lough, Pollacappul Lough, and Kylemore Lough. They get a run of spring salmon from April and grilse and sea trout from June. Boats are available for hire. Enquiries about the fishing should be made to:

◆ *Mrs W. Aspell,* Kylemore, Co. Galway; telephone (095) 41145
◆ *Mrs Nancy Naughton,* Kylemore House, Kylemore,
    Co. Galway; telephone (095) 41143.

LOUGH NA BRACK CAOCH
LOUGH NA CARRIGEEN

These two loughs are at Creeragh and lie south of the Leenaun–Clifden road. Each of them holds brown trout.

CULFIN SYSTEM
Open Season

Salmon: 1 February to 30 September; *sea trout:* 1 June to
30 September; *brown trout:* 15 February to 12 October.

The Culfin River is about one mile long and drains Lough Muck and Lough Feagh into Little Killary Bay. It flows through bogland, and the banks are high. It is worth fishing for grilse, especially in June and July, and gets a run of sea trout in July.

The two loughs lie to the west of the Leenaun–Kylemore road. They hold occasional salmon and get a run of sea trout. They can be fished from June, and there is one boat available on each of them. Enquiries about the fishing should be made to:

◆ *Mrs Ruth Willoughby*, Salruck, Renvyle, Co. Galway; telephone (095) 43498
◆ *Mr Owen King*, Lettergesh, Co. Galway; telephone (095) 43414.

ERRIFF FISHERY
Open Season
Salmon: 1 February to 30 September; *sea trout:* 1 June to 30 September; *brown trout:* 15 February to 12 October.

The Erriff fishery consists of the River Erriff and three loughs: Tawnyard Lough, Derrintin Lough, and Glenawough Lough. The Erriff is divided into nine beats; each beat takes two or three rods. It is owned and managed by the Central Fisheries Board.

The fishery opens on 1 April, and the peak of the spring run is around mid-May, with the grilse beginning to run in early June. It is a productive summer salmon fishery. Fly fishing is the rule, but spinning, worm and shrimp are allowed for a short period each day. The river gets a run of sea trout that are generally taken by anglers fishing for salmon.

Tawnyard Lough is a fair-sized lough that holds salmon and sea trout from July to October. Boats and outboard motors are available for hire. Derrintin Lough is a small, remote lough holding brown trout. It is occasionally stocked with brown trout averaging 1 lb. Bank fishing and a rowing boat are available.

Glenawough Lough is a remote mountain lough and holds only very small brown trout.

Enquiries about the fishing should be made to:

◆ *Erriff Fishery*, Aasleagh Lodge, Leenaun, Co. Galway; telephone (095) 42252.

DELPHI FISHERY

Open Season

Salmon: 1 February to 30 September; *sea trout:* 1 June to
30 September; *brown trout:* 15 February to 12 October.

The Delphi fishery consists of the Bundorragha River and three interconnecting lakes: Finlough, Doolough, and Glencullin. The season opens on 1 February, and usually either the river or Doolough produces the first salmon in the west of Ireland. Three rods are allowed on the river. Spring salmon run in February, March, April, and May, and the grilse begin running in June. The sea trout run begins in late June or early July.

A gillie is available on the river, and gillies, boats and outboard motors are available for hire on the three loughs. Enquiries about the fishing should be made to:

◆ *Mr Peter Mantle,* Delphi Lodge, Leenaun, Co. Galway; telephone (095) 42213; fax (095) 42212.

CARROWNISKY RIVER

Open Season

Salmon: 1 April to 30 September; *sea trout:* 1 June to
30 September; *brown trout:* 1 April to 30 September.

The Carrownisky River flows into the sea south of Louisburgh, Co. Mayo. It is a spate river and gets a good run of grilse from mid-June and holds sea trout from July. It is fly fishing only.

Most of the river is owned and managed by the Western Regional Fisheries Board, and permits are available from:

◆ *Gaffney's Bar,* Louisburgh, Co. Mayo; telephone (098) 66150.

ROONAGH LOUGH

Open Season

Salmon: 1 April to 30 September.

This tidal lough lies about four miles south of Louisburgh. It gets a good run of salmon from late June and has sea trout from mid-July. It is a shallow lough and fishes best after a flood when the salt has been flushed out by the fresh water. Enquiries about the fishing can be made to:

◆ *Western Regional Fisheries Board,* Weir Lodge, Earl's Island, Galway; telephone (091) 63118/63119.

LOUGH NAHALTORA
Open Season
Brown trout: 15 February to 30 September.

Lough Nahaltora is west of the Louisburgh–Delphi road. It holds good stocks of brown trout, and of salmon and sea trout from June. It is usually fished from the bank. Enquiries about the fishing should be made to:

◆ *Western Regional Fisheries Board,* Weir Lodge, Earl's Island, Galway; telephone (091) 63118/63119.

LOUGH NACORRA
Open Season
Brown trout: 15 February to 12 October.

Lough Nacorra is one-and-a-half miles south of Croagh Patrick and west of the Leenaun–Westport road. It holds a big stock of brown trout averaging 0.5 lb. It is fished from the bank, and the banks are fairly good. Permission to fish is not usually required.

MOHER LOUGH
Open Season
Brown trout: 15 February to 12 October.

Moher Lough is five miles south of Westport on the Westport–Leenaun road. It holds a good stock of brown trout averaging 0.5 lb and it is also stocked with brown trout by the fisheries board. It sometimes gets a small run of sea trout from August. It is fly fishing only.

Enquiries about the fishing and boats for hire should be made to:

◆ *Mr Michael McDonnell,* Liscarney, Westport, Co. Mayo; telephone (098) 26638.

BUNOWEN RIVER
Open Season
Salmon: 1 April to 30 September; *sea trout:* 1 June to
30 September; *brown trout:* 1 April to 30 September.

The Bunowen River flows through Louisburgh into Clew Bay. It is a spate river and can get an excellent run of grilse and a run of sea trout from mid-June. Most of the river is owned and managed by the regional fisheries board; permits are available from:

◆ *Gaffney's Bar*, Louisburgh, Co. Mayo; telephone (098) 66150.

BOHEH LOUGHS
These two small loughs lie to the west of the Westport–Leenaun road four miles south of Westport. They hold small brown trout and are occasionally stocked with brown trout. Enquiries about the fishing should be made to:

◆ *Western Regional Fisheries Board*, Weir Lodge, Earl's Island, Galway; telephone (091) 63118/63119.

OWENWEE RIVER
Open Season
Salmon: 1 February to 30 September; *sea trout:* 1 June to
30 September; *brown trout:* 15 February to 12 October.

The Owenwee River is a small spate river that enters the sea west of Westport. It gets a small run of grilse and sea trout from late June or early July, and the last two miles is the most fishable part of the river. Enquiries about the fishing should be made to:

◆ *Mr Vincent Bourke*, Bridge Street, Westport, Co. Mayo.

CARROWBEG RIVER
Open Season
Brown trout: 15 February to 12 October.

The Carrowbeg River flows through Westport, Co. Mayo. It is about ten miles long and holds a fair stock of small wild brown trout, and is sometimes stocked with adult trout to over 1 lb. Enquiries about the fishing should be made locally or to Westport Angling Club.

North-Western Fisheries Region

The North-Western Fisheries Region extends from Pidgeon Point, near Westport, Co. Mayo, to Mullaghmore Point, Co. Sligo. It comprises parts of Cos. Mayo, Roscommon, Sligo, and Leitrim. The predominant underlying rock formations of the area are limestone, lower carboniferous shale, schist, and gneiss.

This is a region that offers the prospect of a wide variety of game fishing in both river and lake. It is probably best known for its salmon fishing. The River Moy is rightly renowned as a salmon river, producing rod catches of up to 11,000 salmon per year; these are made up of spring salmon, grilse, and summer salmon. But the Moy and its tributaries are not alone in the region. The Bonet River, Ballysadare River, Easky River, Owenmore, Owenduff, Owengarve and Newport River all provide salmon fishing. There is good salmon fishing (spring and grilse) in many of the lakes too; the most noteworthy are Lough Gill, Lough Conn, Lough Cullin, Carrowmore Lake, the Burrishoole fishery lakes, and Beltra Lough.

Sea trout are plentiful in the region too and are to be found in the Drumcliff River, Glencar Lough, Easky River, Moy Estuary, Glenamoy River, Carrowmore Lake, Owenmore, Owenduff, Burrishoole fishery, Owengarve, Beltra Lough, and Newport River.

Brown trout are widespread and prolific throughout the region. Lough Conn is one of the premier brown trout lakes in the country; Lough Arrow is famous for its mayfly and sedge fishing. Then there are the small mountain loughs of the Ox Mountains in Co. Sligo and the Nephin Beg range in Co. Mayo, which can offer good sport in quiet, peaceful surroundings. There is a danger, however, that some of these lakes may be cut off or access impeded by forestry development, and enquiries should be made.

The region has its share of river brown trout fishing too. This is mainly confined to the northern part of the region, in the River Moy tributaries and the tributaries of the Ballysadare River.

The headquarters of the North-Western Regional Fisheries Board is at Ardnaree House, Abbey Street, Ballina, Co. Mayo; telephone (096) 22623.

BANGOR DISTRICT

The Bangor Fisheries District comprises north-west Co. Mayo and embraces all the rivers flowing into the sea between Pidgeon Point at Westport and Benwee Head in north-west Mayo.

CLOGHER LOUGH
Open Season
1 May to 30 September.
Clogher Lough lies approximately three-and-a-half miles north-east of Westport. It holds a stock of brown trout with an average size of just over 0.5 lb. The bottom is soft in places, and great care should be taken when wading. There are a number of boats for hire, and enquiries should be made locally. The fishing is regarded as free.

ALTNABROCKY AND NEPHIN BEG LAKES

The Altnabrocky and Nephin Beg lakes are on Nephin Beg Mountain and in the bogland north of this range. Many of the lakes lie within the Nephin Forest. The forest roads all have blocked barriers; anglers can get a key to the barriers by contacting:

◆ *North-Western Regional Fisheries Board*, Abbey Street, Ballina, Co. Mayo; telephone (096) 22623

◆ *Mr Michael Tolan*, Moy Fishery, Ridge Pool Road, Ballina, Co. Mayo; telephone (096) 21332.

Pine plantations are widespread in this area; many of these lakes are now surrounded by a pine forest and may be difficult to find, but in some instances forestry roads have improved access.

LOUGH KEERAN

holds a small stock of brown trout, and the fishing is regarded as free.

LOUGH GALL

holds brown trout averaging 1 lb, but they are not plentiful. The fishing on the west side is private.

LOUGH NABROCK

holds a stock of small brown trout and some sea trout. The fishing is regarded as free.

LOUGH NAMBROCK

also holds small brown trout and sea trout. The fishing is regarded as free.

LOUGH BRACK

holds a stock of brown trout averaging 1.5 lb. Access to this remote lake is difficult.

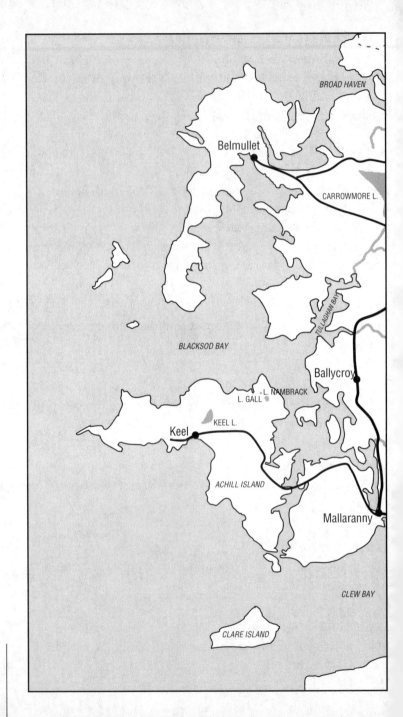

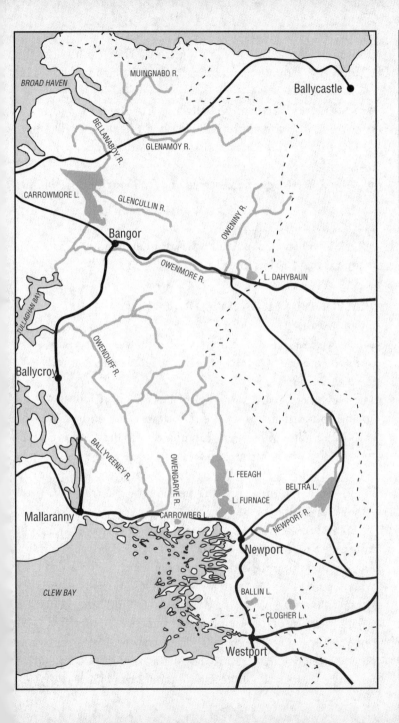

BROAD HAVEN

MUINGNABO R.

Ballycastle

BELLANABOY R.

GLENAMOY R.

CARROWMORE L.

GLENCULLIN R.

OWENINIY R.

Bangor

OWENMORE R.

L. DAHYBAUN

TULLAGHAN BAY

OWENDUFF R.

Ballycroy

BALLYVEENEY R.

OWENGARVE R.

L. FEEAGH

BELTRA L.

L. FURNACE

Mallaranny

CARROWBEG L.

NEWPORT R.

Newport

CLEW BAY

BALLIN L.

CLOGHER L.

Westport

SCARDAUN LOUGH AND BLACK LOUGH

Both hold good stocks of brown trout. They lie high in the Nephin Beg Mountains. Enquiries about the fishing should be made to:

- *Rock House,* Ballyveeney, Ballycroy, Co. Mayo
- *Mr J. R. B. Hewat,* Rathmichael Lodge, Shankill, Co. Dublin.

Corslieve Lough has a stock of small brown trout. The fishing is private; enquiries should be made to:

- *Mr J. R. B. Hewat,* Rathmichael Lodge, Shankill, Co. Dublin.

LOUGH NALAGHAN

holds a good stock of small brown trout averaging 0.75 lb. The fishing is regarded as free.

NEWPORT RIVER AND BELTRA LOUGH
Open Season

Salmon and sea trout: 20 March to 30 September. A bye-law prohibits the use of a gaff at the Burrishoole fishery or on the Newport River.

The Newport River drains Beltra Lough into Clew Bay. The spring salmon run from opening day to the end of May or early June. The grilse begin running on the first flood in early June, and there is a run of fish continuously into the river to the end of the season. It is a fly-only fishery. The sea trout run begins in early July, and the best of the fishing is in July, August, and September.

Beltra Lough lies five miles north-east of Newport and eight miles north-west of Castlebar. It is two-and-a-quarter miles long by about a mile wide, and an outboard motor is essential when fishing the lake from a boat. The lough can be fished for spring salmon from opening day in March until June. The grilse begin to appear in June and the sea trout come in July. It is a fly-only fishery. The lough is divided east and west between Newport House Hotel and Glenisland Anglers' Co-Operative Society; enquiries about the fishing should be made to:

- *Newport House Hotel*, Newport, Co. Mayo;
  telephone (098) 41222
- *Fishery Manager*, Glenisland Anglers' Co-Operative,
  Castlebar, Co. Mayo; telephone (094) 21302.

BALLIN LOUGH
Open Season
1 May to 30 September.

Ballin Lough is south of Newport, Co. Mayo. It is stocked with rainbow trout and brown trout; fly fishing only is allowed. The lough is 54 acres in area and mainly shallow. Anglers are strongly advised not to wade, as it can be very dangerous. Boats are available for hire. Enquiries about the fishing should be made to:

- *Salmon Research Agency*, Newport, Co. Mayo;
  telephone (098) 41107/41171.

LOUGH BEN
Lough Ben is near Glenisland, north of Castlebar. It holds a good stock of brown trout averaging just over 0.5 lb. The banks are reasonably good but difficult in places, and the north shore offers the best prospects for fishing. The fishing is regarded as free.

DRUMGONEY LOUGH
Drumgoney Lough is south of the Newport–Castlebar road. It holds a good stock of small brown trout and is stocked by Newport Anglers' Club. Permits are available from:

- *Mr Bill Geraghty*, Cartoon, Newport, Co. Mayo.

BROAD LOUGH
Broad Lough lies to the east of the Newport–Westport road, about a mile from Newport. It has a good stock of small brown trout with occasional trout to 0.75 lb. They are free-rising.

Enquiries about the fishing or a boat for hire can be made to:

- ◆ *Mr Éamon Kennedy*, Liss, Newport, Co. Mayo; telephone (098) 41229
- ◆ *Mr Tony Gallagher*, Liss, Newport, Co. Mayo.

BURRISHOOLE FISHERY

Open Season

Mid-June to 30 September.

The Burrishoole fishery is north-west of Newport and consists of three lakes: Lough Furnace, Lough Feeagh, and Lough Bunavella. The first two are noted for their salmon and sea trout fishing, and the latter is a brown trout fishery. Lough Furnace and Lough Feeagh offer good salmon and sea trout fishing. The fishing is limited to five boats with engines on each lough, and fly fishing only is the rule. Gillies are available. Enquiries about the fishing should be made to:

- ◆ *Salmon Research Agency*, Newport, Co. Mayo; telephone (098) 41107/41171.

CARROWBEG LOUGH

Open Season

1 May to 30 September.

Carrowbeg Lough lies to the south of the Newport–Mallaranny road. It holds a resident stock of small brown trout and gets a small run of sea trout and salmon. It can be fished off the north bank, and the fishing is regarded as free.

OWENGARVE RIVER

Open Season

Salmon: 1 May to 30 September;

sea trout: 1 May to 12 October.

The Owengarve River holds salmon and sea trout, especially in August and September. It is a fly-only fishery, and fishes best in spate conditions. Permission to fish can be obtained from:

- *Mr T. D. Healy*, Rosturk Castle, Mallaranny, Co. Mayo
- *Mr Peter McGee*, tackle shop, Newport, Co. Mayo
- *Mr Ciarán Moran*, Moynish Guesthouse, Mallaranny, Co. Mayo.

KEEL LOUGH
LOUGH NAMBRACK
LOUGH GALL
Open Season
Salmon: 1 February to 30 September; *sea trout:* 1 February to 12 October; *brown trout:* 15 February to 12 October.

These loughs are on Achill Island. Keel Lough is a big, shallow lough and holds sea trout from June. It can be fished from the shore; a boat is sometimes available for hire if arrangements are made in advance.

Lough Nambrack lies to the north-east of Achill Island and holds a good stock of brown trout averaging just over 0.5 lb. Fly fishing only is allowed.

Lough Gall has a good stock of brown trout averaging 1.5 lb, and fish to 4 lb have been taken in the past. It can be fished from the bank.

Enquiries about the fishing should be made to the honorary secretary of Achill Sporting Club:
- *Mr Roger Gallagher*, Valley House, Bunnacurry, Co. Mayo; telephone (098) 47204.

LOUGH GALL
Lough Gall lies to the east of the Mallaranny–Achill road, and it can be approached on the bog road. It holds a stock of small brown trout. Enquiries about the fishing should be made to:
- *Rock House*, Ballyveeney, Ballycroy, Co. Mayo; telephone (098) 49137.

BALLYVEENEY RIVER
Open Season
Salmon: 1 February to 30 September;
sea trout: 1 February to 12 October.

This small river offers over a mile of sea trout fishing.
Enquiries about the fishing should be made to:
◆ *Rock House,* Ballyveeney, Ballycroy, Co. Mayo;
   telephone (098) 49137.

OWENDUFF RIVER
Open Season
Salmon: 1 February to 30 September;
sea trout: 1 February to 12 October.

This is an exceptionally prolific salmon and sea trout river,
draining into Tullaghan Bay, a few miles north of Ballycroy,
Co. Mayo. It holds spring salmon and grilse. The fishing rights
are all privately owned, except for the estuary below the weir
at Srahnamanragh Bridge. There is about a mile of free fishing
in this estuary. A recently formed angling club hopes to
acquire some fishing rights on the river. Enquiries should be
made locally.

Upriver there are five private fisheries and three fishing
lodges. Occasionally, a week becomes available in one of the
lodges; details of the fishing are available from:
◆ *Mr Roy Craigie,* Owenduff, Celbridge, Co. Kildare
◆ *Rock House,* Ballyveeney, Ballycroy, Co. Mayo
◆ *Mr Colm Ó Briain,* New Park, Stillorgan Road, Dublin 18.

■ OWENMORE RIVER SYSTEM

Open Season
Salmon and sea trout: 1 February to 30 September.

The Owenmore River drains a large area of north-west Mayo
into Tullaghan Bay. The river holds spring fish from February.
The grilse come in early June, and the river gets a good run of

autumn fish from late August. It gets a good run of sea trout from mid-June to the end of September. Fly fishing only is permitted upstream of a line across the river from the juncture of the townlands of Goolamore and Tristia to the townland of Ballina.

Much of the fishing is private and not let. A four-mile stretch in the middle reaches is leased by Bangor Sporting Club; a limited number of day tickets is available (not at weekends) from:

◆ *Mr Séamus Henry*, Bangor Sporting Club, Bangor, Co. Mayo; telephone (097) 83487/83461.

OWENINY RIVER

The Oweniny River is a tributary of the Owenmore, and joins the main river at Bellacorick Bridge. The river holds spring salmon from April, grilse from June, and sea trout from July.

The fishing rights are fragmented. The Glenalt syndicate and the Office of Public Works have about a quarter of a mile of fishing upstream from the confluence that is not let. Upstream from here, permission to fish can be obtained from:

◆ *Mr John Gillespie, Dominick McLoughlin, John Ruddy, Bord na Móna, Tony Cosgrave,* and *Michael McGrath*, at Srahnakiely, Bellacorick, Co. Mayo.
  For information on gillies, contact:
◆ *Mr Barry Seagrave*, Cloonamoyne Fishery, Enniscoe House, Castlehill, Co. Mayo; telephone (096) 31112
◆ *Val or Martin Irwin or Jackie Conway*, Srahmeen, Garranard, Co. Mayo.

SHESKIN RIVER

This small river joins the Oweniny from the west. It is a spate river and gets a run of fish in August and September on a flood. Enquiries about the fishing should be made to:

◆ *Mr Pat Mullarkey*, Srahnakiely, Bellacorick, Co. Mayo.

LOUGH DAHYBAUN

Open Season

Brown trout: 15 February to 30 September.

This is a large lough lying off the Crossmolina–Bangor road about two miles east of Bellacorick. It has a small stock of brown trout, some up to 2 lb, and is usually stocked with rainbow trout. Fishing permits may be obtained from:

◆ *The Alpine Hotel*, Enniscrone, Co. Sligo;
   telephone (096) 36144.

CARROWMORE LAKE

Open Season

Salmon and sea trout: 1 February to 30 September.

Carrowmore Lake lies two miles north-west of Bangor, Co. Mayo. It is four miles long and nearly three miles wide. It holds spring salmon from opening day and sea trout from late June, and it has a good resident stock of brown trout. It is one of the premier spring salmon fishing loughs in the country.

Bank fishing is not allowed: fishing methods are spinning and fly fishing to 31 March, and thereafter fly fishing only; trolling is not permitted at any time. This lake is shallow, and boats should take great care to avoid submerged rocks.

Enquiries about the fishing and about boats and gillies should be made to:

◆ *Mr Séamus Henry*, Bangor Sporting Club, Bangor, Co. Mayo;
   telephone (097) 83487/83461.

GLENAMOY RIVER

Open Season

Salmon: 1 May to 30 September;
sea trout: 1 May to 12 October.

The Glenamoy flows into Sruwaddacon Bay in north-west Mayo. It gets a run of grilse from June and can provide good fishing in suitable water right to the end of the season. It also gets quite a good run of sea trout from July. Permits can be obtained from:

◆ *Mr Séamus Henry,* Bangor Sporting Club, Bangor, Co. Mayo; telephone (097) 83487/83461.

MUINGNABO RIVER
BELLANABOY RIVER
GLENCULLIN RIVER
Open Season
Salmon and sea trout: 1 February to 30 September.
These three small spate rivers are also in north-west Mayo. Some hold salmon and sea trout; some are sea trout only. You can expect to find fish in any of them after a spate from June.

The Muingnabo River is just nine miles long and joins the Glenamoy Estuary about two miles west of the village of Glenamoy. The Bellanaboy River flows into Carrowmore Lake from the north, and the best fishing is from the last bridge down to the lake. The Glencullin River flows westwards into Carrowmore Lake. It holds a good stock of sea trout and salmon after a flood.

Enquiries should be made to:

◆ *Mr Séamus Henry,* Bangor Sporting Club, Bangor, Co. Mayo; telephone (097) 83487/83461.

BALLINA DISTRICT

The Ballina Fisheries District comprises parts of Cos. Mayo and Sligo and embraces all rivers flowing into the sea between Benwee Head, Co. Mayo, and Cooanmore Point, Co. Sligo.

CLOONAGHMORE (PALMERSTOWN) RIVER
Open Season
Salmon: 1 June to 30 September;
sea trout and brown trout: 1 June to 12 October.

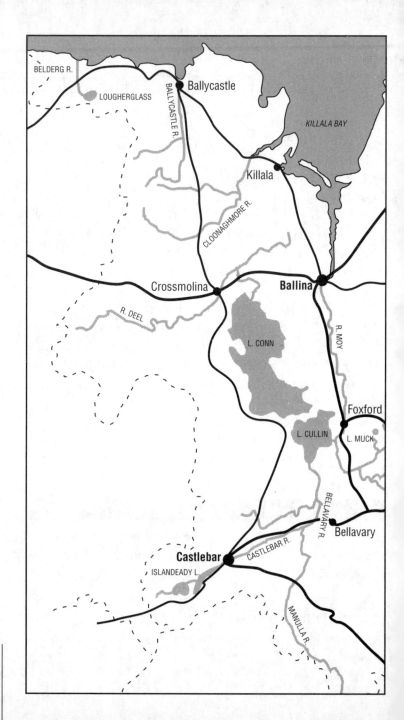

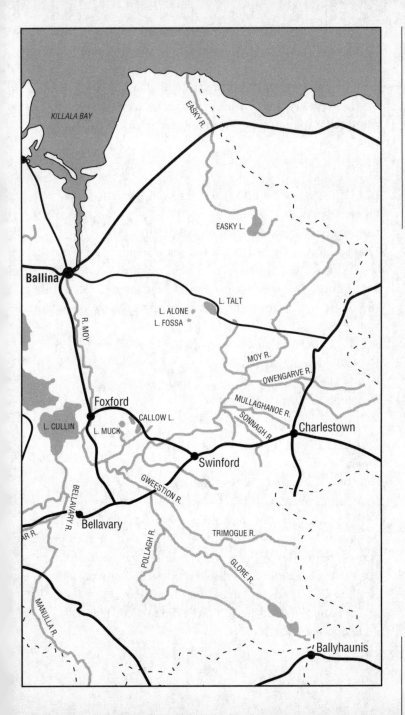

KILLALA BAY

EASKY R.

EASKY L.

Ballina

L. TALT

R. MOY

L. ALONE
L. FOSSA

MOY R.

OWENGARVE R.

MULLAGHANOE R.

Foxford

CALLOW L.

SONNAGH R.

L. CULLIN

L. MUCK

Charlestown

Swinford

GWEESTION R.

BELLAVARY R.

Bellavary

POLLAGH R.

TRIMOGUE R.

GLORE R.

AR R.

MANULLA R.

Ballyhaunis

A short stretch just above Palmerstown Bridge is leased by Ballina and Cloghans Angling Club, and the fishing on this stretch is reserved. The rest of the fishing is regarded as free. The river also gets a run of sea trout, and spinning for sea trout on the tidal waters of Rathfran can be productive. The best chance of a salmon is late in the season in Doobehy, high up on this system.

BELDERG RIVER AND LOUGHERGLASS
Open Season
Sea trout and brown trout: 1 June to 12 October.

This small river, which joins the sea at Belderg, gets a run of sea trout, while Lougherglass at the top of the system holds a small stock of brown trout. Access to the lake is over a mile of rough ground. Permits for both river and lake can be obtained from:

◆ *Ms Deirdre McDonnell*, secretary, Belderg Fishing Club, Belderg, Co. Mayo
◆ *Ms Mary McAvock*, Belderg, Co. Mayo; telephone (096) 43044.

BALLYCASTLE (BALLINGLASS) RIVER
Open Season
Salmon: 1 February to 30 September;
sea trout: 1 February to 10 October.

This river, which flows into the sea at Ballycastle, Co. Mayo, gets a run of sea trout and occasional salmon from July to the end of the season. Fishing rights over a large part of the river are leased from the fisheries board by Ballina and Cloghans Angling Club. Permits can be obtained from:

◆ *Mr Séamus Barrett*, Barrett Ltd, Ballina, Co. Mayo; telephone (096) 21177

■ RIVER MOY SYSTEM

Open Season

Salmon: 1 February to 30 September; *sea trout:* 1 February to
10 October; *brown trout:* 15 February to 10 October. Under
various bye-laws, the minimum size limit for salmon and trout
on Lough Conn and on the Moy Estuary is 10 inches, and
elsewhere in the Ballina District, 7 inches. The use or
possession of a gaff on the Moy or its tributaries is prohibited.
Angling on the tidal waters of the Moy downstream of the
Upper Bridge in Ballina is not permitted until 17 April
each year.

The River Moy is probably the most prolific salmon river in the
country. The Department of the Marine purchased the former
Moy fishery and operates draft nets in the tidal waters and
salmon traps at Ballina.

A major arterial drainage scheme was carried out on the
river in the 1960s, whose effects were to destroy the natural
character of the river; and most of the famous old salmon pools
no longer exist in their original form. The runs of salmon,
however, remain good. The surroundings in which anglers fish
are no longer as pleasing as in former times: the banks are high
and difficult, much of the river is wide, canal-like, and
featureless, and much of the old natural pool-stream sequence
is missing. Nevertheless, it produces big numbers of salmon,
and big catches are reported every season.

Fish can be taken from opening day at certain points along
the river if conditions are suitable. If conditions are not
suitable, the fishing picks up as soon as the water drops. A run
of small spring salmon goes through in April, and the peak of
the spring salmon fishing is usually between 1 and 20 April.
The grilse begin running in early May, with the peak of the run
being about the middle of May, continuing until about the end
of July.

Low water tends to prevent fish from running past the traps
in Ballina in August, with the result that there is often a build-

up of fish in the estuary. The first good flood in late August or September brings more fish upriver and can give excellent autumn fishing, with plenty of fish in the 7 to 9 lb range. The average weight of the spring fish is 9 lb, and the grilse range from 2 to 7 lb. The sea trout average about 0.75 lb.

All legitimate fishing methods are allowed on most of the fisheries, except natural prawn and shrimp, which are not allowed on most fisheries and are prohibited by by-law on the tidal waters. The sea trout fishing is mainly confined to spinning on the estuary and a short stretch at Foxford, which can sometimes be productive to fly.

Boats for sea trout fishing on the Moy Estuary are available for hire from:

◆ *Mr J. Ruane,* The Quay, Ballina, Co. Mayo;
   telephone (096) 22183.

Moy Fishery

The Moy fishery controls both banks downstream of the weir in Ballina and a short stretch of the left bank above the weir. For angling purposes, the fishing can be divided into six sections: (a) the Ridge Pool; (b) between the bridges; (c) the Wells; (d) the Ashtree Pool; (e) the Point; and (f) the Moy Estuary. Enquiries about the fishing should be made to:

◆ *Fishery Manager,* Moy Fishery, Ridge Pool Road, Ballina,
   Co. Mayo; telephone (096) 21332.

Ballina Salmon Anglers' Association has about three miles of double-bank fishing extending upstream from Ballina. Enquiries about the fishing should be made to:

◆ *Mr Billy Egan,* Barrett Street, Ballina, Co. Mayo
◆ *North-Western Regional Fisheries Board,* Ardnaree House,
   Abbey Street, Ballina, Co. Mayo; telephone (096) 22623
◆ *Moy Fishery,* Ridge Pool Road, Ballina, Co. Mayo
or to local fishing tackle shops.

Mount Falcon Salmon Fisheries

Mount Falcon Salmon Fisheries has extensive fishing rights on the Moy, including the Mount Falcon Castle Water, Scott's fishery, and Baker's fishery. The company has five private beats that are let with a gillie. It also lets day tickets and weekly permits on its association water, on which a season ticket is also available. Enquiries about the fishing should be made to:

◆ *Mount Falcon Salmon Fisheries*, Mount Falcon Castle, Ballina, Co. Mayo; telephone (096) 71296/21172

◆ *Gillie Angling*, Grasshopper Cottage, Dooras, Cornamona, Co. Galway; telephone (092) 48165.

Alpine Hotel Fishery

This fishery consists of about half a mile of single-bank fishing. It is a deep stretch and has good holding water. Enquiries about the fishing should be made to:

◆ *The Alpine Hotel*, Enniscrone, Co. Sligo; telephone (096) 36144.

Armstrong's Fishery

Armstrong's fishery is approximately one mile of single-bank fishing and has about 300 yards of nice fly water. A limited number of season tickets is issued, and the remainder of the fishing is let by day tickets. Enquiries should be made to:

◆ *Mr George Armstrong*, Ballina Road, Foxford, Co. Mayo; telephone (094) 56580.

Béal Easa Fishery
Leckee Fishery

The Béal Easa fishery is one mile of left-bank fishing a short distance north of Foxford. It is all good holding water, and there is a nice stretch for fly fishing. The Leckee fishery is one-fifth of a mile long on the right bank south of Foxford. Limited numbers of season tickets are let, and day tickets are available. All enquiries should be made to:

◆ *Mr P. Gannon*, Foxford Post Office, Foxford, Co. Mayo; telephone (094) 56101.

Foxford Salmon Anglers' Association

This fishery consists of about one mile of double-bank fishing upstream of Foxford. Part is suitable for fly fishing, and the rest is dead heavy water. Enquiries about the fishing should be made to:

♦ *Mr Jack Wallace,* Swinford Road, Foxford, Co. Mayo; telephone (094) 56238.

Clongee Fishery

Clongee fishery is upstream of Foxford at the confluence of the Cross or Lake River, which flows out from Lough Cullin. The fishery offers over two miles of fishing on the right bank of the Moy as well as fishing on the left bank of the Cross River. Day tickets only are available, and there is no limit to the number of rods allowed on the fishery. The Cross River can give good brown trout fishing, especially at mayfly time. Enquiries about the fishing should be made to:

♦ *Mr Michael Ruane,* Clongee, Foxford, Co. Mayo; telephone (094) 56634.

East Mayo Anglers' Association

The East Mayo Anglers' Association water stretches upstream of the Clongee fishery on both banks for about eight miles. Permits are available on a daily, weekly or seasonal basis. There is spring salmon fishing here from early April, and the grilse fishing can be good in June. It is not an easy river to fish at this point: wading is necessary but can be difficult and dangerous. Enquiries about the fishing should be made to:

♦ *Mrs Florence Wills,* Ballylahan Bridge, Foxford, Co. Mayo; telephone (096) 56221

♦ *Boland's Lounge,* Bridge Street, Swinford, Co. Mayo; telephone (094) 51149.

UPPER MOY

The Upper Moy is uncharted and undeveloped. There are said to be some nice fishing stretches up as far as Banada. It is overgrown in places with bushes.

CULLENTRAGH AND DERRY LOUGH

Derry Lough is about two miles south of Knock, Co. Mayo. It is stocked with brown trout. Bank fishing is difficult, but boats are usually available for hire. Cullentragh Lough is about two miles west of Knock and is also stocked with trout. Enquiries about the fishing should be made to:

◆ *Mr Bart Dennedy*, Prague Ville, Churchfield, Knock, Co. Mayo; telephone (094) 88187.

LOUGH CULLIN
Open Season
Salmon: 1 February to 30 September;
trout: 15 February to 10 October.

Lough Cullin is adjacent to the Foxford–Pontoon road. It is a shallow lough of over 2,000 acres, and access to it is from the north shore only. Lough Cullin holds an excellent stock of brown trout averaging 0.75 lb. It gets a big run of salmon, both spring and summer fish – in fact all the fish heading for Lough Conn must pass through Lough Cullin. The best trout fishing area is in the northern half of the lake. The trout are free-rising, and the best of the fishing is between April and mid-June. The lake becomes weeded and very shallow and the fishing tapers off from mid-June. The fishing is free.

Boats and boatmen are available for hire at:

◆ *Healy's Hotel*, Pontoon, Foxford, Co. Mayo; telephone (094) 56443
◆ *Pontoon Bridge Hotel*, Pontoon, Foxford, Co. Mayo; telephone (094) 56120.

PONTOON BRIDGE

This fishery is in the short channel between Lough Conn and Lough Cullin. It is highly regarded as a lie for spring salmon; some of the first spring salmon on the Moy system are often taken here. The grilse fishing can be especially good in May. The fishing is free.

LOUGH CONN

Open Season

Salmon: 1 February to 30 September;
brown trout: 15 February to 10 October.

Lough Conn is a lake of 14,000 acres, measuring nine miles from north to south and between two and four miles in width. It is regarded as a free-taking lake for brown trout. The lake is managed by the regional fisheries board, and, because of the healthy state of the wild trout stocks, it has never been stocked with trout of any kind. There is access to the lake shore at Gortnorabbey Pier near Crossmolina, Errew Pier, Phiulawakhouse Bay, Gillaroo Bay, Pontoon, Knockmore Bay, Brackwansha, Sandy Bay, and Cloghans Bay.

Salmon are taken mainly by trolling from the end of March to July, and the best areas to concentrate on are in the northern end of the lake and at Cornakillew, Maasbrook, and Castlehill Bay. The trout fishing begins to pick up in April and reaches its peak with the mayfly hatch from late May and June. The wet fly fishing can be very good from late August to the end of the season.

The shallows on Lough Conn are all well marked with marker bars, and the best fishing areas are along the shores in the shallow bays and on the shallows in the middle of the lake.

There are plenty of boats and outboard motors for hire, and some professional boatmen. Boats, outboards and boatmen can be arranged through:

- *Pontoon Bridge Hotel*, Foxford, Co. Mayo;
  telephone (094) 56120
- *Healy's Hotel*, Pontoon, Foxford, Co. Mayo;
  telephone (094) 56443
- *Mr Pádraic Kelly*, Newtown, Cloghans, Ballina, Co. Mayo;
  telephone (096) 22250
- *Mr Joseph Moffatt*, Kilmurray House, Castlehill, Ballina, Co. Mayo; telephone (096) 31227
- *Mr Barry Seagrave*, Cloonamoyne Fishery, Enniscoe House, Castlehill, Co. Mayo; telephone (096) 31112

◆ *North-Western Regional Fisheries Board,* Abbey Street, Ballina, Co. Mayo; telephone (096) 22623

or through any of the hotels and guesthouses around the lough.

DEEL RIVER

The Deel River forms part of the headwaters of the Moy. It rises in north Mayo and flows through Crossmolina to Lough Conn.

The river holds salmon and brown trout. There is good spring salmon fishing early in the season from Deel Castle downstream to the river's mouth. The grilse fishing begins in June. The river holds a good stock of brown trout, ranging upwards from 0.5 lb. There is about two miles of good trout fishing at Knockglass House, north-east of Crossmolina; five miles of trout fishing from Ballycarron House, upstream past Richmond Bridge and Carrowgarve Bridge; and a further mile of fishing immediately upstream of Deel Bridge. The fishing is free.

A gillie service is available through:

◆ *Mr Barry Seagrave,* Cloonamoyne Fishery, Enniscoe House, Castlehill, Co. Mayo; telephone (096) 31112.

BELLAVARY RIVER
CASTLEBAR RIVER
MANULLA RIVER

The Bellavary River is about two miles long. It begins at the confluence of the Castlebar and Manulla Rivers and joins the Clydagh River north of the village of Bellavary. The spring salmon fishing begins at the confluence of the Castlebar River and the Manulla River and extends downstream for about three-and-a-half miles. There is another stretch of about a mile upstream of Lough Cullin.

All three rivers hold good stocks of trout and offer good dry fly fishing possibilities. On the Castlebar River the best fishing is around Windsor Bridge, while on the Manulla the stretch downstream of Moyhenna Bridge is best. On the Bellavary the area above and below Chancery Bridge provides good fishing.

The regional fisheries board has opened up a lot of fishing on these rivers by erecting stiles and footbridges.

Enquiries regarding permits should be made to:

◆ *Canning's Lounge*, Bellavary, Co. Mayo.

ISLANDEADY LOUGH
Open Season
15 February to 10 October. There is a statutory 10 inch size limit and a six-trout daily bag limit.

Islandeady Lough is north of the Westport–Castlebar road and is 1,000 acres in size. There is good access, with a car park and jetty. The lough is managed by the regional fisheries board. It holds wild brown trout averaging 1 lb with some to 3.5 lb, and it is stocked annually with two-year-old brown trout. Fly fishing only is permitted. The fishing is free.

A bye-law prohibits the use of any lure other than artificial fly. There is a minimum size of 10 inches for brown trout and 11 inches for rainbow trout, and a maximum daily bag limit of six brown trout and four rainbow trout on the Castlebar lakes.

Boats are available for hire from:

◆ *Mrs Helen O'Malley*, Church Road, Islandeady, Co. Mayo; telephone (094) 21317.

LOUGH NASPLEENAGH
Lough Naspleenagh is about four miles north-west of Castlebar. It holds a small stock of trout averaging 0.75 lb. The shoreline is difficult to fish and dangerous in places. The fishing is regarded as free.

LOUGH NA GCEARC
Lough na gCearc is about a mile north of Castlebar. It holds a small stock of brown trout averaging about 1 lb. The banks are good, and the lough can be fished all round. The fishing is regarded as free.

LOUGHANAVEENY

Loughanaveeny is about four miles north of Castlebar. It holds a good stock of brown trout averaging around 0.5 lb. The banks are good and easy to fish, but planting has taken place in recent times, and in the future it will be difficult to fish this lough from the shore. Access is also difficult. The fishing is regarded as free.

GWEESTION RIVER
POLLAGH RIVER
GLORE RIVER
TRIMOGUE RIVER

The Gweestion River is a tributary of the Moy, and the Pollagh, Glore and Trimogue Rivers are tributaries of the Gweestion. The Gweestion lies between Swinford and Bohola and is a limestone river that holds both grilse and a good stock of brown trout. Stiles and bridges have been erected along the banks.

The Pollagh River holds a good stock of trout from Bushfield Bridge downstream. The Glore River consists of fast-flowing water with occasional pools. The brown trout average 0.5 lb. The Trimogue River holds a good stock of trout up to 0.75 lb from the confluence up to Kinaff Bridge. It also is overgrown.

SONNAGH RIVER

The Sonnagh River rises south-west of Charlestown and joins the Moy downstream of Bellanacurra Bridge. It holds stocks of trout up to 1.5 lb.

MULLAGHANOE RIVER

The Mullaghanoe River rises near Charlestown and flows west to the Moy upstream of Bellanacurra Bridge. It holds good stocks of trout to 1.5 lb.

OWENGARVE RIVER

The Owengarve River flows through the village of Curry and joins the Moy downstream of Cooleen Ford. The three-mile stretch downstream of Curry holds a good stock of small brown trout. The banks are developed, with stiles and bridges.

LOUGH TALT

Open Season

Brown trout: 15 February to 10 October.

Lough Talt is a lake of about 200 acres, ten miles east of Ballina in a valley in the Ox Mountains. It holds a big stock of small, free-rising brown trout. Boats can be hired at the Lough Talt Inn on the lake shore. The fishing is free.

LOUGH MUCK

Open Season

Brown trout: 15 February to 10 October.

Lough Muck lies two miles east of Foxford, and access is relatively easy. The lough holds a big stock of small brown trout averaging 0.5 lb. The best of the fishing is on the north-eastern end. It can be fished from the bank, but a boat is desirable. The fishing is regarded as free.

CALLOW LOUGHS

Open Season

Brown trout: 15 February to 10 October.

The Callow Loughs lie south of the Foxford–Swinford road. There are three lakes here, and they hold good stocks of small brown trout; the northern part probably holds the biggest stock. The fishing is free.

There is a jetty on the southernmost lough, where it is possible to launch a boat. Bank fishing is not possible. Boats are available for hire from:

◆ *Mrs Deacy*, Callow, Foxford, Co. Mayo;
  telephone (094) 56266.

LOUGH FOSSA
Open Season

Brown trout: 15 February to 10 October.

Lough Fossa is high in the Ox Mountains in Co. Sligo. There is a steep climb up to the lake. The trout are not plentiful, but the average size is good. The fishing is free.

LOUGH ALONE
Open Season

Brown trout: 15 February to 10 October.

This lake is in the Ox Mountains. It holds a good stock of small trout, although gaining access involves a long walk. The fishing is regarded as free.

EASKY RIVER
Open Season

Salmon: 1 February to 30 September;

sea trout: 1 February to 12 October.

The Easky River is primarily a salmon river and gets a good run of grilse and summer salmon. It is eighteen miles long, and its catchment includes Easky Lough. It has been opened up recently by the regional fisheries board, and stiles and footbridges have been erected. The grilse start running in late June, and a prolific run of fish enters the river on every flood right to the end of September.

There is a draft net fishery in the tidal section. From the bridge in Easky upstream to Fortland Falls, a distance of about a mile, is private water. Most of the rest of the river is controlled by Easky Salmon Anglers' Association. Permits are available from:

◆ *Forde's Shop*, Easky, Co. Sligo.

EASKY LOUGH
Open Season
Brown trout: 15 February to 12 October.
Easky Lough is also in the Ox Mountains in Co. Sligo, but the road runs alongside the lake, making access easy. It holds brown trout, but they are very small. The fishing is regarded as free.

TULLYVILLIA LOUGHS
These loughs lie high in the mountains. The trout are free-rising and come about three to the pound. Access is very difficult, with only a mountain pass leading from the nearest road to the lakes. The fishing is free.

SLIGO DISTRICT

The Sligo Fisheries District comprises parts of Co. Sligo and Leitrim and includes all rivers flowing into the sea between Cooanmore Point, near Easky, and Mullaghmore, Co. Leitrim.

■ BALLYSADARE RIVER SYSTEM

Open Season
Salmon and sea trout: 1 February to 30 September.
The Ballysadare River, together with its tributaries the Unshin, the Owenmore, and the Owenbeg, drains a large catchment area, which includes Lough Arrow and Templehouse Lake, into Ballysadare Bay, Co. Sligo. The fishing rights of the migratory fish in the system were vested in the Cooper family by an Act of Parliament in 1837; the Cooper family then built fish passes at the impassable Ballysadare Falls, and introduced salmon to the system.

The salmon fishing takes place mainly in the pools at the bottom of the Ballysadare Falls and in the stretch just above the falls. The river gets a small run of spring salmon from April, and a big run of grilse, which peaks in June and early July. The river above the falls is being developed for salmon fishing.

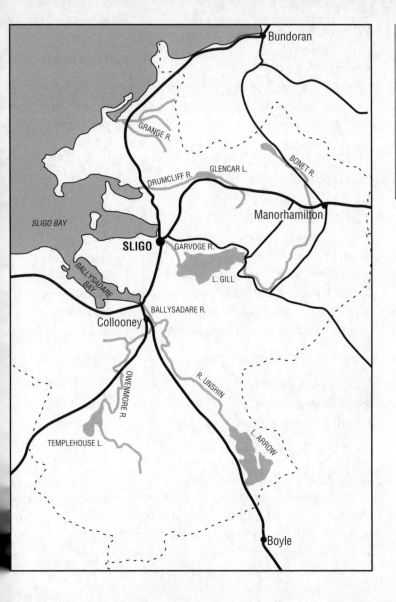

Enquiries about fishing should be made to:

◆ *Fishery Office*, Ballysadare

◆ *Markree Castle*, Collooney, Co. Sligo; telephone (071) 67800.

RIVER UNSHIN

Open Season

Brown trout: 1 March to 30 September.

The Unshin joins the Ballysadare River at Collooney. It is overgrown immediately downstream of Lough Arrow and has a lot of deep water. Further down, the banks are more open, and here it holds good stocks of brown trout. The best of the fishing is from the end of April to mid-June, and it has a mayfly hatch.

OWENMORE RIVER

The Owenmore River rises near Gorteen, Co. Sligo, and flows through Templehouse Lake to join the Ballysadare River at Collooney. It holds small trout, and the banks are clear downstream of the confluence of the Owenbeg. It is best known, however, as a coarse fish river. There are also trout in a stretch upstream of the bridge at Ardkieran, ranging from 0.5 lb to 1 lb.

LOUGH BO

Open Season

1 April to 30 September. There is a 9 inch size limit for trout and a bag limit of six trout.

Lough Bo is four miles to the east of Riverstown and two-and-a-half miles north-east of Lough Arrow. It holds a small stock of wild brown trout and is stocked annually by the regional fisheries board. The trout average about 1 lb. Bank fishing is possible, with a road running along by the lake shore. There is also a boat for hire.

Fisheries board permits and information on a boat for hire are available from:

◆ *Miss E. McDonagh,* public house, Lough Bo, Riverstown, Co. Sligo; telephone (071) 65325.

LOUGH ARROW

Open Season
Brown trout: 1 March to 30 September.

The trout in Lough Arrow average 1.5 lb, and fish to 5 or 6 lb are taken every season. The lake is four miles north-west of Boyle, six miles from Ballymote, and three miles from Ballyfarnon. This is a limestone lake, and it is mainly spring-fed. There is good public access around the shore; the principal access points are Brick Pier, Ballinafad Pier, and Rinnbawn Pier.

The duckfly hatches in late March and early April, and the olives begin hatching around mid-April and last until mid-May. The mayfly season generally begins about 17 May and lasts until the second week of June. The spent gnat fishing is one of the great attractions of Lough Arrow. The fishing is free.

Enquiries about boats, outboard motors and boatmen can be made to:

- *Mr Finian Dodd*, Ballindoon, Co. Sligo; telephone (071) 65065
- *Mr Chris Tighe*, Cromlech Lodge, Ballindoon, Co. Sligo; telephone (071) 65155
- *Mr Rudolf Acheson*, Andersna House, Carrigeenroe, Co. Roscommon; telephone (079) 66181
- *Rock View Hotel*, Ballindoon, Co. Sligo; telephone (079) 66073
- *Mr Thomas Flynn*, Arrow Cottage, Ballindoon, Co. Sligo
- *The Mayfly Inn*, Ballinafad, Co. Sligo
- *Mr Joseph Gray*, Ballindoon, Co. Sligo.

■ GARVOGE RIVER SYSTEM

Open Season
Salmon and sea trout: 1 January to 30 September; *brown trout:* 15 February to 30 September (except between 600 yards upstream of New Bridge and the Lodge). From the Weir up to the Park Gates opens on 1 February for salmon fishing. From the Weir down to the Silver Swan Hotel opens on 1 June for salmon, sea trout and brown trout fishing.

The Garvoge River drains Lough Gill through Sligo, and is about three-and-a-half miles long. It produces occasional spring salmon, and the grilse fishing can be good in June and July. Salmon, sea trout and brown trout can be taken from the Silver Swan Hotel up to Bective; the best of the sea trout fishing is downstream of Victoria Bridge.

COLGAGH LOUGH
Open Season
Brown trout: 15 February to 12 October.

Colgagh Lough lies three miles east of Sligo on the Manorhamilton road. It has a good stock of brown trout averaging nearly 1.5 lb. There are no boats for hire, and bank fishing is not practical. There is a problem about access, and enquiries about this should be made locally.

LOUGH GILL
Open Season
Salmon and sea trout: 1 January to 30 September;
brown trout: 1 March to 30 September.

Lough Gill is a large lake, nearly six-and-a-half miles long and two-and-a-half miles wide. There is public access to the lough from a pier on the south shore at the mouth of the Garvoge River, at Inishfree Pier, and at Shriff Bay.

Lough Gill holds brown trout and salmon. It gets a big run of spring salmon, and has produced salmon on opening day in recent years. Most of the salmon fishing is done by trolling, and February and March are regarded as the best months. Lough Gill also holds a good stock of brown trout, but they tend to be difficult and slow to take a fly, except during the mayfly hatch, when fishing can be good. Boats and outboards motors are available for hire from:

◆ *Mr Peter Henry,* The Blue Lagoon, Sligo;
   telephone (071) 42530.

Permission to fish the north shore of the lake can be obtained from:

◆ *Mrs White*, Shriff Bay, Newtownmanor, Dromahair,
   Co. Leitrim
◆ *Mr James McCarney*, honorary secretary, Sligo Anglers'
   Association, Annelen, Cornageeha, Sligo;
   telephone (071) 62385
◆ *Mr Barton Smith*, tackle shop, Hyde Bridge, Sligo.

A permit is not usually required to fish the south shore of the lake.

BONET RIVER
Open Season
Salmon: 1 February to 30 September;
brown trout: 15 February to 30 September.

The Bonet River rises in Glenade Lough, Co. Leitrim, and flows past Manorhamilton and Dromahair into Lough Gill. It gives excellent salmon fishing in spring, summer, and autumn, and holds good stocks of brown trout.

There are six distinct fisheries on the river. The principal ones are those of Manorhamilton Angling Club, Dromahair Lodge, and Stanford's Inn; of the other three fisheries, Dromahair Angling Club has half a mile at Glebe House, and information on this fishing is available from:

◆ *Mr Seán Ward*, Drumlease, Dromahair, Co. Leitrim.

There is one-and-a-half miles of syndicate water downstream of Dromahair, which is private, and Sligo Angling Club has a stretch above Lough Gill. Neither of these two stretches is available to the public.

Manorhamilton Angling Club Water

This consists of about seven miles of single- and double-bank fishing. The fishery holds spring salmon from mid-March, and grilse start running in late June or early July. There is some good brown trout fishing on this stretch too. Enquiries about the fishing should be made to:

◆ *Mr A. Flynn*, Manorhamilton Post Office, Manorhamilton,
   Co. Leitrim; telephone (072) 55001

- *Mr John McDonnell*, 2 Church Street, Manorhamilton,
  Co. Leitrim; telephone (072) 55217
- *Mr Harold Sibbery*, The Waterfall, Glencar, Co. Leitrim.

Dromahair Lodge

Dromahair Lodge has about nine miles of fishing. The salmon fishing season is as for Manorhamilton, with perhaps even better spring salmon fishing in March and April. There are good stocks of brown trout here too. The fishing is reserved for residents staying at Dromahair Lodge and at:
- *Breffni Holiday Cottages*, Dromahair, Co. Leitrim;
  telephone (071) 64103.

Stanford's Inn

Stanford's Inn, Dromahair, has three-quarters of a mile of double-bank fishing with three good pools. There is good spring salmon fishing here in April, and grilse fishing in June and July. Enquiries about the fishing should be made to:
- *Mr Thomas McGowan*, Stanford's Inn, Dromahair,
  Co. Leitrim; telephone (071) 64140.

DRUMCLIFF RIVER AND GLENCAR LOUGH
Open Season

Salmon: 1 February to 30 September; *sea trout:* 1 February to 12 October; *brown trout:* 15 February to 12 October. Bye-laws prohibit the use of gaffs and tailers on the Drumcliff River, and fly fishing only is permitted below the Drumcliff Bridge.

The Drumcliff river is four miles long and drains Glencar Lough into Drumcliff Bay. It gets a small run of spring salmon from February, and the grilse run in June and July. It also gets a run of sea trout that begins in early July. The sea pools downstream of Drumcliff Bridge can provide good sea trout fishing to the fly. Fishing on this tidal stretch is free.

Enquiries about the fishing on the freshwater portions of the river should be made to:

◆ *Mr Harold Sibbery,* The Waterfall, Glencar, Co. Leitrim
◆ *Mr A. Flynn,* Manorhamilton Post Office, Manorhamilton,
   Co. Leitrim; telephone (072) 55001.

Glencar Lough lies to the north of the Manorhamilton–Sligo road, five miles from Sligo. The lake holds a big stock of small brown trout and gets a good run of sea trout from July, and has a good stock especially of grilse. The average size of the sea trout is 1.5 lb, and these fish are said to be quite free-rising, especially when fresh. Fly fishing and dapping are the only methods allowed on the boats, but spinning is allowed from the shore.

Enquiries about the fishing should be made to:

◆ *Mr John McDonnell,* honorary secretary, Manorhamilton
   Anglers' Club, 2 Church Street, Manorhamilton,
   Co. Leitrim; telephone (072) 55217
◆ *Mr James McCarney,* honorary secretary, Sligo Anglers'
   Association, Annelen, Cornageeha, Sligo;
   telephone (071) 62385
◆ *Mr Harold Sibbery,* The Waterfall, Glencar, Co. Leitrim.

There is one boat for hire, from Mr Harold Sibbery, as above.

GRANGE RIVER
Open Season
Salmon: 1 February to 30 September; *sea trout:* 1 February to 12 October; *brown trout:* 15 February to 12 October.

The Grange River is a small stream that drains through Grange, Co. Sligo, to the sea. It is primarily a sea trout fishery, and the banks are quite overgrown. Access is on the main road at Grange.

Northern Fisheries Region

The Northern Fisheries Region stretches from Mullaghmore in Co. Sligo to Malin Head in the north of Co. Donegal. It comprises West Donegal, part of Leitrim and Sligo and then extends in a south-easterly direction to part of Cos. Cavan, Longford and Monaghan.

The underlying rock formation is complex, with a lot of granite and quartzite in Donegal, and Cavan and Monaghan have silurian and ordovician strata.

The Northern Region has a variety of game fishing on offer with something to suit all tastes. The Donegal, Leitrim, Sligo part of the region has salmon, sea trout and brown trout. The River Drowes is probably the best known salmon river of the area with a big reputation for producing early spring salmon and frequently gives up the first salmon of the new season. The River Leannan and Lough Fern also have a big reputation for spring salmon. The Lackagh River has salmon and grilse. The Ray River, the Tullaghabegley River, the Clady River, the

Crolly River, the Gweebarra River, the Owenea River, the Glen River, the Eany Water, the River Eske and the Duff River all get runs of grilse.

Sea trout are plentiful in all the rivers along the Donegal coast and give good sport in many of the smaller loughs of Donegal where they can gain access. Glen Lough, Lough Beagh and the many lakes in the Rosses as well as Lough Eske are all noteworthy.

Brown trout in the Donegal/Leitrim area are found mostly in lakes. Lough Melvin is probably the premier brown trout lake of the area. Some of the smaller hill lakes hold good stocks of medium-sized trout and a lot of development work has been carried out in recent years in the Pettigoe, Ardara and Dunglow areas.

The Erne system drains Cavan and Monaghan to the sea at Ballyshannon. The Erne Estuary is noted for the quality of its sea trout fishing from the shore or from a boat. The Upper Erne and tributaries such as the Annalee River, the Bunnoe River and the Laragh River offer good sport for brown trout with both the wetfly and the dry fly. There are a number of stocked trout lakes in this area too.

The headquarters of the Northern Regional Fisheries Board is at Station Road, Ballyshannon, Co. Donegal; telephone (072) 51435.

BALLYSHANNON DISTRICT

The Ballyshannon district comprises that part of the River Erne catchment which lies on the southern side of the border and all the rivers entering the sea between Mullaghmore in Co. Sligo and Rossan Point in Co. Donegal.

■ RIVER ERNE AND TRIBUTARIES

Open Season

Salmon: 1 March to 30 September; *sea trout:* 1 March to
30 September; *brown trout:* 1 March to 30 September.

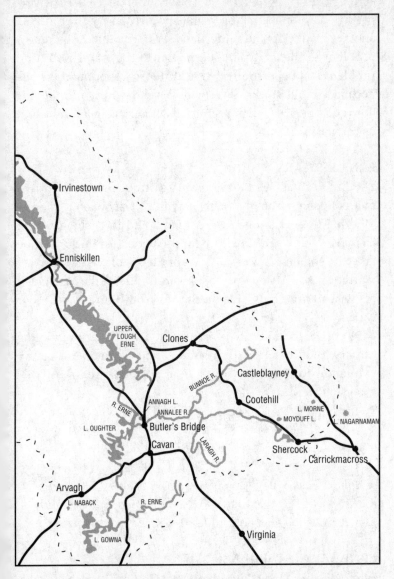

The River Erne rises in Co. Cavan and flows 64 miles through Loch Gowna, Lough Oughter and Upper and Lower Lough Erne to the sea at Ballyshannon. It is a river that has seen many changes. A hydro-electric power station and dam was commissioned in 1950 and the dam has a serious effect on the passage of salmon. The roach first appeared in the river in 1963 and the trout population declined. Water pollution became a problem in the 1970s. In recent times, the water pollution problem has been controlled and the roach population has declined. Trout stocks have made a good return and there is now good fishing in many stretches of both the main river and its tributaries.

ERNE ESTUARY

The Erne estuary is an important sea trout fishery with two miles of fishing from the Mall Quay in Ballyshannon to the Bar Mouth. The season opens on 1 March and the fishing is best from May, through June, July and August. The trout can be taken by spinning, spoons, Toby's or Mepps or on the fly.

Access is at Abbey Road on the north side, at the Mall Quay or by walking across Tullan Strand from Bundoran at low water.

A special local licence is required to fish for sea trout in the estuary and anglers with a valid salmon licence can get an extension to that licence for a small fee. Agents for this extension are:

◆ *Mr Tom Waters*, Drowes Bridge, Tullaghan, Co. Leitrim
◆ *Mr Jack Phillips*, West End, Bundoran, Co. Donegal
◆ *Rogan's*, Fishing Tackle Shop, Bridge End, Ballyshannon, Co. Donegal
◆ *Imperial Hotel*, Ballyshannon, Co. Donegal
◆ *Regional Fisheries Board Office*, Station Road, Ballyshannon, Co. Donegal; telephone (072) 51435.

ERNE SALMON FISHING

Salmon lie below the Power Station at Cliff in a stretch of water about a quarter of a mile long. The best fishing is when the station is generating through July and through September. Access is off the Knakher Road.

Permits are available from:

◆ *E.S.B. Shop*, Castle Street, Ballyshannon, Co. Donegal.

BELTURBET

Belturbet Trout Anglers' Club have carried out extensive improvements to the river in a three-quarter-mile stretch upstream from Kilconny Bridge. The fishing is for both wild and stocked trout. It is fly fishing only. There are reported to be other good stretches for trout fishing upstream at Cornadara, Pogue's Ford and Baker's Bridge.

MIDDLE ERNE

The Middle Erne is that part of the river between Sallaghan Bridge near Lough Gowna and Bellahillan Bridge near Crossdoney. The trout stocks have made a good recovery along this eight-mile stretch and the best fishing is said to be to the wetfly early in the season.

UPPER ERNE

This is a stretch of water extending from the source of the river to Lough Gowna. A drainage scheme is 1989 destroyed many of the pools upstream of Carrigan's Bridge. The trout stocks are said to have recovered downstream of Carrigan's Bridge and the trout fishing can be good in spring as far as Legwee, Killadoon and Kilsarn. It is very overgrown and anglers will find the banks difficult to negotiate.

ANNALEE RIVER

The Annalee River rises in Co. Monaghan and flows via Cootehill, Ballyhaise and through Butler's Bridge to join the Erne at Urney. Trout fishing on the river can be divided into two parts. Upstream of Cootehill, the river is recovering and holds some nice trout, especially in the vicinity of Knappagh. From Cootehill to Butler's Bridge, trout stocks have recovered well. There are big trout at Deredis, and some nice stocks of trout at Butler's Bridge. There are moderate stocks of trout from Ballyhaise upstream towards Cootehill. The fly hatches have recovered well. The banks are very overgrown in places but local angling clubs have plans to improve this situation.

Enquiries about the fishing should be made to:

◆ *Mr Seán Young*, 66 Main Street, Cavan
◆ *Mr Patrick McCaul*, Scotshouse, Co. Monaghan.

LARAGH RIVER

The Laragh River flows through Clifferna to join the Annalee at Rathkenny. The fishing on the river is managed by Laragh Angling Club. There are good stocks of trout to 3 lb and good hatches of the usual river flies. The best fishing is early in the season.

Enquiries about the fishing should be made to:

◆ *Mr Gerry O'Grady*, Stradone, Co. Cavan
◆ *Mr Phelim Donohoe*, Clifferna, Stradone, Co. Cavan.

BUNNOE RIVER

This is an excellent little stream that flows south from Newbliss to join the Annalee near Lisboduff. There is an active angling club on the river that keeps the banks well serviced with stiles and footbridges. The best of the fishing is from the confluence up to Magheratemple. The club has a 'fly fishing only' rule on certain stretches.

Enquiries about the fishing should be made to:

◆ *Mr Patrick McCaul*, Scotshouse, Co. Monaghan
◆ *Mr Séamus Hughes*, Lisboduff, Bunnoe, Cootehill, Co. Cavan.

LOUGH NAGARNAMAN

Lough Nagarnaman is managed by the Carrickmacross Trout Angling Club. It is situated nearly five miles north-west of Carrickmacross. It is entirely dependent on artificial stocking with trout. There is a bag limit of four trout and fly fishing and worm fishing are the methods that are allowed. The banks can be fished all around.

Enquiries about the fishing should be made to:

◆ *Mr Gordon Sweetnam*, Main Street, Carrickmacross, Co. Monaghan; telephone (042) 61219

◆ *Carrickmacross Sports Shop*, Main Street, Carrickmacross,
   Co. Monaghan.

LOUGH MORNE

Lough Morne is managed by the Lough Egish Rod and Gun
Club. It holds a good stock of wild brown trout and is also
artificially stocked by the club. There is a 10 inch size limit and
a six-trout bag limit.

Enquiries about the fishing to:

◆ *Mr Eugene McMahon*, Lough Egish, Co. Monaghan.

LOUGH NABACK

Lough Naback lies to the east of the Arva-Longford road and
holds a good stock of wild brown trout with an average weight
of 1 lb. It also holds char. There is both access to the water's
edge and a car park. The fishing is free.

LOUGH GOWNA

Lough Gowna lies midway between Arva in Co. Cavan and
Granard in Co. Longford. There is good public access to the
lough with a car park and boat slip at Dring, Dernaferst Bridge
and at Cloone. Lough Gowna holds a moderate stock of brown
trout. It has a good Duckfly hatch and a Mayfly hatch. The
fishing is free.

MOYDUFF LAKE

Moyduff Lake is off the Cootehill-Shercock road. The season
runs from 1 May to 30 September and there is a six-trout bag
limit and a 10 inch size limit. The lough is stocked annually
with rainbow trout.

Permits are available on the lake shore from:

◆ *Mr Peter Smith*, Moyduff, Shercock, Co. Cavan.

ANNAGH LAKE

Annagh Lake is situated along the Butler's Bridge-Belturbet road. It is stocked annually with rainbow trout and brown trout. The angling season runs from 1 May to 30 September and there is a 10 inch size limit and a six-trout bag limit.

Butler's Bridge Trout Angling Co-op Ltd operate the fishery. Permits and boats are available from:

◆ *Mr Seán O'Hare*, Hackelty, Butler's Bridge, Co. Cavan; telephone (049) 32490.

SANDY LOUGH

Sandy Lough is situated in the hills four miles north of Manorhamilton. It holds trout averaging 0.5 lb and can be fished all around. The fishing is regarded as free.

RIVER DUFF

Open Season

Salmon and sea trout: 1 February to 30 September;
brown trout: 15 February to 30 September.

The River Duff drains into Donegal Bay. It is a spate river that gets a run of grilse and summer salmon. The peak of the run is in early July. Most of the fishing is done in a pool below the waterfall at the sea. There is a two-fish-per-day bag limit on anglers fishing this pool.

Tickets are available from:

◆ *Mrs McGloin*, The Shop, Bunduff Bridge, Tullaghan, Co. Leitrim.

ABBEY RIVER

Open Season

Salmon: 1 March to 30 September;
sea trout and brown trout: 1 March to 9 October.

The Abbey River drains into the Erne Estuary west of Ballyshannon. A lot of pools were destroyed by an arterial drainage scheme and the banks are very overgrown and difficult to fish. It gets a run of sea trout in July and August and fishes best with a worm after a flood. The fishing is regarded as free.

RIVER DROWES
Open Season
Salmon and sea trout: 1 January to 30 September;
brown trout: 15 February to 30 September.

The River Drowes is a good spring and summer salmon fishery. Sea trout only run in small numbers, but it holds good stocks of brown trout.

The spring salmon season opens on 1 January and fish are usually taken on opening day. The peak of the spring run is in April and the fishing is always good in May with the peak of the grilse run taking place in June. The fishing usually picks up again in September. The number of rods allowed to fish on the river at any one time is not limited.

All legitimate fishing methods are allowed.

The brown trout fishing can be good, especially on summer evenings, but it is largely unused because of fishermen's preoccupation with the salmon.

Permits: All of the left bank from Lough Melvin to Bundrowes Bridge and most of the right bank is owned by:

◆ *Mr Thomas Gallagher*, Edenville, Kinlough, Co. Leitrim, telephone (072) 41208.

Permits are available at:

◆ *The Fishery Office*, Lareen, Kinlough, Co. Leitrim; telephone (072) 41055

◆ *The Drowes Bar*, Bundrowes, Tullaghan, Co. Leitrim

◆ *Barrett's Fishing Tackle Shop*, Bundoran, Co. Leitrim

◆ *Mr Jack Phillips*, Westend, Bundoran, Co. Donegal

◆ *Mr Patrick Bradley*, Magheracar, Bundoran, Co. Donegal, who issues permits for a short stretch on the right bank.

LOUGH MELVIN

Open Season

Salmon and sea trout: 1 February to 30 September;
brown trout: 15 February to 30 September.

Lough Melvin is eight miles long and nearly two miles wide. It is by far the most important trout and salmon fishing lake in Leitrim/Donegal. It straddles the border. Its north-eastern corner from near Dernaseer to the County Bridge is in Northern Ireland, while the major part of the lake lies in Co. Leitrim. The angling activities around the lake are centred mainly at Kinlough, Garrison and Rossinver.

Lough Melvin is rightly noted for its trout and salmon fishing. The salmon season opens on 1 February. The quality of the trout fishing can be very good. In addition to salmon and trout, the lake holds char and perch. There is a minimum trout size of 10 inches.

Public access to the lake is good with boat jetties at Kinlough Pier, Stracomer, Breffni Pier, Dernaseer and Garrison. Boats, and in some cases boatmen and outboard motors, are available for hire from:

◆ *Mr Thomas Kelly,* Kinlough, Co.Leitrim;
  telephone (072) 41497
◆ *Mr Thomas Gallagher,* Edenville, Kinlough, Co. Leitrim;
  telephone (072) 41208
◆ *Mr John Hill,* Dernaseer, Askill, Ballyshannon, Co. Donegal.
◆ *Mr Terence Bradley,* Eden Point, Rossinver, Co. Leitrim;
  telephone (072) 54029
◆ *The Carlton Park,* Information and Fishing Centre, Belleek, Co. Fermanagh
◆ *Mr Michael Gilroy,* Garrisson P.O., Co. Fermanagh.

Fishing permission: The fishing on the south-western side from Rooskey Point to Kinlough is regarded as free. Other permissions required: for Lareen Bay:

◆ *Mr Thomas Gallagher,* Edenville, Kinlough, Co. Leitrim;
  telephone (072) 41208

and for the Rossinver Fishery:

◆ *Mr Terence Bradley*, Eden Point, Rossinver, Co. Leitrim; telephone (072) 54029.

A Northern Ireland Game Fishing permit is required to fish the Northern Ireland part of the lake.

MURVAGH RIVER
Open Season
Salmon: 1 March to 30 September;
sea trout and brown trout: 1 March to 9 October.

The Murvagh River, with its tributaries, the Bridgetown River and the Ballintra River, drain into Donegal Bay. They hold salmon, sea trout and brown trout. The peak of the salmon run is towards the end of July and through the month of August. This is said to be an excellent sea trout fishery too and the fish begin running at the end of June.

The Bridgetown River is regarded as a better sea trout river than the Ballintra River and sea trout are taken up as far as Rath Mill. There are no stiles or footbridges and the banks are badly overgrown.

The fishing is regarded as free.

LOUGH NAGEAGE
Lough Nageage is in south-east Donegal. It lies about six miles to the north-east of the village of Pettigoe. It holds a good stock of brown trout averaging 0.5 lb. The banks are fishable all around.

PETTIGOE ANGLERS' ASSOCIATION LAKES
The Pettigoe Anglers' Association have developed a number of lakes in the Pettigoe area for brown trout fishing. The lakes offering the best prospects of sport are: Lough Avehy, Lough Laghtowen, Lough Namnemurrive, Lough Ultan, Drumgun Lough and Banus Lake.

Enquiries about the fishing should be made to:

◆ *Mr Kevin Mangan*, Pettigoe Anglers' Association, Main Street, Pettigoe, Co. Donegal; telephone (072) 61672.

LOUGH AGHVOG
COLMCILLE LOUGH

These two small lakes are located about two miles north of Belleek on the Cashelard road. Lough Aghvog holds brown trout averaging 0.5 lb and Colmcille Lough holds fewer trout but they are slightly bigger. Both of these lakes can be fished from the banks. Permission is not usually required.

LOUGH UNSHIN
LOUGH MCCALL

Lough Unshin lies to the north east of Ballyshannon. There is a road running by the lough shore. The banks are safe and the trout average about 7 ounces.

Lough McCall is close by. It too can be fished from the shore and the trout are slightly bigger than in Lough Unshin.

Permission to fish is not usually required.

LOUGH SHIVNAGH
LOUGH ACAPPLE

Lough Shivnagh lies to the north of the secondary road that runs from Ballintra to Pettigoe in south Donegal.

Lough Acapple lies on the opposite side of the road from Lough Shivnagh. It holds brown trout up to 0.75 lb and the bank is three-quarters fishable. Pike were introduced to these lakes some years ago and the fears are that the trout stocks have suffered as a result.

LOUGH NATRAGH

This little lough holds a good stock of brown trout, averaging 0.5 lb. The banks are good. It lies off the Pettigoe-Donegal road and involves a half hour walk from the roadside.

The fishing is regarded as free.

LOUGH NADARRAGH

Lough Nadarragh lies along the Pettigoe-Donegal road. It holds wild brown trout and is sometimes stocked with brown trout and rainbow trout. It is bank fishing only.

Enquiries about permission to fish should be made locally.

RATH LOUGH

Rath Lough is three miles east of Ballintra in south Donegal. It holds a good stock of brown trout averaging 0.5 lb. The fishing is regarded as free.

LOUGH NARATH

Lough Narath is a small lough south-east of Ballintra. It holds some trout but it also has pike and perch which were introduced in recent years.

The fishing is regarded as free.

DURNASH LOUGH

Durnash Lough is tidal and the level is controlled by flood gates. Part of the shoreline is free fishing but the part by Kelly's property is private and angling is not allowed. The average size of the brown trout is 0.5 lb and it gets a run of sea trout in July. Boats are available for hire, but only to residents of:

◆ *The Sand House Hotel*, Rossnowlagh, Co. Donegal; telephone (072) 51777.

LOUGH GOLAGH

Lough Golagh lies seven miles north-east of Donegal town. It holds a good stock of brown trout averaging 0.5 lb with some better fish. It fishes well early in the season and also in July, August and September. The banks are good all round.

The fishing is regarded as free.

RIVER ESKE

Open Season

Salmon: 1 March to 30 September;
sea trout and brown trout: 1 March to 9 October.

The River Eske is about three-and-a-half miles and drains Lough Eske into Donegal Bay at Donegal town. It gets a small run of grilse in June and the main run of salmon goes through in August and September. The banks are mainly overgrown and the river itself is said to be lightly fished.

Enquiries about the fishing should be made to:

- ◆ *Mr C. Doherty,* Fishing Tackle Dealer, Main Street, Donegal town.

LOUGH ESKE
Open Season
Salmon: 1 March to 30 September;
sea trout and brown trout: 1 March to 9 October.

Lough Eske is 900 acres. It lies a few miles north of Donegal town. It holds small brown trout, sea trout and gets a run of spring salmon, grilse and autumn fish. It fishes best from a boat. Access to the lough is at a point at the north-west side but there is a possibility that other access points may be opened up. The late season is the best time to fish Lough Eske. Boats and gillies can be arranged through Harvey's Point Hotel, Lough Eske, Co. Donegal.

Enquiries about the fishing should be made to:

- ◆ *Northern Regional Fisheries Board,* Station Road, Ballyshannon, Co. Donegal; telephone (072) 51435
- ◆ *Mr C. Doherty,* Tackle Dealer, Main Street, Donegal town.

ST PETER'S LOUGH
Open Season
Brown trout: 1 March to 9 October.

This lough lies on the Mountcharles-Killybegs road near the village of Mountcharles. It holds a stock of wild brown trout averaging about 1 lb. There is a bag limit of four trout and it is bank fishing only.

GLENCOAGH LOUGH
Open Season
Brown trout: 1 March to 9 October.

This is a small lough over a mile north-west of the village of Mountcharles. It holds a stock of small brown trout and is occasionally stocked with rainbow trout. Enquiries about the fishing to:

- ◆ *Mr John Wilson,* Mountcharles, Co. Donegal; telephone (073) 35032.

EANY WATER

Open Season

Salmon: 1 April to 30 September;
sea trout and brown trout: 1 April to 9 October.

The Eany Water is about fifteen miles long and drains into Inver Bay in south Donegal. It is owned by the Central Fisheries Board and controlled by the Northern Regional Fisheries Board. The grilse run peaks at the end of July and continues into August and there can be good salmon fishing in September. This is a typical spate river. Fly fishing, worm and spinning are all allowed, but the use of prawn and shrimp is prohibited. It has a bag limit of three fish per day. The river gets a run of sea trout and the peak of the sea trout fishing is in early July.

Enquiries about the fishing should be made to:

◆ *Kelly's Bar*, Frosses, Co. Donegal
◆ *Mr C. Doherty*, Fishing Tackle Dealer, Main Street, Donegal town
◆ *Northern Regional Fisheries Board*, Station Road, Ballyshannon, Co. Donegal; telephone (072) 51435.

LOUGH DIVINE

Open Season

Brown trout: 1 March to 9 October.

Lough Divine lies to the south of the road from Glencolumbkille to Meenamevry. It holds a good stock of brown trout averaging 0.5 lb.

Enquiries about the fishing should be made locally.

GLEN RIVER

Open Season

Salmon: 1 March to 30 September;
sea trout and brown trout: 1 March to 9 October.

The Glen River drains the mountains of west Donegal into Donegal Bay. It gets a run of salmon in May and a good run of grilse in early July. There is a run of summer salmon in August.

The Yellow River shares the same estuary as the Glen River. It gets a good run of summer salmon and is well worth fishing in August and September when conditions are right.

The fishery has been leased by the Slieve League Angling Association and permits are available from:

◆ *Séamus McGinley*, Central Store, Carrick, Co. Donegal.

LOUGH AGH, LOUGH AUVA, LOUGH UNNA
Salmon: 1 March to 30 September;
sea trout and brown trout: 1 March to 9 October.

These loughs are on the Glen River system. Lough Agh holds a good stock of brown trout averaging 0.5 lb. Lough Unna has small brown trout but holds a good stock of sea trout and occasional grilse from July. Lough Auva holds small brown trout and occasional sea trout from mid-August.

The fishery has been leased by the Glen Angling Association and permits are available from:

◆ *Séamus McGinley*, Central Store, Carrick, Co. Donegal.

LETTERKENNY DISTRICT

The Letterkenny Fisheries District comprises part of north-west Co. Donegal and embraces all the rivers flowing into the sea between Rossan Point and Malin Head.

LOUGH ANNA
Open Season
15 February to 12 October.

Lough Anna is in the hills two miles south-east of the town of Glenties in Co. Donegal. The access to the lake shore is difficult. It has a good stock of brown trout averaging 0.5 lb and it can be coarse fished from the shore.

Permission to fish is not usually required.

RIVER BRACKEY, RIVER DUOGH
Open Season
Salmon: 2 February to 30 September;

sea trout: 2 February to 12 October;
brown trout: 15 February to 12 October.

These two small rivers enter the sea about a mile south of the village of Ardara. Both of them get a run of sea trout and grilse in the months of July, August and September.

The fishing is regarded as free.

OWENTOCKER RIVER
Open Season
Salmon: 1 April to 30 September;
sea trout and brown trout: 1 April to 30 September.

The Owentocker River is an extreme spate river. It gets a run of grilse on a spate between June and September and is heavily fished when the fish are in the pools.

Permits to fish are available from:
- *The Hatchery,* Glenties, Co. Donegal
- *Kennedy's Filling Station,* Glenties, Co. Donegal
- *Maguire's Filling Station,* Ardara, Co. Donegal
- *Doherty's Bar,* Ardara, Co. Donegal.

LOUGH NACROAGHY, KILTOORIS LOUGH, DOON LOUGH

Ardara Anglers' Association has fishing on a number of lakes in the vicinity of Ardara. Lough Nacroaghy holds nice brown trout averaging 0.5 lb and the banks are three-quarters fishable. Kiltooris Lough is approximately five miles north-west of Ardara and is reputed to hold a good stock of trout with an average size of 0.75 lb. There are boats for hire from J. McLoone by the lake shore.

Doon Lough is approximately a mile south of Portnoo. It holds a fair stock of brown trout averaging 0.5 lb. There is a boat for hire from Mr Kevin McHugh and the banks are safe for fishing.

Enquiries about the fishing should be made to:
- *Mr John McGill,* Hon. Secretary, Ardara Anglers' Association, Ardara, Co. Donegal.

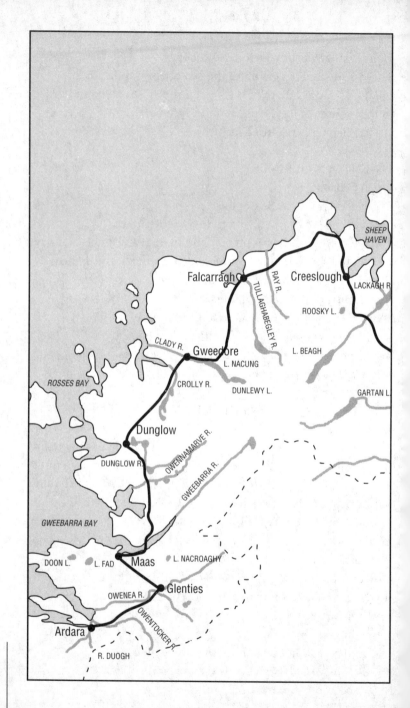

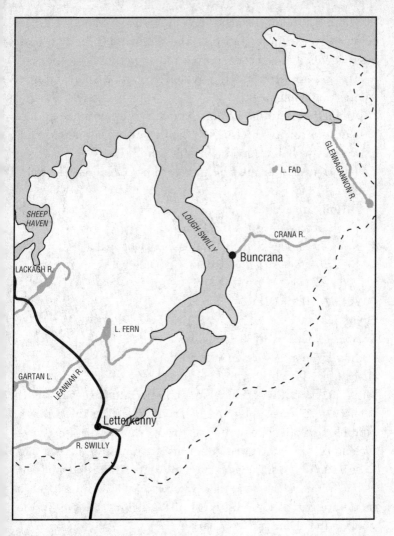

OWENEA RIVER
Open Season
Salmon: 1 March to 30 September; *sea trout:* 1 April to
30 September; *brown trout:* 15 March to 30 September.
The Owenea is one of the best salmon and sea trout rivers in
Co. Donegal. It is a spate river and drains a large catchment of
mountain and farmland into the sea a mile north of Ardara.

There is a run of spring salmon in April and May. The grilse begin to run in June, and July and August are the two best months with a prospect of sport in September.

The sea trout run in late July and give good sport through August and September.

All methods are allowed on the river, except in a one-and-a-half mile stretch which is fly fishing only. The banks are reasonably well developed with stiles and bridges.

The river is managed by the Northern Regional Fisheries Board.

Permits are available at:

◆ *The Hatchery*, Glenties, Co. Donegal
◆ *Kennedy's Filling Station*, Glenties, Co. Donegal
◆ *Doherty's Public House*, Ardara, Co. Donegal.

GWEEBARRA RIVER
Open Season
Salmon: 2 February to 30 September;
sea trout: 2 February to 12 October;
brown trout: 15 February to 12 October.

The Gweebarra River drains Lough Barra into Gweebarra Bay. It is about 25 miles long and is heavily fished in the summer months for both salmon and sea trout. The spring fish run at the end of April, the grilse run from late June and there is said to be a run of big summer salmon in August and September.

The sea trout arrive in the Gweebarra River in July. It gets a moderate run of fish and most of the fishing is done in the pools in the vicinity of Doocharry.

The fishing is regarded as free.

OWENNAMARVE RIVER
Open Season
Salmon: 2 February to 30 September;
sea trout: 2 February to 12 October;
brown trout: 15 February to 12 October.

The Owennamarve River drains a dozen small loughs into the sea south of Dunglow. It gets a run of salmon and sea trout. The best of the fishing is from July to September. Access is at the bridges.

Enquiries about the fishing should be made to:

◆ *Mr C. Bonner*, Rosses Anglers' Association, Fishing Tackle Shop, The Bridge, Dunglow, Co. Donegal; telephone (075) 21163.

DUNGLOW RIVER
Open Season
Sea trout: 2 February to 12 October.

This is a small river that drains several of the loughs in the Rosses area. It is fished for sea trout in the summer months.

Enquiries about the fishing to:

◆ *Mr C. Bonner*, Rosses Anglers' Association, Fishing Tackle Shop, The Bridge, Dunglow, Co. Donegal.

RIVER CLADY
RIVER CROLLY
Open Season
Salmon: 2 February to 30 September;
sea trout: 2 February to 12 October.

The River Clady gets a moderate run of salmon. The main run of grilse comes in June and the Whit weekend can be an excellent time to take salmon if the water is right. There are good runs in July and some big fish run in August and September. It also gets a moderate run of sea trout and the best of this fishing is in August.

The Crolly River drains Lough Anure and many other lakes in the area. The grilse run begins early in June and fish enter the river with every spate right through to September.

Enquiries about the fishing on both of these rivers should be made to:

◆ *Mr C. Bonner*, Rosses Anglers' Association, Fishing Tackle Shop, The Bridge, Dunglow, Co. Donegal.

THE ROSSES FISHERY

The Rosses Anglers' Association has fishing on over 130 lakes in west Donegal. The town of Dunglow is the centre from which the angler makes his way to fish the various loughs. These lakes hold salmon, sea trout and brown trout and all of them are within a five-mile radius of the town. Permits to fish and boats can be arranged.

A detailed angling map and guide is available. Enquiries about the fishing should be made to:

◆ *Mr C. Bonner*, Rosses Anglers' Association, Fishing Tackle Shop, The Bridge, Dunglow, Co. Donegal;
   telephone (075) 21163.

LOUGH NACUNG LOWER
LOUGH NACUNG UPPER
DUNLEWY LAKE

This is really all one piece of water and is nearly five miles long, stretching from Cung Dam to Dunlewy. It holds small brown trout and gets a run of sea trout and salmon from mid-June. Bank fishing is permitted and fly fishing and dapping is the rule. Anglers may use their own boats but a fee will be charged. Outboards motors over 4 H.P. are not allowed. There are seven boats with outboard motors for hire from the Lakeside Centre, Dunlewy. A full list of angling regulations is available from the Fisheries Manager.

Enquiries about the fishing to:

◆ *Lakeside Centre,* Dunlewy, Co. Donegal; telephone (075) 31699.

TULLAGHABEGLEY RIVER
Open Season

Salmon: 2 February to 30 September;
sea trout: 2 February to 12 October;
brown trout: 15 February to 12 October.

The Tullaghabegley River is an eight-mile river that enters the sea west of Falcarragh. It drains Mount Errigal and Lough Altan. It gets a moderate run of grilse and sea trout. The bottom part of the river is very heavily fished after a spate.

Fishing permits are issued by Cloughaneely Anglers' Association and are available from:

◆ *Mr Sean Meehan*, Newsagent, Falcarragh, Co. Donegal
◆ *Mr Michael Sweeney*, Fishing Tackle Shop, Falcarragh, Co. Donegal.

RAY RIVER
Open Season

Salmon: 2 February to 30 September;
sea trout: 2 February to 12 October;
brown trout: 15 February to 12 October.

The Ray River joins the mountains of west Donegal into the sea west of Horn Head. It is eight miles long. This river gets a small run of spring fish and the grilse run from mid-June. It gets a run of fish on every spate from mid-June to the end of the season. It is a river that is very heavily fished.

Permits are issued on the river by Cloghaneely Anglers' Association and are available from:

◆ *Mr Sean Meehan*, Newsagent, Falcarragh, Co. Donegal
◆ *Mr Michael Sweeney*, Fishing Tackle Shop, Falcarragh, Co. Donegal.

LETTERKENNY AND DISTRICT ANGLERS' ASSOCIATION WATER

The Letterkenny and District Anglers' Association have fishing rights on a number of lakes in the Letterkenny area. These lakes include: Columbkille Lough, Lough Fern, Gartan Lough, Glen Lough, Lough More, Lough Agannive and Drumaneany Lough. These lakes offer a mixture of brown trout fishing, sea trout fishing and occasional salmon.

Enquiries about the fishing should be made to:

◆ *Mr Gerard McNulty*, Hon. Sec., Letterkenny and District Anglers' Association, Hawthorn Heights, Letterkenny, Co. Donegal.

DUNFANAGHY ANGLERS' ASSOCIATION WATERS

The Dunfanaghy Anglers' Association develops a number of brown trout lakes in the Dunfanaghy area. These are Sassiath Lough, New Lake and Port Lough. All of these loughs hold wild brown trout and are occasionally stocked. Boats are available for hire. Enquiries about the fishing should be made to:

◆ *Dunfanaghy Anglers' Association*, c/o Arnold's Hotel, Dunfanaghy, Co. Donegal; telephone (074) 36218.

ROOSKY LOUGH
LITTLE ROOSKY LOUGH

These two small loughs lie west of the village of Creshlough. The former holds a small stock of brown trout averaging 1 lb and the latter holds a moderate stock of 0.5 lb brown trout.

Enquiries about the fishing to:

◆ *Lafferty's Supermarket*, Creshlough, Co. Donegal.

LACKAGH RIVER
Open Season

Salmon and sea trout: 1 January to 30 September;
brown trout: 15 February to 30 September.

The Lackagh River is a short river of less than two miles and drains Glen Lough into the sea. It is noted for its run of spring salmon, grilse and sea trout. The spring run peaks in March and there is a moderate run of grilse in June and July. The sea trout fishing can be very good from mid-July to the end of the season.

Creshlough and District Angling Club issue permits on the left bank of the Lackagh, upstream of the tide to Glen Lough. The permits are available at:

◆ *Doherty's Supermarket*, Creshlough, Co. Donegal.

LOUGH BEAGH

Lough Beagh is nearly four miles long by about half-a-mile wide. It holds a good stock of small brown trout, occasional salmon and can hold a moderate stock of sea trout in August. It is fished for its sea trout and the best of the fishing is through

August and September. Bank fishing is not allowed. There are boats for hire and enquiries about the fishing should be made to:

◆ *Mr James McGinley or Mr Bernard Gannivan,*
   Glenveagh National Park, Churchill, Co. Donegal;
   telephone (074) 37090.

RIVER LEANNAN
Open Season
Salmon: 1 January to 30 September; *sea trout:* 1 January to 30 September; *brown trout:* 15 February to 30 September.

The River Leannan rises in north Donegal and flows through Gartan Lough and Lough Fern to the sea at Lough Swilly. The best of the spring fishing is usually in the months of February and March. The grilse come into the river in late June and the best fishing takes place in the month of July.

The fishery downstream of Drumonahan Bridge at Rathmelton is the property of the Rathmelton Fishery Company and the fishing is not let.

The fishing on the rest of the river is regarded as free.

RIVER SWILLY
Open Season
Salmon: 2 February to 30 September;
sea trout: 2 February to 12 October;
brown trout: 15 February to 12 October.

The River Swilly is nearly 26 miles long and drains into Lough Swilly near the town of Letterkenny. It has very few deep stretches and the water runs off quickly after a flood. The grilse run in good numbers about the second week of June and the sea trout come in August. It is heavily fished by local anglers when the fish are running.

The fishing is regarded as free.

CRANA RIVER
Open Season
Salmon: 1 March to 30 September;
sea trout: 1 March to 12 October.

The fishing on the Crana River is controlled by the Buncrana Angling Association. The river flows into Lough Swilly north of the town of Buncrana. It holds both salmon and sea trout and is well worth fishing from late June to the end of the season. Fishing methods are confined to fly and worm in low water and spinning is allowed in high water.

Enquiries about the fishing should be made to:

◆ *Mr Tom Sreenan*, Westbrook, Buncrana, Co. Donegal
◆ *Mr Leo Burke*, Westbrook, Buncrana, Co. Donegal.

GLENNAGANNON RIVER
DONAGH RIVER
Open Season

Salmon: 2 February to 30 September;
sea trout: 2 February to 12 October.

The Glennagannon River flows from Lough Inn to Trawbreaga Bay. It gets a moderate run of salmon and sea trout and is regarded as the best river on the Inishowen Peninsula. The sea trout arrive in July and the salmon fishing is best in August and September.

The Donagh River is nine miles long and flows through the village of Carndonagh into Trawbreaga Bay. It holds sea trout from July and gets a small run of grilse from mid-August.

Enquiries about the fishing to:

◆ *Mr Conn Smyth*, 134 Ardcolgan, Carndonagh, Co. Donegal
◆ *The Tourist Office*, Carndonagh, Co. Donegal.

LOUGH FAD
LOUGH NAMINA
Open Season

Brown trout: 15 February to 12 October.

These loughs lie to either side of the Buncrana-Carndonagh road. Both of them hold a good stock of small brown trout.

The fishing is regarded as free.

Index